JAGUAR
SALOONS

GRACE, SPACE AND PACE

CHRIS HARVEY

The Oxford Illustrated Press

© 1991, Chris Harvey

ISBN 0 946609 48 9

Published by: The Oxford Illustrated Press,
Haynes Publishing Group, Sparkford, Nr Yeovil,
Somerset BA22 7JJ, England

Printed in England by: J.H. Haynes & Co Limited,
Sparkford, Nr Yeovil, Somerset

British Library Cataloguing in Publication Data:
A catalogue record for this book is available from the
British Library

Library of Congress Catalog Card Number:
90 – 85836

Contents

Acknowledgements

Half my life seems to have been spent at the wheel of a Jaguar. Much of that time has been in saloons which have known no equal, only the E type sports car matching my other great love, Porsche RS grand touring cars. These affairs of the heart started long before I could drive: as I dodged in and out of London traffic on my bicycle, dreaming of designing cars, I was transfixed by one of the most graceful that could be imagined: a Mark VII saloon. There was nothing quite like it in 1950.

Five years later a snowbound Monte Carlo Rally was rendered unforgettable by my first sight of a Mark I Jaguar although it would be 10 years before I could afford to indulge my passion in a 3.8-litre Mark 2 modified by my local dealer, John Coombs. At that time it was one of the fastest cars on the road and served me well travelling Britain as a newspaper and television reporter before I transferred to an E type.

Eventually the Coombs was replaced by a smooth, sweet, Daimler saloon, surely the best-handling Mark 2 with its lightweight V8 engine and beautifully-weighted manual steering. As my family expanded, so did the Daimler, into a Sovereign based on the Jaguar S type, and then a 2.8-litre XJ6. Pistons pinging, that was updated to prove uncommonly good at ploughing through snow with its low rear axle ratio as the main car became the best-ever, a Jaguar XJ6 4.2-litre automatic. Wild excursions in a shortwheelbase XJ12 confirmed that it used even more fuel than a Carrera RS, so it had to go.

All the other Jaguars have belonged to someone else, as a career in London's Fleet Street turned into motoring journalism and motor racing photography. For these experiences, I must thank Alan Hodge, Dave Crisp, and later, David Boole, at Jaguar—who along with secretary Tina Kennedy—provided much information and even more valuable pictures. Wise words in my ear from Sir William Lyons and John Egan were much appreciated, and a visit to one of my favourite countries, Austria, proved even more enlightening in a priceless interview with Lofty England.

Such contacts had been fostered by Paul Skilleter, one of our greatest modern automotive authors, who talked me into using a camera, rather than telling other people what I needed. Andrew Whyte tried to persuade me to stick to writing, but photography took over and now it's a major occupation.

All along I've had the invaluable support of Jane Marshall, of Oxford Illustrated Press, and John Haynes, the supremo who is one of the most dependable men I have ever met in publishing. Few people realise the patience they have shown in waiting years for another book . . . other than my wife, Mary Harvey, who is a proper photographer: she not only takes pictures, and sells them, but she does all the laboratory work which is such a mystery to me.

None of this would have been possible had it not been for the continuing support of colleagues like Tony Dron, editor of *Classic Cars* magazine, associate editor Lionel Burrell, and former deputy Jeremy Coulter. Books alone cannot support a freelance, but colleagues can.

Wander where I may, all round the world, from San Francisco to the South of France, I never fail to be grateful for the support of Jaguar club members such as David Harvey of the Jaguar Car Club, Rikki Bideleux and David Hames of the Drivers' Club, Les Hughes with *Australian Jaguar*, and that eternal *Jaguar Enthusiast*, Nigel Thornley, for keeping in touch with the grassroots.

Thanks to everybody, named and unnamed, who have waited so long for yet another Chris Harvey car book.

August 1991   Hethe, Oxfordshire

The Greatest Jaguars

For nigh on a century, Britain produced the best cars in the world. Jaguar was just a jungle cat when Rolls-Royce first laid claim to the title. Then the son of an Irish musician, William Lyons, began to make lovely cars that moved so well they easily adopted a feline image. It was easy to visualise a D type sports racer, or the glamorous E type it spawned, as his greatest cars until you examined the reality: in post-war years, the best Jaguars have always been the saloons. Sometimes they have been better than any other car in the world, Rolls-Royce included.

Big and voluptuous as it was, the Mark VII was in a class of its own when it first appeared in 1950. It was more than a match for a Rolls-Royce in almost every department, especially price. The smaller Mark I saloon that followed in 1955 would be merely a taster for the lithe and nimble Mark II four years later that appealed not only to the wealthy, but to the equally discerning ordinary buyer. As if that was not a hard act to follow, the XJ introduced in 1968 was still being proclaimed the best car in the world—bar none—ten years later. Inevitably, Lyons grew old, and had to relinquish control of the company he founded. But his wonderful saloon cars carried Jaguar through years of corporate decline into the 1990s with such a reputation that a massive injection of multinational cash from Ford made sure that the marque will carry on as Britain's only major luxury car maker, and quite possibly, continue to make the best car in the world.

The Mark VII was a trendsetter because it combined the XK engine—of such advanced design that only racing car makers had been able to attain before—with an evocative streamlined body. The range that followed became ever more competent, building on the success of sports racing cars like the Le Mans-winning D type, to scoop ever larger por-

tions of a lucrative export market. But these cars were too big to sell in large numbers anywhere other than the United States, so the medium-sized saloons that followed became the backbone of Jaguar's continuing growth. Lyons, by then Sir William Lyons, was at the height of his powers as an inspired stylist and businessman when he lost his only son in the year that the Mark I saloon was launched. Hardly recovered from his personal tragedy, he actively motivated his workforce to throw off the effects of a factory fire in 1957 which might have fatally wounded a less-determined operation. Within a couple of years, a Mark II version of the smaller saloon became Jaguar's greatest profit-maker, alongside the even more fabulous-looking E type sports car, developed from the D type.

As Jaguar entered the Swinging Sixties, growth was hampered by planning restrictions. They could not move into high-volume production because there was little land available near their base in Coventry. And they could not move out of Coventry because there was not sufficient skilled labour elsewhere. So Lyons had to concentrate on making small numbers of big cars and sports cars, on which there were traditionally big profit margins. This meant that, as a low-volume producer, Jaguar could not afford the massive investment needed to produce their own bodies. They would always be at the mercy of a larger manufacturer that could fund such operations from high-volume car sales, plus sub-contract work from smaller businesses like Jaguar.

Lyons tried every trick of the trade, buying up weaker companies for the extra factory space he needed. Meanwhile, his new big car, the Mark X, misjudged its market. It was conceived at a time when American cars were truly gargantuan, and had to carry on into an age when they became smaller

The long graceful lines, sheer performance, and exceptional value for money made Jaguars like Graham Button's Mark VII – pictured at the Brands Hatch Festival of Yesteryear in 1984 – a sure winner throughout the world.

and more compact. Once more, Jaguar was a victim of economic factors beyond its control. They had survived, and prospered, during an era when cars made in America—their largest export market—were produced in such quantities that manufacturers like Ford could afford to change their appearance dramatically every year. Jaguar was just about viable because Lyons styling was so brilliant that he could keep his basic design in production far longer, thus containing development costs, and keeping his relatively low-volume product competitive. But not even his flowing lines could mask the sheer size of the Mark X and 420G that followed; happily, however, the popularity of the Mark II saloon and various developments, masked that hole in his economic armour.

The Mark X was not a total disaster. It had a lot of good points that Lyons and an inspired engineering team led by William Heynes were able to weld together into a car that capitalised on the success of the Mark II. This was the XJ6 that set standards of excellence so far ahead of the opposition that Jaguar were able to live off it for a decade or more. A grand touring development, the XJ-S, had features so sophisticated that it enjoyed a new sales boom ten years after it was launched!

It may well have been that Lyons had to devote so much time to design that his long-term business strategy was weakened. As the XJ6 was nearing production in 1968, he merged Jaguar—in two steps—with the British Motor Corporation, who produced his bodies, in an attempt to ensure its survival in an ever more competitive market. His lieutenants were able, but like Lyons, they were ageing. With no obvious heir, Jaguar was in decline as the newly-formed British Leyland group strug-

Colin Chapman, the genius behind the British Lotus sports and racing makers, battles in a 3.8-litre Mark II saloon with race ace Jack Sears at Silverstone in 1960. Chapman won by 0.2 second – little knowing that he would eventually come close to having to sell his company to Jaguar!

gled in vain to hold their own as a high-volume producer.

But there was still the impetus from the most innovative years of the engineering team that Lyons created. Their new V12 engine was so good, even if it was thirsty, that it survived the world's first prolonged energy crisis to scoop the world's best car title from Rolls-Royce in the face of intense opposition from German and American rivals such as Mercedes, BMW and Cadillac. Partly through the grim determination of men like engineering wizard Bob Knight, partly through a basic integrity of design, Jaguar survived appalling problems with British Leyland-inspired quality control, until they were saved by modern management in the form of troubleshooter John Egan.

He attacked Jaguar's problems with such vigour, and roused such support from his work force, that they were able to exploit a booming economy to break free from the millstone of debt that British Leyland had been forced to accumulate during the bad years. As a newly-privatised company, profits boomed not so much from the cars that Jaguar made, but from inspired dealings on the money market. But they created enough financial power to keep the XJ6 competitive in a world rapidly being starved of individualism as ever bigger conglomerates gobbled up smaller fry.

Inevitably, all bubbles burst. Just as the world's economy, and demand for luxury cars, had boomed with each decade, it came close to collapse with the 1987 American stock market crash. Egan, by now Sir John, kept Jaguar afloat long enough for Ford to have to pay so much for the prestige it could never acquire elsewhere that it would be foolish to dilute such investment by turning Jaguars into ordinary cars. As Egan bowed out in 1990, virtually ten years to the day after he took over, he left Jaguar in better shape than at any time since, to carry on making the greatest luxury cars . . . which means, not just sports cars, or racers that win at Le Mans, but saloon cars.

The magnificent Mark X saloon was so big it could be likened to a dinosaur . . . yet its technology was so advanced it spawned a whole new breed of Jaguars.

The XJ6 became not only Jaguar's top-selling saloon but it was so far ahead of any opposition that it became the best car they ever made.

Daimler versions of Jaguar saloons featured prominently in the British marketplace, and in Double Six form, provided the basis for what would be recognised as the best car in the world.

Jaguar survives into the 1990s on Ford finance and a unique range of open and closed cars.

Grace, Space and Pace

The Jaguar Mark VII was like a dream come true: a sensational saloon that could seat five people in comfort and outrun most of the sports cars of the day. As if that was not enough, it had timeless lines which made it one of the best-looking cars of the 1950s.

Even its most conservative aspect, the chassis, was well advanced when it was introduced at the London Motor Show in October 1950. In essence, it had been carried over from the earlier Mark V saloon which had bodywork with long, flowing, separate wings and was a longer edition of that used in the XK120 sports car of 1948. The chief components were two massive 6.5-inch deep box section side members, splayed out from a narrow frontal aspect to almost the full width of the car at the back. Weight was saved by tapering the extremities to a 3.5-inch depth at the point where they swept up and back in an arc to support the rear spring hangers. Substantial cross-bracing was used in front and behind the rear axle, in a cruciform section around the gearbox, and across the front of the engine bay. The idea was to make the whole structure more rigid than earlier efforts. This allowed the use of softer suspension because the chassis, on a long 10-ft wheelbase, did not whip so much as before, with the result that the ride was better and the handling improved with more wheel movement.

The front suspension comprising wishbones and torsion bars had become established Jaguar practice while the rear, with half-elliptic leaf springs, was common practice at the time. The spring rates were relatively soft, however, which meant that an anti-roll bar had to be used at the front, with telescopic shock absorbers which were less prone to fade under the considerable weight of the engine. Traditional lever arm shock absorbers were used on the more lightly-loaded Salisbury live rear axle. The front track, at 4ft 8ins, was slightly narrower than the 4ft 9.5-inch back.

The British considered that the Burman steering box had a relatively low ratio of 4.75 turns from lock to lock, although American cars of that era habitually used 5 turns. To Jaguar, it was the best compromise because they had moved the engine 5 inches further forward in the chassis than on the Mark V to liberate more room in the cabin: a higher ratio would have made the steering unacceptably heavy at parking speeds.

The engine had already achieved fame in the XK120 sports car which had only really been built as a mobile test bed. But not only did it look good, it went so well that the XK had become an immediate race-winner. Even more important, the classic dimensions of an 83-mm bore allied to a long 106-mm stroke gave it such good torque that the substantial Mark VII, weighing more than two tons laden, still displayed remarkable acceleration and flexibility. As an in-line six-cylinder, it had 3,442cc giving 150bhp on a 7:1 compression ratio—needed in areas where the quality of petrol was poor—or 160bhp at 5,200rpm with 195lb/ft of torque low down at 2,500rpm in a higher, 8:1, compression ratio form.

The most important part of the engine was the cylinder head, which weighed only 50lb against 120lb for a more normal cast iron equivalent. The weight saving was important because the engine had been moved forward, which concentrated more of its mass over the front wheels. But there were equally-important side effects. Because the cylinder head used twin overhead camshafts for ultimate efficiency, it had to have a relatively bulky cast-

The cars that Jaguar used to make, such as the Mark V, in drophead form, provided a backbone for the new Mark VII saloon.

ing. Had the cheaper cast iron been used, it would not have dispersed the heat generated so well, making the engine less efficient. It would also have concentrated a heavier mass relatively high in the car, making it roll more while cornering. The use of iron for the cylinder block could be defended because its weight was carried low down, and with no camshafts to support what was a reasonably slim casting. It also absorbed more sound than aluminium. Individual timing chains were used for each camshaft to reduce the whine set up by using one long one.

The heart of the engine was a seven-bearing crankshaft with massive 2.75-inch main bearings which proved near-indestructible. Power was enhanced by a low-pressure lubrication system which reduced oil drag, and lightweight valve gear that operated direct from the camshafts through bucket tappets for ultimate efficiency. The only compromise to efficiency could be seen in the use of 0.3125-inch lift cams, rather than ones of 0.375ins. This was because contemporary fuel created a lot of carbon and necessitated frequent decokes. Few mechanics had ever worked on such an advanced engine at the time, and it was envisaged that the valves might be bent when the cams were turned during a decoke if a higher lift been adopted.

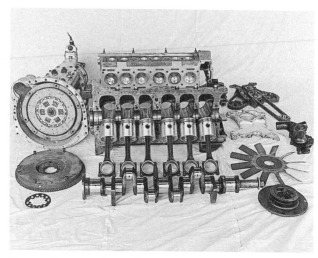

The new Jaguar engine – pictured in exploded form – had already undergone a thorough test in the XK120 sports car by the time it was fitted to the Mark VII saloon.

The only real problem with the engine was that the cooling system, which used a relatively small front radiator for styling reasons, was hard put to cope with prolonged use in heavy traffic in hot areas. This was ironic because style-conscious Southern California would become one of Jaguar's biggest markets.

Two 1.75-inch SU carburettors were used, linked to one SU electric fuel pump in each of two petrol tanks, contained in each rear wing to make as much space as possible for luggage in between. An electric enrichment device cut in for cold starting. The gearbox was driven by a 10-inch single dry plate Borg and Beck clutch, hydraulically-operated on all except the first 55 cars. Like the four-speed transmission, it was exceptionally strong, which mitigated its heavy change and the relatively weak synchromesh on the top three ratios. A far higher proportion of motorists—especially in Europe—had learned to drive without synchromesh at the time, and found this cumbersome gearbox no handicap. But it hastened the need for an automatic variant in the United States

The lines of the Mark VII saloon followed the pattern established by the XK120 sports car – pictured in fixed-head form on Jaguar's favourite promotional spot, the football ground beside their Brown's Lane factory in the background.

where there was already a generation that had never used primitive straight-cut gears. The standard ratios of 14.4, 8.48, 5.84 and 4.27:1 were wider than those on the XK120 which had a similar transmission that could be specified for competition. The drive to the hypoid bevel rear axle was by a Hardy Spicer propeller shaft, divided to allow a flat floor which increased passenger space. The standard axle ratio was 4.27:1, although a lower 4.55:1 unit gave better acceleration in competition.

The brakes were typical of their day in that they suffered from an on-going trend towards using all-enveloping bodywork, cheaper, easier-to-clean disc wheels, and smaller tyres. Pre-war cars normally had large narrow wheels, often with wire

The interior of the Jaguars was so luxurious it could be readily adapted as a limousine.

spokes, covered by long flowing wings which let in—and equally important—let out a lot of cooling air. When more efficient streamlined bodies like that of the Mark VII came in, the wheels were far more shrouded. At the same time manufacturers started switching to smaller and cheaper wheels and tyres—without spokes. An additional advantage of these wheels and tyres, of 16ins diameter with a 6.70 section, was that they improved handling because there was not so much unsprung weight. But, in company with voluminous bodywork, they played havoc with the braking. Not only did the brakes suffer from inadequate cooling, but the drums in use at the time were reduced in diameter to fit inside the smaller wheels. Jaguar tried to counter these problems by fitting a twin trailing shoe system to the more heavily-loaded front brakes. The earlier twin leading shoe variants had worked well with their inherent self-servo effect, but suffered badly once the linings overheated. The trailing shoes gave a more consistent braking effect, but needed more pedal pressure, so a Clayton-Dewandre servo was fitted. The shoes were also made self-adjusting, which helped a lot when the linings and drums heated up. The existing one leading shoe, one trailing, system was retained at the back with 12-inch drums all round. Nevertheless, the best thing that could be said about this system was that American rivals suffered from far more fade . . .

The standard four-door body was the biggest step forward for Jaguar. It retained a family resemblance to the Mark V and its predecessors in the rounded rear quarters of the roofline. But the wings were totally new, high and sweeping like those pioneered by the XK120 sports car, complete with spats to cover the rear wheels. Items such as a sunroof and foglights that were often extra-cost options on other cars were fitted as standard. Massive chrome bumpers reflected the taste of the vital American market, but the otherwise restrained use of chrome plating made the Jaguar look quite different to the contemporary Detroit iron. Lyons used timeless elegance in this way to contain production costs because he did not have to keep updating chrome embellishments like his rivals.

In the same way the interior featured lavish leather and walnut in such a traditionally British manner that it did not date. In fact, a great deal of development went into the interior to make the Jaguar fully competitive with outwardly bigger American cars. As in previous Jaguars, the driver and front passenger had massive bucket seats. It was found possible, however, to accommodate three passengers in the back by using a bench seat. Jaguar had found a a vital five inches extra shoul-

der room within the restrictions of a conventional 5ft 3-inch overall height by re-arranging major components in the car. The new full-width body provided part of the extra space with the rest being liberated by moving the engine forward. This gave an extra three inches of legroom even when the rear seat squab was moved forward by a couple of inches to clear the wheel arches and provide more hip room. It also had the effect of dramatically increasing the size of the luggage boot behind, which—at nearly 2ft 6ins deep, and 4ft long and 3ft 8ins at its widest point—was comparable to America's biggest sedans. But the Mark VII was still shorter in overall length, at 16ft 4½ins, and wider at 6ft 1ins, because Lyons avoided excesses of overhang in his styling. The benefits were never better felt than in the way that the lack of over-hanging weight improved the ride and handling.

Detail improvements were made to fittings as a result of the Mark VII saloon, with the XK120 sports car, proving a popular mount in competition. This example, crewed by Colin McMeekin, Denis Bell and James Ross-Tomlin, is pictured starting from Glasgow in the 1990 Monte Carlo Challenge.

Despite the bulk of the big saloon – pictured in contemporary Mark VIIM form – it handled well on what now seem tall, narrow, tyres.

There was such a demand for the Mark VII that few changes were needed during the first years of production—which was fortunate because Jaguar desperately needed more space and were busy moving into new premises at Brown's Lane, Coventry. But the extremes of temperature in export markets revealed hidden flaws. Jaguars in general, not just the Mark VII, soon gained a reputation for overheating, especially when snarled up in traffic jams in their biggest market, Southern California. This problem was partly alleviated late in 1951 by replacing the original cast aluminium cooling fan with a steel one which ran at a higher speed. At the same time, the cylinder block was adapted to take an element to keep the water warm during very cold nights. But nothing was done to counter complaints that the heater's output was inadequate: Lyons habitually wore an overcoat for winter motoring!

However, better fittings found their way into Jaguars when accessory manufacturers were able to offer them at competitive prices: two-speed wipers and windscreen washers appeared in 1952. Other changes were incorporated that year as a result of competition work with the XK sports cars. The front of the camshaft covers received additional studs to stop oil leaks, and the valve and tappet guides were modified so that 0.375-inch high-performance camshafts could be fitted. The gearbox casing was also strengthened. Uprated Girling dampers became optional equipment in many countries and standard in areas where rough roads were the norm. Stronger and wider, 5.5-inch rim, wheels were fitted all round. Although the standard of Jaguar's finish was very high by immediate post-war standards, it was improved by switching from cellulose to synthetic enamel late in the year.

But by 1953 the option of automatic transmission had become a necessity in the vital Ameri-can market where already a generation had grown up without ever using a manual gearbox. British rivals Rolls-Royce and Bentley were also offering it, which made the need more acute. Lyons took the view that it was not worth spending a lot of money and time developing his own transmission when it was not something you could see—like the engine—and there were perfectly good units on offer from independent manufacturers. So an American Borg-Warner transmission was modified to suit the XK engine's torque curve, with a kick down switch under the accelerator pedal to provide a change-down into the intermediate of three speeds below 60mph for overtaking. There was also a bottom gear lock-up for loose surfaces or emergency braking, an anti-creep device that operated the back brakes at idle, and an American-style parking pawl which could lock the output shaft. Take off in the normal Drive option was distinctly

Jaguar's first quantity-production saloon, seen here in Mark VIIM form with owner Dennis Blanch lapping Brands Hatch at the Festival of Yesteryear in 1984, proved durable to the extreme.

The Mark VII certainly provided dignified appeal . . . Britain's Queen Mother retained this example so long that she had it updated with Mark IX running gear.

leisurely, however, because it still used the intermediate ratio that favoured the low-revving, slugging, American engines, rather than the higher-revving XK unit.

These functions could be overridden by a quadrant selector on the dashboard which allowed Jaguar to follow the normal American practice of fitting a bench seat at the front, and so made the automatic Mark VII a six-seater. The handbrake had to be moved from its place between the front seats to under the dashboard in this case and lost a lot of its efficiency as a result. But Jaguar reckoned that was acceptable: most of the early automatic Mark VIIs were destined for America where the parking pawl was commonly used . . .

More sporting drivers could specify quite a lot of the tuning equipment developed for the XK sports cars on the Mark VII. Now that high-quality petrol was readily available, 9:1 compression ratio pistons could be fitted, along with a modified distributor and carburettors. At the same time, a C type cylinder head with oversize valves bolted straight on, with 2-inch SU carburettors. Closer-ratio gears used in the contemporary XK120 could be fitted, with a higher-ratio steering box and uprated springs, torsion bars and dampers.

More efficient telescopic dampers replaced the lever arm units at the back from August 1953, which necessitated an extra crossmember for the top mountings. Around the same time, further attempts were made to improve the cooling. An eight-bladed fan was fitted, with a more efficient pump and an expansion tank for the radiator. But

Jaguar found that costs could be cut by using a pressed-steel sump rather than the earlier alloy casting. It had to be enlarged, however, to disperse as much heat, so the anti-roll bar mountings were moved down to the lower wishbone arms to make way. Minor improvements included stronger valve springs, twin throttle return springs and metal to protect the brake servo from road debris.

Few markets enjoyed such cheap petrol as the United States, so Jaguar offered the option of an overdrive on the manual gearbox cars from January 1954. This higher ratio gave more economical cruising with the standard 3.54:1 rear axle or better acceleration without sacrificing too much economy with a 4.55:1 ratio. This immediately became popular in Europe whereas most American cars retained the lazier, less-economical, automatic transmission.

The general availability of high-octane fuel enabled Jaguar to uprate the big saloon as the Mark VIIM in September 1954. This had the higher-lift camshafts as standard on the normal 8:1 compression ratio model, which was now rated at 180bhp. The closer-ratio gearbox and stiffer torsion bars were fitted in keeping with its sprightlier performance, along with a stronger Salisbury axle. The gearbox in automatic versions was modified to take-off more quickly in first gear rather than intermediate.

Outwardly, the Mark VIIM received detail changes to give it a closer family resemblance to Jaguar's new XK140 sports car. These included new Lucas headlights, wider-spaced foglights, and even more comprehensive bumpers. New horn grilles were also fitted with revised road wheel trims as clear glass flashing indicator lights replaced the old-fashioned semaphore swinging arm trafficator. The steering wheel also got a neater and safer horn push. The heater output was raised at the same time, but not by enough to upset anybody wearing an overcoat . . .

But it was not possible to phase in all the improvements that Jaguar wanted in one month. People who ordered 7:1 compression ratio engines had to wait till early 1955, when stocks of early camshafts were sufficiently low, before the higher-lift versions were fitted as standard; at the same time the lubrication system on all power units was improved. This involved fitting a new oil pump and crankshaft seal with better timing chain tensioners.

The early white indicator lights enjoyed only a short production run before changing regulations forced Lucas to switch to amber from February 1955, at which point the rev counter's red warning sector was also moved from 5,200rpm–5,500 to 5,500–6,000 in keeping with the higher-performance engines. And once Borg-Warner could supply enough Jaguar-specification transmissions, the automatic option was extended to Britain late that year. It immediately became popular because Jaguar had also introduced a smaller, more sporting, saloon that appealed to manual gearbox users.

The trend continued so that the vast majority of big Jaguars built from 1956 had automatic transmission. These included the revised Mark VIII model launched in October that year. It had a modified C type cylinder head that was confusingly called the B type: Jaguar's reasoning was that the original 160bhp castings should now be known as the A type; the 190bhp B type was the new production head; the original C (for competition) type unit was derived from sports racing Jaguars which had 210bhp; and now there was a D type (so-called because it followed the C type) producing up to 300bhp. At any rate, the new B type head—which used gas-flow techniques developed to produce more power for the C type—was better for the heavy, chiefly automatic, Mark VIIIs because it continued to use the smaller A type port throats, which gave an improved 203lb/ft of torque at 3,000rpm. A new twin exhaust system was part of the package.

The automatic gearchange controls were further modified so that a dashboard-mounted switch could be used to hold the intermediate ratio or switch down to it for overtaking. This was achieved through a solenoid fitted to the gearbox's rear oil

The massive Mark IX might have weighed a lot . . . but it was still unusually spritely, as Mario Marconi and Anthony Vorley were about to demonstrate after starting from Tower Bridge on the 1989 Classic Marathon.

pump. Two-tone paint with a chrome strip dividing the top colour from the bottom made standard Mark VIIIs easy to distinguish from the earlier cars.

They also had cutaway rear-wheel spats that blended in with the swage line and a larger, more prominent, radiator grille.

Advances in glass-making technology also enabled Jaguar to replace the old split windscreen with a modern one-piece pane. The interior was made slightly more luxurious by increasing the thickness of the Dunlopillo rubber seat cushioning, and moulding the rear bench to suggest two individual buckets. Fold-down picnic tables were provided in the backs of the front seats with cigar lighters and ashtrays let into the doors. When a bench front seat was fitted it had a pocket in the middle and integral electric clock facing the back seats. All told, the Mark VIII weighed 1cwt more than the Mark VII, but performed just as well because of the B type head.

There were few changes during the Mark VIII's short production run. Along with other Jaguar cars, the camshafts were drilled for quieter cold starting from early 1957 and first rubber, then nylon, membranes were used to insulate the rear spring leaves to prevent squeaks. Money was also saved by using aluminium alloy rather than brass in the radiator casing.

In company with automatic transmission, power-assisted steering had long been a feature of luxurious American cars, and made its debut on some left-hand-drive Mark VIIIs in April 1958. Jaguar opted for a high degree of hydraulic pressure from the pump operated from the back of the dynamo to suit the transatlantic market which favoured featherlight steering. They tried to retain some of the old feeling in the steering by reducing the number of turns from lock to lock to 3.5, but

still raised little enthusiasm in Europe. Reutter reclining front seats were offered as an option from July 1958 before a new model, the Mark IX, was launched alongside the Mark VIII in October that year. This had power-steering as standard with vastly superior servo-boosted disc brakes all round—12.125ins in diameter at the front, 12.375ins rear—like the contemporary XK150 sports car. For the first time, Jaguar's big saloon had stopping power to fully match its performance. It was just as well because a bored-out version of the XK engine was fitted, chiefly to provide more torque, 240lb/ft at 3,000rpm, although at the same time it gave extra power, 220bhp at 5,500rpm. The capacity increase to 3,781cc was achieved by using a new cylinder block with 87-mm liners rather than 83mm. Detail changes included fitting an uprated heater and a single 12-volt battery to replace the earlier twin six-volts. But apart from a discreet Mark IX badge on the bootlid, the new car looked exactly like the Mark VIII, which stayed in production until December 1959. The Mark IX then carried on until late in 1961 with few changes. Larger ball joints were fitted to the front suspension during 1958, and new 'quick-change' disc pads from January 1959. In keeping with other Jaguars, the XK engine was modified to run with a half-inch fan belt and pulley and fitted with lead-indium crankshaft bearings midway through 1959, at which time the rev counter switched to electric operation.

Then all XK engines got an improved water pump early in 1960 along with a modified crankshaft rear cover to improve sump sealing on the 3.8-litre unit. A combined handbrake and low brake fluid warning light appeared at the same time before the heater's capacity was further uprated, along with larger rear lights, in 1961. But by then, a sensational new all-independently sprung Mark X was about to be launched.

Businessman's Express

A smartly-dressed executive stepping from a steaming express train presented a popular image of a businessman in the Britain of the 1950s. That image was about to disappear, however, when Jaguar introduced their new medium-sized saloon in September 1955. Suddenly such people discovered that there was a car that could convey them as fast from door to door as the traditional train and in as much comfort: small wonder the new Jaguars rapidly became known as the businessman's express. In time they would also become genuinely classless cars as bank robbers found their performance equally appealing . . .

But it was economy more than performance that was the theme of the first of these cars, because demand was still exceptionally strong for the big Jaguar saloons. As a result, it had a smaller version of the original XK engine, with the stroke shortened to 76.5mm to give it a capacity of 2,483cc. This affected the engine in a number of ways. It was more compact with an overall height 3ins shorter than the 3.4-litre unit, which weighed 50-lb more, and needed only a 9-inch single dry plate clutch. Because of the shorter stroke, it could be revved harder, producing 112bhp at 5,750rpm with an A type cylinder head and twin Solex carburettors. It also had softer 0.3125-inch- lift camshafts which helped produce 140lb/ft of torque low down at 2,000rpm. But none of this did much for the fuel consumption, which was about the same as an overdrive Mark VII—20mpg on average.

Nevertheless, the early Mark I saloon, as it was known, was far more nimble than the bulky Mark VII and became more appealing to the sporting motorist. It was notably smaller than the Mark VII, with an 8ft 11.375-inch wheelbase, overall length of 15ft 0.75ins, width of 5ft 6.75ins and height of 4ft 9.5ins. Oddly, the front track, at 4ft 6.625ins, was a good deal wider than that at the rear which was 4ft 2.125ins. This crab-tracked layout had been dictated by Lyons's insistence on using full-sized wheelspats like those on the Mark VII. Steel wheels with a 4.5-inch rim width were fitted as standard.

The body itself represented a breakthrough for Jaguar in that it was their first really modern one. It featured unitary construction in which the bodyshell took over the role of the traditional chassis, providing the mounting points for all the running gear besides accommodating the occupants. The chief advantages were that it provided a far stiffer and more efficient backbone to the car, which meant that softer suspension could be used for an improved ride and handling. It also helped enable the overall weight of the Mark I to be reduced considerably to 27cwt. The disadvantages were that unitary bodyshells cost more to prepare for production, which meant that the styling could not be changed too often. Lyons, however, was confident that his styling—which showed a strong frontal resemblance to the equally-new XK140 sports car with influences of the big saloon and sports car at the back—was good enough to stay in production for a long time. This was certainly true with these new saloons.

One of the main problems in designing such a bodyshell was that engineers did not know what they could get away with—so they made the first ones far heavier than they need have been because they did not want anything to fail under stress. This fear of the unknown was particularly well illustrated on the Mark I saloons by the extreme thickness of the roof pillars, and the fact that a sunroof was never offered as a factory option.

In essence this brave new bodyshell retained a

The early Mark I saloon was distinguished by a slim radiator grille. This example, driven by Roger Hurt, was pictured winning class B in the Pre-1965 Classic Saloon Car series at Castle Combe in May, 1985.

perimeter chassis in that two channel sections ran from the front of the car to the rear wheel arches, with transverse crossmembers, and the steel floorpan welded to them to make a rigid platform. The roof, supported by its substantial pillars, with inner wings, front and rear, and connecting box section sills, then provided a sturdy frame for the outer panels, which further stiffened the structure.

The front suspension was basically the same as that on the Mark VII except that it used coil springs rather than torsion bars because Jaguar's engineers were not confident that they could provide a sufficiently strong anchorage for the bars in a unitary bodyshell. The coils were located in steel turrets which provided the top wishbone mountings, and seated on the bottom wishbones which were also linked to an anti-roll bar. The turrets were part of a massive subframe which included the bottom wishbone mountings and

spread the load over a wide area of the floorpan. The recirculating ball steering gear was also carried on this subframe.

Jaguar were jealous of their reputation for building smooth, sweetly-performing cars, and feared that the unitary bodyshell might react to sound and vibration like a big steel drum. So apart from using a lot of soundproofing material, they used rubber blocks to insulate any moving parts from the shell. These blocks were used to support the engine, transmission and front subframe and meant that the steering column had to incorporate two universal joints so that the subframe could move. Happily, this also allowed the steering column to fold up under severe frontal impact, anticipating modern safety legislation by many years.

The rear springs were also mounted in rubber insulating blocks—but in a thoroughly unconventional manner. Again Jaguar's engineers were worried about the stresses involved with a unitary shell. So, rather than risk problems between the two widely-separated points needed for conventional half-elliptic springs, they turned the springs upside down and clamped half their length to the false chassis in the floorpan ahead of the rear axle. This made the springs effectively quarter-elliptic and meant that radius arms and a Panhard rod—again rubber-mounted—were needed to locate the axle. Similar mountings were used for Girling telescopic shock absorbers located by the axle casing and the tops of the wheelarches.

The interior trim was substantially the same as that which would be introduced on the Mark VIIM and was only noticeably smaller at the back.

The original Mark I radiator grille was based on that of the XK140 sports car produced at the same time, which had also adopted the heavier bumpers that made their debut on the Mark VII.

The headroom was virtually the same as that in the big saloon although the new car was far lower and more aerodynamic because its body did not have to sit on top of a chassis.

Two Mark I models were listed, a standard edition and a Special Equipment. Few, if any, standard cars were made because demand was so strong that customers were willing to pay extra for the special equipment: a rev counter, rear armrest, screen washers, foglamps, cigar lighter and heater. Overdrive also became a popular option, which, in conjunction with the 4.55:1 Salisbury rear axle, gave an overall ratio of 3.54:1.

Although the Mark I sold well in its 2.4-litre form outside the United States, there was a strong demand for tuning gear to improve its performance.

Despite its slim tail, the Mark I saloon had a good-sized luggage boot, as demonstrated by Ron Faulkner's 3.4-litre version in the 1958 RAC Rally.

The interior of the Mark I saloon – in this case an early 2.4-litre left-hand-drive version – was furnished along the traditional lines established by the contemporary Mark VIIM.

Initially, the factory listed a stage one conversion with improved carburettor settings—made standard in November 1956—and a straight-through silencer which 119bhp; a stage two with high-lift cams and a new distributor which produced 131bhp, and stage three, with the B type head, 1.75-inch SU carburettors, the stage two distributor, and a dual exhaust which was good for 150bhp. A stronger clutch was needed with stage three, and close-ratio gears, stiffer dampers, a stiffer anti-roll bar, and a high-ratio steering box were also available.

Detail modifications included reinforcements to the Panhard rod mountings by dealers from May 1956 after a spate of breakages on hard-driven cars. Complaints of high fuel consumption on non-overdrive cars were countered the following month by raising the rear axle ratio to 4.27:1, although overdrive cars retained the existing 4.55:1 crown wheel and pinion. Jaguar also began to offer after-market overdrive conversions as a complete kit. Then, in July 1956, cars ordered with an overdrive—which meant practically every one— were fitted with closer gearbox ratios to improve acceleration. The shock absorbers were uprated at the same time and a crankshaft damper fitted the following month, costs which were alleviated by fitting a cheaper steel sump from November 1956.

Although the 2.4-litre Mark I was well received in Europe, it did not get the same reception in the vital American export market. Fuel consumption was less important there than whether or not a car had automatic transmission—which was not considered suitable by the manufacturers

at that time with the high-revving 2.4-litre engine. So Jaguar decided to produce a 3.4-litre Mark I with the American market specifically in mind. When the car made its debut in February 1957, it performed so well they found they had a runaway success in all markets!

The engine, carburettors, 10-inch clutch and choice of manual or automatic transmission, were lifted direct from the Mark VIII saloon, with an adaptation of its twin exhaust system. Automatic transmission had not been offered initially on the 2.4-litre Mark I because of a potentially embarrassing lack of performance when compared with

Later versions of the 2.4-litre Mark I used the same bodyshell as the 3.4-litre variant introduced in 1957, which featured a new, wider, radiator grille. This car, driven by Colin Lane in the Pre-1957 Classic Saloon Car race at Brands Hatch in November 1977 leads one of its contemporary rivals, the Mercedes 220S of Philip Wicke.

the 3.4-litre cars. As it was, a new rear axle had to be made up for the 3.4-litre Mark I from the heavier Mark VIII centre section with 2.4-litre ends and the 3.54:1 ratio as standard, or a 3.77 for overdrive cars, with an optional close-ratio gearbox on either model. The automatic gearbox was longer than the manual edition, which meant that a divided propeller shaft had to be fitted.

A larger radiator was used because of the more restricted space underbonnet raised the engine operating temperature. As a result, the front end of the car was restyled around a wider radiator grille that made it look very much like the new XK150 sports car. Such changes usually start a chain reaction, and in this case it meant abandoning the built-in foglights.

Divided bench type front seats were fitted as

The wider grille used on the later model Mark I saloons was based on that introduced at the same time on the XK150 sports car – which assumed an almost identical appearance from the front. These examples of the XK150 were pictured at an American concours during the 1970s.

standard on cars with the automatic transmission and as an option on models with a manual gearchange. An interesting detail feature was the use of a quadrant mounted in the centre of the parcel shelf to house the automatic gearbox controls. The idea proved attractive to Jaguar as a money saver

The Mark I saloon's traction was improved when the optional limited-slip differential was fitted. Despite being hurled round the famous original Woodcote corner at Silverstone on the limit of adhesion in 1961, wheelspin is not evident on these hard-pressed cars. The leading car, a Mark I, can be easily distinguished from the Mark II that followed *(left)* by the thicker windscreen pillars, and sidelights mounted in the middle of the front wings rather than on top.

because they did not have to change the controls for left-hand-drive and right-hand-drive cars. It was just the sort of thing you would expect to find in a large American sedan where gearbox controls were a distinct afterthought.

As it turned out, the use of this sort of control was a total misjudgment because Jaguar Mark I buyers, whether or not they opted for an automatic gearbox expected their new car to look like a sports saloon.

They also expected it to stop like one and it was soon discovered that now the Mark I was capable of 120mph, it ran into severe brake cooling problems. Jaguar tried to alleviate this problem initially by fitting cutaway spats (standardised on both models) and offering the option of 60-spoke

wire wheels, which had a wider, competition-orientated, 5-inch rim width. But they did not do enough to cool the brakes and the disc brakes fitted all round on the XK150—and later the Mark IX—soon became an option. In fact, the disc brakes were so much better that very few 3.4-litre Mark Is were fitted with drums.

As supplies of the original narrow-radiator front wings ran down, production costs were reduced by standardising on the 3.4-litre bodyshell for both models from September 1957. Then, as the higher-powered Mark I began to dominate saloon

Eventually firms such as Vicarage, based in the Midlands, found it worthwhile to almost completely remanufacture the Mark II saloon, it was held in such high regard by classic car enthusiasts.

Daimler's neat little V8 engine soon found a home in the Mark II bodyshell to give Jaguar another marketing option.

car racing a Thornton Powr-Lok limited-slip differential was offered as an option from mid-1958; this did a lot to improve traction. In company with the other Jaguars, larger ball joints were fitted to the front suspension during 1958, with stronger 72-spoke wire wheels when that option was specified. Dunlop had not considered it worth their while tooling up for such wheels earlier, until they had a big enough market with the powerful new Jaguar saloon and sports cars, and the Austin-Healey 100-Six.

Then eventually, towards the end of the year, the 2.4-litre Jaguar was also offered with automatic transmission.

New 'quick-change' disc pads were fitted to all models from January 1959 and the standard XK engine modifications—a half-inch fan belt and pulley and lead-indium crankshaft bearings—appeared on all Mark Is midway through 1959, along with the electric rev counter.

But by then the stage was set for a far more dramatic transition in October to one of Jaguar's greatest classics, the Mark II saloon. Quite simply, it kept everything that was good about the Mark I and improved everything that could receive atten-

tion at the time. The two most obvious changes could be seen in the far greater glass area that resulted from using slimline roof pillars, and the much wider, 4ft 5.375-inch track, rear axle. Rapidly advancing research into unitary body stressing had revealed that the slimmer pillars were just as strong as the wider ones and highly-desirable because they improved vision so much. New door pressings were needed, so the opportunity was taken at the same time to make the windows between 1.25ins and 1.5ins deeper, which made the interior far more airy.

Now that Sir William Lyons had been persuaded that full-size spats were not a vital styling aid, the rear track could be increased by 3.5ins increase to make the car look far better as well as improve stability. The front suspension's roll centre was also raised to a point 3.25ins above ground level, which, in keeping with the wider rear axle, made the Mark II a good deal more manageable than the earlier car. Detail styling revisions included a slightly different radiator grille, a reversion to built-in foglights, and sidelamps on top of the front wings.

The interior followed established Jaguar practice, although the dashboard, in particular, was completely redesigned to site the speedometer and rev counter ahead of the driver, rather than in the centre, and the automatic gearchange controls assumed a far more sporting position on the steering column. This was the first time that Jaguar had been able to use a far more logical layout in a production car because of the necessity of saving money by using as many common parts as possible in export and home markets. Happily, the heater was given a greater volume at the same time.

A choice of three engines was offered in 2.4-litre, 3.4-litre and 3.8-litre capacities. They all used B type heads, which took the 2.4 up to 120bhp at 5,750rpm with 144lb/ft of torque at 2,000rpm, the 3.4 remaining at 190bhp and the 3.8 giving 220bhp at 5,500rpm with 240lb/ft of torque at 3,000rpm in keeping with the Mark IX. A Powr-

Detail styling changes – such as the radiator grille and badges – were all that distinguished the new Daimler saloon from the Mark II Jaguars, although the difference could rarely be felt from behind the wheel, especially in the handling.

Lok limited-slip differential was fitted as standard to the 3.8-litre car (with a slightly higher first gear ratio) and remained an option on the others. Power-assisted steering, like that fitted to the Mark IX, was also offered as an option on export cars before making its home debut in the Mark II a year later. There was such a performance gap between the 2.4-litre cars now they had a heavier bodyshell, however, that Jaguar stopped exporting them to the United States, along with the 3.4-litre Mark II. There was sound marketing logic here: Jaguars sold on their exclusivity in America as

Economy measures led to the adoption of slimline bumpers for all Mark II variants from late in 1967. This 340 was typical in that it retained the old twin foglights, which were normally deleted on the cheaper, but visually similar, 240.

much as their performance and character, and top-of-the-range models were more profitable than the economy editions.

Fittings were constantly updated on the Mark II range, although there were few major changes in the first six years. The 3.4-litre and 2.4-litre engines proved well-developed, so they remained substantially the same, while the 3.8-litre needed a lot of detail attention to combat a high oil consumption. These included fitting the revised rear crankshaft cover, shared with the Mark IX, from January 1960 to improve sump sealing and the new water pump. The combined handbrake and low brake fluid warning light appeared at the same time. Stiffer shock absorbers were fitted to all

The 340 retained the earlier dual exhaust, whereas the cut-price 240 had a single-outlet system.

models soon after, followed by an oil pressure gauge with revised readings specially applicable to the XK engine from March 1960. The recalibration moved the normal running mark of 40psi nearer to the middle than its earlier position around the bottom.

The first signs of California's clean-air campaign were also seen in the replacement of the SU carburettor cars' oil bath air filter with a modern paper element, and the re-routing of crankcase breathers into the carburettors.

The indicator switch and overdrive stalk—where applicable—swopped sides to a more conventional left and right-hand location in June 1960, and then the heater was further modified to prevent unwanted hot air entering the interior when it was turned off! The width of the standard disc wheels was increased to 5in three months later.

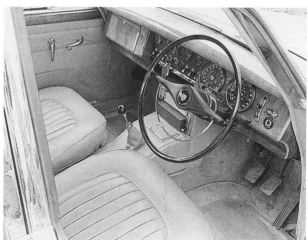

More rigid ribbed cam covers were fitted to the new range of Mark II variants, as in the case of this 240 engine.

For all its price-cutting measures, the interior of the 240 lost little of its traditional Jaguar appeal.

Then the accelerator pedal was changed to an organ type in November and the steering column lowered to give more room for adjustment. The power steering pump and SU fuel pump were also updated, along with the brake fluid reservoir, which was now made from plastic rather than glass.

Problems with oil loss from XK engines in cars parked facing up steep hills—like those in the prime export territory of San Francisco—led to a modified crankshaft rear cover being fitted from January 1961.

Handling received attention the following month with the standardisation of the stiffer anti-roll bar and the substitution of more rigid forged wishbones for the former pressed items. The engine oil dipstick then got a tubular guide before the lubrication system generally was improved in June 1961 with a larger oil pump and new sump. Further attempts were made to reduce oil leakage six months later by using an asbestos rope rear crankshaft seal before the 3.8-litre engine's consumption was cut dramatically by fitting the pistons with Brico Maxiflex scraper rings from September 1962. Nevertheless, it proved possible to improve it further with another new sump and oil pump in January 1964, and revised pistons in the 3.8-litre engine

that eased the passage of oil back to the sump.

Meanwhile the handbrake had been made more effective in August 1961 by incorporating a self-adjusting mechanism, with water deflectors for the front hubs at the same time. Larger and stronger universal joints appeared in the propeller shaft from December that year before sealed-for-life units were adopted in September 1963. Seat belt mounting points had been welded into the bodyshell in January 1962, and a high-output dynamo, available as an option chiefly on police cars, was fitted as standard from October 1963. Drilled camshafts were adopted for all engines from May 1962 to reduce noise when starting from cold.

A further option on the Mark II theme then became available in November 1962. Jaguar had taken over the British Daimler company two years earlier when they needed to expand production but could not get permission to extend the Brown's Lane factory. Part of the package was a 2.5-litre V8 engine used in the Daimler Dart sports car. This was an especially interesting unit because it produced more power and torque than the 2.4-litre XK, and weighed 1.25cwt less, because it was far more compact and used a lot of aluminium alloy in its construction. The only real disadvantage was

The upholstery remained as sumptuous as ever in appearance, despite the substitution of synthetic Ambla material for the now-optional leather.

that it needed heavy investment in new tooling if it was to be produced in large numbers. So the decision was taken to market it as a more exclusive version of the 2.4-litre Mark II, using the same bodyshell and similar running gear.

The engine, inspired by a very successful Triumph vee-twin motor cycle unit, was based on a 90-degree cast iron cylinder block with a bore and stroke of 76.2mm by 69.25 giving 2,548cc. Aluminium alloy was used for the lower half of the crankcase and for the cylinder heads, which carried pushrods and rockers operated from a single camshaft high in the centre of the block. Ultralightweight valve gear enabled it to use 7,000rpm, producing 140bhp at 5,800rpm and 155lb/ft of torque at 3,600rpm on twin SU carburettors, nestling, with the dynamo in between the cylinder heads. Few modifications were needed to accommodate the engine in the Mark II bodyshell, simply a reshaped sump to clear the front suspension crossmember and set bolts rather than studs to secure the cylinder heads so that they could be removed while the engine was in the car. The only

real problem could be seen in the very complex twin exhaust system, which ran from the outside of the cylinder banks all around the Mark II's floorpan.

A new and more sophisticated automatic transmission was fitted as standard because the model would retail at a price bracket between that of the 2.4-litre saloon and the 3.4-litre. This was the Borg Warner Model 35, which provided full engine braking in each gear range although it suffered from rather jerky engagement. This more compact gearbox not only saved weight, but it was more compact than the earlier gearbox, which meant that a smaller transmission tunnel could be fitted. This allowed the Daimler's front seat to be extended forward to form a split bench which could accommodate three people at a pinch. Legroom at the back was increased by making the new front seat squabs thinner and deleting the picnic tables.

There was now far less weight over the front wheels, so softer springs and dampers were fitted, making the manual steering variants the best-handling cars in the Mark II range. They had a 52/48 per cent weight distribution against the 55/45 of the 2.4-litre Mark II and 58/42 of the 3.4-litre. The high-revving engine allowed Jaguar's 4.55:1

Detail fittings such as the opening rear quarter light frames and catches were still chromium-plated.

And the door handles and window winders were works of engineering art compared to the plastic fittings which followed on later cars.

optional rear axle to be fitted as standard and helped make the acceleration notably better than that of the 2.4-litre Jaguar Mark II. Otherwise, apart from a traditional Daimler fluted radiator grille, different badges and colour schemes, and the designation Daimler 2½-litre V8, the models were identical.

All right-hand-drive cars had received sealed beam headlights in September 1962 and a weak point, the body's Panhard rod mounting bracket, was further strengthened in January 1963. At the same time, rear-seat footroom in the Jaguars was improved by paring away the bottoms of the front seats and the centre button on the steering column of all Mark IIs was made to work with the horn ring from October 1963.

Renewed attempts to improve the XK engine's cooling had been started in March 1963. First the blow-off pressure of the radiator cap was increased to 9psi, then, when a more efficient water pump was fitted from September 1963, it reverted to 7psi. Further modifications resulted in a 4psi cap in May 1964 before a new radiator and fan cooling appeared in December 1965.

In the meantime, the Daimler V8 had been made much more economical by fitting the 2.4-litre Jaguar's higher, 4.27:1, rear axle ratio from January 1964 at the expense of some of the superior acceleration. Later that year, a new, more sophisticated Borg Warner model 35 gearbox was fitted across the entire range, offering Drive One and Drive Two ranges that gave the option of a sporting performance using all three ratios in the first range or a very smooth one using just the top two in the second range.

Detail changes to all Mark IIs at this time included fitting nylon washers in the front suspension and grease nipples to the front wheel bearings of disc-wheeled cars.

The Mark II saloons—with the exception of the Daimler—then came in for a major change when they were brought into line with the rest of the Jaguar range by substituting a new all-synchromesh four-speed gearbox for the earlier Moss unit. This had a much lighter and more pleasant gearchange which was matched by a diaphragm clutch with a self-adjusting slave cylinder.

Only normally-unseen items like the jack on the 240 began to look mundane.

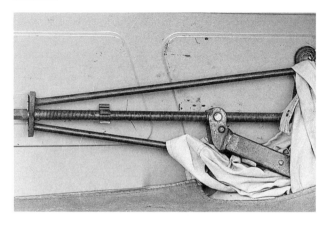

Jaguar's proud mascot still sat on the bonnet top of the 240.

By 1966, however, Britain was in the grips of a credit squeeze and Jaguar sales looked vulnerable. Cost-cutting exercises resulted in Ambla plastic upholstery being used as standard on the Mark II from September 1966, with leather as an extra—although very few of the higher-priced Daimlers had Ambla. Marles Varamatic steering for power-assisted models was a definite improvement from July 1967, however. The overall ratio varied from 4.25 turns from lock to lock in the straight ahead position to only half that at half lock, making it feel more like a car with conventional steering.

Major revisions were then made two months later when the 3.8-litre Mark II was dropped—there was, by now, a similar 4.2-litre all independently-sprung Jaguar saloon—and the 2.4-litre, 3.4-litre and Daimler became the 240, 340 and V8 250. Outwardly, the chief difference between these cost-cutting models were cheaper slimline bumpers and grilles to replace the foglights on the Jaguars and pressed steel wheels as standard.

Suddenly the economy model became a front-line sales proposition especially as it could be priced at £1,300 or so against the £1,700–£1,900 it would cost for a larger model. Performance needed to improve, however, so Jaguar did it the cheapest way they could, using existing components. The 240's engine was taken nearer to the Daimler V8's output by fitting a straight-port head like that of the 4.2-litre, with twin 1.75-inch SU carburettors and a twin exhaust. This saved money on development and took the engine up to 133bhp at 5,500rpm with 146lb/ft of torque at 3,700rpm by courtesy of a twin-pipe exhaust system.

A more modern negative earth electrical system with an alternator replacing the dynamo appeared on all models with new ribbed cam covers for XK engines, along with a paper element air filter for the 240 and twin air filters for the Daimler to improve carburettor accessibility.

Automatic 240s and 340s also received the Borg Warner 35 transmission and, from February 1967, a few V8 250 Daimlers were fitted with the all-synchromesh manual Jaguar gearbox. These were invariably fitted with overdrive as an optional extra, so that they could use the earlier 4.55:1 final drive to improve acceleration without compromising top speed and fuel consumption. At the same time, the Daimler's trim was brought more into line with that fitted to other models with that badge by using a padded top rail on the dashboard, heated rear screen and reclining front seats. These seats and the other features, which were not available on the more basic 240, established the Daimler as a more upmarket model.

A dozen or so customers also managed to obtain 340s fitted with 3.8-litre engines, and a variety of extras like limited-slip differentials, by special order from the factory, although these variants were never listed. The 240 and 340 then stayed in production until they were replaced by the sensational new XJ6 in 1968 and the Daimler variant lingered for another year in right-hand-drive form until there was a Sovereign version of the XJ.

The Luxury liners

By the late 1950s, it became evident that the existing big Jaguar saloons were becoming too dated in concept to sell well in their most important market—North America. Rival cars from Detroit were becoming ever longer and lower, which meant that Jaguar had to follow suit. Sir Williams Lyons' answer was one of his most adventurous cars, the controversial Mark X. Not only was it 5.5ins longer at 16ft 10ins, on the same 10-ft wheelbase, but it was 3ins wider, the overall width of 6ft 4ins making the widest car produced in Britain at the time. The effect was made all the more dramatic by the fact, at 4ft 6.75ins, it was far lower. Many Europeans tended to find such dimensions intimidating, although Americans were expected to love them.

The Mark X was the most technically-advanced car Jaguar had produced when it was launched in October 1961, and it heralded a new range of saloons that would continue into the 1990s. Apart from the unitary bodyshell, the chief new feature was the rear suspension. This was an independent system that had been developed in the E type sports car introduced seven months earlier. Although the track was far wider, at 4ft 10ins, the basic layout was the same. It used double-jointed shafts from a final drive mounted centrally in a subframe as the top links, with a tubular wishbone underneath linking the central mounting to hub carriers. Single radius arms each side provided additional location, with coil spring damper units in front and behind the driveshafts linking the wishbones and top of the transverse subframe. Brake discs were mounted inboard on either side of the final drive to reduce unsprung weight. The differential contained in the final drive was a Powr-Lok like that used in the Mark II saloon, although the casing was new. The subframe and forward ends of the radius arms were attached to the body by rubber mountings which insulated the shell from noise and vibration. This new suspension was an essential advance, not only in that it improved the ride and handling, but because it would be capable of efficiently transmitting far more power and torque. Jaguar were already visualising V8 and V12 engines as American competitors produced ever more powerful units.

The Coventry factory took advantage of the Mark X's great width to provide an engine bay that could take almost anything, even two XK units mounted in V-formation on a common crankcase. Once it had been decided that the accent would be on power rather than economy—America was still enjoying very cheap fuel—overall weight was of secondary importance. So the Mark X's bodyshell was massively strong, based around two sills 7in deep and 7ins wide. They were connected by a floorpan braced by equally-strong box sections and a deep transmission tunnel, further reinforcement being provided by a boxed-in front bulkhead and rear seat pressing. The rear suspension's subframe was supported by massive rear wheel arches linked by the luggage boot floor with hefty box-sections running forward to support the engine and front suspension mounting beam. These parts were reinforced by inner wings and passenger footwells to make a structure so strong that the roof was of little importance and the door openings could be exceptionally generous. The width of the doors, 3ft 4.5ins at the front and 2ft 7.5ins at the back, helped compensate for the depth of the sills.

The opportunity was taken when designing this new bodyshell to improve the heating system by ducting in fresh air from a scuttle vent past a Marston heat exchanger and out through four vents, two at the front and two at the back. A cooling effect was

The sheer size of the Mark X is well illustrated by this picture of a prototype being assembled at Jaguar's Brown's Lane factory before the model was launched in 1961.

possible when the air was diverted past the heat exchanger, but it was still not possible to vary the actual heating output. But two electric fans were used to boost the throughput with opening quarter lights for additional ventilation.

In common with the Mark II, the outer body panels were welded to the inner structure, but they had a far more futuristic look. Although the low flowing wing lines marked a complete departure from the earlier styling, a Jaguar family resemblance was maintained by the roofline, windows and wide radiator grille. A neat four-headlamp system and new slim-line bumpers helped break up the mass of bodywork. An exceptionally large luggage boot, with petrol tanks either side concealed in the wings, was aimed directly at the American market. Sir William Lyons also achieved considerable satisfaction by incorporating elements of his original full-sized rear spats in the rear wheel arch line, finally arriving at an exceptionally neat compromise between the conflicting demands of fashion and practicality. The low lines of the Mark X were also made more practical by the use of new 14-inch wheels with unusually wide 5.5-inch rims, fitted with 7.50-14 tyres.

Because the engine bay was so wide it was possible to fit the E type's 3.8-litre XK engine equipped with three 2-inch SU carburettors, a feat which could only be achieved in the Mark 2 series by cutting away the offside inner wing. This engine was rated at 265bhp, giving the two-ton Mark X a very good performance for its day: around 120mph flat out with a 12-second 0–60mph time, achieved at the expense of 14mpg. Manual transmission was offered as an option to the normal Borg-Warner automatic change, the four-speed box being normally fitted with an overdrive.

Wishbones and coil springs like those of the Mark II saloon were used at the front, but mounted in a subframe, like the new back suspension, to reduce noise and vibration. The braking system was based on that of the E type, using 10.75-inch discs at the front with 10-inch ones at the back with a servo made by Dunlop under licence from Kelsey-Hayes in America using a bellows to exert mechanical pressure on the master cylinder. The hydraulic circuits were doubled up for safety. Power-assisted steering was carried over from the Mark IX with a ratio that gave 4.5 turns from lock to lock.

The interior followed the new lines established by the Mark II although everything, like the dashboard, was on a far grander scale. Strong American influences were shown in the front seats, however, which amounted to a split bench with reclining backrests. They were fine while the Mark X was cruising sedately, but provided little support when it was driven vigorously. Traditional Jaguar touches included picnic trays and vanity mirrors let into the backs of the front seats and new features took in the option of electric window lifts with individual controls on each door, with grouped switching for the driver on the centre console.

Detail specifications were changed throughout the production run along with the Mark II saloons and the E type. But the first individual change was a heated rear window from January 1962. Larger wheel cylinders were fitted to the hard-pressed brakes from July 1962 with thicker discs in January 1963. The brakes had proved perfectly capa-

The new big Jaguar was as long and low as it was wide – as can be seen from this profile shot of the later 420G version (outwardly the same as a Mark X except for the chrome swage line strip frequently added to earlier models).

ble of arresting two tons, but would now last longer. Larger capacity dampers were fitted at the same time for the same reason and an improved radiator two months later after premature failures. New heater controls were also fitted in March 1963 which meant that the scuttle vent could now be opened separately.

In the meantime, Jaguar was trying to cater for European tastes by developing a more luxurious version of the Mark II saloon, effectively combining many of the new features of the Mark X in the existing package. These new S type saloons introduced in October 1963 with twin carburettor versions of the 3.4-litre and 3.8-litre engine used the new independent rear suspension, a narrower edition of the Mark X tail, Mark X interior features and the slim-line bumpers.

Active attempts were made to promote the S type as a new exclusive form of Jaguar in the United States by substituting the 3.4-litre Mark II for the 3.8-litre and exporting only 3.8-litre editions of the S type, often embellished with extras like wire wheels and whitewall tyres.

Outwardly, the S types looked very much like a Mark II with an enlarged boot to give an overall length of 15ft 7ins against 15ft 0.75ins. But the new rear suspension had a slightly wider track, at 4ft 6.25ins, partly because the wheels were fatter, with 5.5-inch rims. Less obvious changes to the bodyshell included a revised roofline that gave more headroom in the back and needed a more upright rear window. Thinner seats and more reclined rear squabs created more room in the back at the same time. Sheet metal changes included extending the box section beams on which the Mark II's back springs were mounted over the wheel arches and under the luggage boot floor. The boot floor was reinforced along with the wheel arches in the manner of the Mark X with further stiffening being provided by built-in wheel fairings, rather than detachable spats, on the outer panels. The rear suspension, final drive and brakes that bolted in with their subframe were of identical layout to the Mark X and E type, varying only in dimensions, spring and damper rates. The front suspension came directly from the Mark II, however, although the steering ratio was decreased to 3.5 turns from lock to lock when power-assistance was specified. This was to make it feel 'more European in character'.

Although the S types weighed around 3 cwt more than the equivalent Mark II, they shared the same gear ratios, because it was felt that the people who bought them would rate comfort before ultimate performance. All the same, the 2.4-litre engine was not offered as an option because the performance would then suffer too much.

The cooling system of the Mark X came in for more development in January 1964 when another new radiator was fitted, with a separate header tank like that in the E type, and revised plumbing, after air lock problems were experienced in hot climates. Sealed-for-life units replacing the driveshaft grease nipples were fitted at the same time, with parallel modifications to those in the

Once more, the interior of the Mark X was so vast that it could be readily adapted for a limousine version.

3.8 litre Mark II engine and cooling system after that.

The Mark X was then fitted with a 4,235-cc variant of the XK engine from October 1964, to provide more torque in competition with ever-bigger American engines. It used the same straight port cylinder head, but the block was modified to increase the bore to 92.07mm. This was quite a squeeze and was achieved only by staggering the bores around the original centre line. Besides new pistons, the engine needed a new crankshaft and although the power output remained the same as

The Jaguar S type used not only the new rear suspension pioneered by the Mark X and a similar bodyshell to that of the Mark II saloons, but styling features, such as the later slim line bumpers, and the small eyebrow cowls, sidelights and indicators from the Mark X. This example, driven by Dave and Veronica Woodgate, is competing in the Coronation Rally at Eppynt in 1984.

that of the 3.8-litre engine at 265bhp, total torque was raised by 23lb/ft to 283.

Despite the repeated radiator changes, over-heating could still a problem, so the internal pro-file of the water jackets was improved when the block was modified, and another revised cooling system incorporated a more efficient water-heated inlet manifold. A viscous coupling fan was also fitted, which saved 14bhp at 3,000rpm.

The new all-synchromesh gearbox was phased in at the same time, at first on the Mark X and E type only. But it was listed as an option on the S type from December 1964, and fitted as standard from March 1965 when supplies had built up. All automatic versions of the Mark X received the new Borg Warner Model 8 transmission from October 1964, however, with the Varamatic power-assisted steering that eventually appeared on the Mark II in 1967. A more modern negative earth electrical

system using an alternator was fitted at the same time, with a pre-engaged Lucas starter motor for improved operation in cold weather. This had been available earlier, but could not be fitted until the gearbox casting had been revised. A conventional servo operating direct on the hydraulic lines replaced the Kelsey-Hayes unit which had been heavily criticised outside America for removing all feeling from the brake pedal. Stronger calipers with a larger pad area further improved braking, and the road wheels had to be slightly reshaped to clear the necessary new plumbing.

The Mark X's heating was much improved by modifying the controls so that hot air and cold could be mixed, with a new option of full air conditioning. This was provided by a Delaney Gallay system using an evaporator unit in the luggage boot

The similarities between the S type and Mark II saloons can be readily seen from these two 3.4-litre cars, driven by Robin Rudderham (right), and Dave Woodgate in the Jaguar Drivers' Club Pre-1968 Challenge at Silverstone in March 1987.

The Daimler limousine, based on the 420G floorpan and running gear, continued being made for 20 years after the original car went out of production.

The chief mechanical difference between the 420G and the Daimler limousine could be seen in the use of a twin-carburettor version of the 4.2-litre XK engine like that which powered the first Sovereign and 420.

with a refrigerator under the engine's radiator—which had to be of larger capacity with a different fan. By March 1966, this radiator and fan had become standard fittings on the Mark X, with the S type receiving the Mark II's revised radiator and fan cowling four months earlier.

The space this needed led to a lot of restyling when the range began to be rationalised around the 4.2-litre straight port engine from October 1966. The S types got a new frontal treatment along with the larger engine in twin carburettor 245-bhp form as the Jaguar 420, or Daimler Sovereign, while the Mark X—which already had plenty of room for the radiator—was slightly facelifted as the 420G (for Grand). But they all ended up looking very much alike with a four-headlamp system and square-shaped grilles, Daimler's traditional fluting being retained on the Sovereign. Jaguar could not afford to spend too much on these cars, however, with a completely new one on the way, so the 420 and Sovereign kept the Mark II bonnet.

But their interiors were revised along the Mark X lines transferred to the 420G, and Varamatic power steering was offered as an option, with air conditioning on all three. Changes for the bigger car were few: the 420G simply received chrome strips along the sides, indicator repeating lights and a grille like that of the 420. The wheel trims were modernised and the interior revised slightly in keeping with the changes to the 420 and Sovereign, while all models got an electric rev counter rather than the old cable-driven device.

Changes after that were few, being confined to those shared with the 240 and 340 engines, although the 420G's front suspension was mounted on a subframe from July 1968 in company with the new XJ6, which was about to be phased in. When it appeared two months later, the 420 disappeared, although the Sovereign stayed in production till August 1969 when stocks of a Daimler version of the XJ6 had built up enough to supply specialist dealers. The 420G carried on until June 1970, when XJ6 production got into full swing, but its floorpan and much of its running gear would live for 20 years or more.

This was because it would form the basis for a new limousine to replace special versions of the 420G, Daimler's Majestic Major—a throwback to days before the Jaguar takeover—and Austin's Princess, which was made by the same group when Jaguar became part of British Leyland in 1968. Before that, Jaguar's limousines had simply been top-of-the-range saloons with every optional extra, plus a division, and maybe a cocktail cabinet, let into the space liberated by a thinner front bench seat.

In 1968, however, Pressed Steel Fisher, which made the 420G bodyshell and had become part of British Leyland, sent floor pressings, the front bulkhead and wheelarches to Motor Panels, in Coventry, where an extra 1ft 9-inch section was let into the floorpan and sills behind the centre door pillar to give a wheelbase of 11ft 9ins. The floor was reinforced at the same time so that the sills could be

Jaguar enthusiast Graig Hinton's Classic Cars of Coventry concern received an enthusiastic response for open versions of the Mark X or 420G in the late 1970s but were unable to find enough donor cars and eventually Hinton relocated his operation in Florida.

cut down by 1.75ins around the rear doors to make entry and exit easier. The front bulkhead was extended upwards so that a new body, as big as that of the old Austin Princess, could be fitted to the floorpan. The latest through-flow ventilation was incorporated, with a separate header for the rear compartment. The running gear, except for an extended propeller shaft, came from the 420G, with other expensive items, like the bumpers, carried over from the standard bodywork. The overall dimensions—18ft 10in long, 5ft 3.75ins high, and 6ft 6.5ins wide—made the new eight-seater 43-cwt Daimler limousine one of the largest cars on the road.

It was painted and trimmed by the Vanden Plas coachworks in London, which has been responsible for the Austin Princess.

But at around one quarter the cost of a Rolls-Royce limousine, it was a bargain and an average of 10 per week were built.

Production was transferred to Coventry when Vanden Plas closed in 1979.

Classic Jaguar saloons – such as the Mark I, Mark II and S type – were cheap and plentiful in the late 1970s and early 1980s, so much so that many firms began to market bodyshells to enable the mechanical components to be used to make replicas of the sports racing cars which were rare and fetched far more money than the average enthusiast could dream of raising. Many of the kits were poorly designed and made, but one, made by Copycat, at Bolton, Lancashire, and pictured in 1984, was of exceptionally high quality. The replica space frame was so good that a moderately skilled person could fit the reconditioned running gear from an S type to make a car that was hard to tell apart from a real Jaguar C type and handled better because it had independent rear suspension. Eventually, supplies of scrap S types dwindled and Copycat adapted their kit to accept XJ6 parts, and moved into D type replicas ...

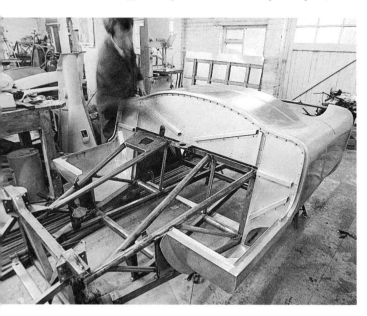

XJ for Excellent Jaguar

The XJs which replaced the rest of the range from September 1968 rapidly became the most successful saloons ever made by Jaguar. At the time of writing more than half a million had been made against 164,000 of the earlier medium-sized saloons and 72,000 larger ones. The concept of a slimmed-down 420G was the result of 50 years' work by Sir William Lyons. Not only was the styling and performance honed to a fine degree, but for the first time it was matched by the refinement of the ride and handling.

Most of the development work went into the bodyshell because this was the first new Jaguar since the Mark X, all other models having been adaptations of an earlier theme. The chief problem was that it had to be lower than the previous saloons for better air penetration and more modern styling. At the same time, ground clearance could not be reduced and the rigidity afforded by deep sills could not be sacrificed. Somehow Lyons and his engineers produced a package 1.625ins lower, 1.25ins longer and 3ins wider than the 420, making the overall dimensions 15ft 9.5ins long, 5ft 9.25ins wide and 4ft 6 ins high on a 9ft 0.75in wheelbase. Although the resultant car weighed 12 per cent less than the Mark X at 3,389lb dry (in the case of early models), it was even more rigid. This was achieved by treating the roof as a stressed member, well illustrating how much they had learned about unitary construction since the first relatively-clumsy efforts with the Mark I bodyshell 13 years earlier. Other aspects of the bodyshell layout were essentially the same as those on the 420G, especially in the area of the engine bay, which was wide enough to accept a V12 engine that had been under development for 20 years although the lower bonnet line needed a bulge to clear the XK unit's cam covers.

But the detail design was considerably different.

The centre section was made as strong as possible with equally massive side members, scuttle and rear seat pan pressings. But now the front and back extremities were not so rigid. This meant that an impact from either end was likely to leave the passenger area intact as the nose or tail crumpled. In addition, the engine was now mounted further forward, which meant that in the event of a severe head-on collision, it would be deflected downwards and away from the passenger cabin. The strong side members and doors—with burstproof locks—also helped protect the occupants, with fuel pipes routed well away from potential sources of impact. The twin 11.5-gallon petrol tanks were again contained in their own rear wing compartments, with recessed anti-burst filler caps.

It was also possible to fit a far more modern heating system in the new bodyshell. It incorporated face-level variable-direction and volume air ducts of a type that had been pioneered by Ford four years earlier. Extractor vents were fitted in the low pressure area below the rear window although front quarter lights were retained, officially for smokers, but, in reality in case anybody still complained about not being able to get enough fresh air without opening the main windows. In addition, automatic temperature control was maintained by a heat sensor, operated from the centre console.

Just as much effort went into the running gear. The rear suspension with its inboard disc brakes were almost identical to the 420G, with a track of 4ft 10.5ins only fractionally narrower. Although the front suspension followed similar lines to that of the 420 and 420G, it was now mounted on a large box section subframe like the rear, to reduce noise, vibration and harshness. This beam also supported the majority of the engine's weight, which further

Jaguar were proud of their heritage, which could be traced to the dawn of motoring following the acquisition of the Daimler marque and – with its use of the trendsetting XJ6 range – showed that they were also in the vanguard of technological development.

dampened road noise. It meant that anti-dive geometry had to be built into the front suspension now that it directly supported 53 per cent of the weight of what was a 32-cwt car, but resulted in the chassis engineers being able to reduce the front spring rates by 25 per cent to further improve the

ride. The tubular shock absorbers were also re-mounted outside the front coil springs to allow greater displacement and, consequently, better damping.

The far more efficient rack-and-pinion steering that had been used on the E type sports car since 1961 at last found its way into a Jaguar saloon. This was adapted by its makers, Adwest, to incorporate elements of the Varamatic system although it still came in for a lot of criticism from Europe in that it was far too lightly weighted towards American tastes. The actual rack ran behind the notional axle line for safety, which was enhanced by universal joints and a collapsible section built into the steering column.

Braking was further improved by fitting front calipers with triple cylinders to reduce fade and prolong pad life while the back remained the same with twinpot calipers and a separate caliper for the handbrake.

The most noticeable change from the outside—next to the revised lines—could be seen in the wheels and tyres. They were the largest yet seen on a Jaguar saloon with 6-inch rims and a 15-inch diameter. Dunlop had developed a special E70VR radial ply tyre from their SP Sport range which not only contributed immensely to the road-

holding, but remained reasonably quiet because it had a circumferentially irregular tread pattern which broke up resonance. Rivals like Mercedes and Rolls-Royce were left standing when Dunlop and Jaguar capitalised on the inherently better handling qualities of large radial ply tyres, and reduced noise and vibration to historically low levels at the same time.

Initially the XJ6 was listed with two engines, a 4.2-litre like that used in the 420 and a new 2.8-litre version to fall within tax laws in Europe which militated against larger capacities. Both engines had received a lot of attention to the cooling system, with a larger impeller for the water pump using a smaller pulley so that it turned faster, with revised passages in the straight port cylinder head aimed at evening out the temperature around inlet and exhaust valves.

Twin Zenith-Stromberg 175CD carburettors replaced the SUs in North American versions to meet new exhaust emission regulations. They were fitted with a complex anti-emission system involving the use of two inlet manifolds and throttles. This meant that when the car was driven at part-throttle, the fuel mixture went through the primary throttle, to a primary mixture pipe, by-passing the second throttle. Then it was warmed in a water-heated chamber before being returned to the intake manifold just downstream of the secondary throttle. At higher engine speeds, a bypass allowed a full charge of unheated mixture to enter the cylinders. This system ensured that the air and fuel mixture remained constant when delivered to the combustion chambers. It made it possible for a leaner mixture to be used and prevented the presence of wet fuel in the intake manifold, a major cause of exhaust fumes. An unfortunate side effect was that the engine ran hotter as a result. A transmission-controlled ignition retarder was also fitted to contain those obnoxious smells, along with

Great care went into making the front bay of the XJ6 wide enough to accept almost any engine, especially the proposed 12 cylinder power unit.

Innovative American safety legislation was at its height while the XJ6 was being designed and resulted in smooth-contours for crash protection in a revised interior.

Opening quarter lights were retained to improve ventilation, but were now fitted with twist-grip knobs near the recessed doorhandles to provide better protection for the occupants.

Electric window lifts became common fittings to the XJ saloon range. Operating switches were kept well out of harm's way, chiefly to meet American safety regulations.

a sealer tank system filtering vapour through a charcoal canister. Although Jaguar quoted a similar power output—246bhp at 5,500rpm—to that of 4.2-litre engines fitted with the simpler SU system, the reality would seem to indicate nearer 168bhp at 4,500rpm. This figure, although recorded on revised modern ratings, would still indicate that these engines were well down on power as a result of the emission equipment.

The 2,791-cc engine—built only for Europe—followed traditional XK patterns, being based on the old 2.4-litre unit rather than the 3-litre engine which had been raced with a conspicuous lack of reliability in the late 1950s. The problem with the 3-litre unit, which produced as much as 315bhp by dint of a competition head and high revs, was that the connecting rods ran at too wide an angle with an 88-mm stroke and 85-mm bore: so the time-honoured 83-mm piston diameter was retained on the new 2.8-litre engine to avoid the connecting rod trouble, along with a still rather long 86mm stroke.

This meant that revs had to be restricted to 6,000, with the result that it produced only 180bhp under the old ratings—with 182lb/ft of torque at 3,750rpm on twin 2-inch SU carburettors. Nevertheless, it was felt that this rather gutless engine would still be a vital attraction where road tax was high . . .

The lengths to which Jaguar had gone to reduce noise and vibration was well illustrated by the exhaust system on the car. The manifold downpipes fed into a siamese main pipe which eliminated the engine's characteristic beating note before entering two separate systems involving four silencers looped either side of the rear suspension. The overall result rivalled a Rolls-Royce for silence and sophistication . . .

The effort which had gone into improving the cylinder head cooling was reflected externally in a larger diameter bypass pipe leading to a new crossflow radiator with a separate header tank to help keep down the bonnet line. The 12-bladed plastic cooling fan was driven by a viscous coupling which allowed it to freewheel above 2,500rpm—by which time the radiator would be subject to ram air pressure. Cars fitted with automatic transmission had an oil cooler built into the bottom of the water radiator.

The relative lack of torque produced by the 2.8-litre unit led to a Model 35 Borg-Warner transmission being fitted to early automatic cars because it used all three ratios in the normal Drive option; whereas the Model 8 specified for the 4.2-litre cars used just the top two ratios for a smoother take-off. A 4.27:1 final drive ratio was offered on the 2.8-litre automatic cars to pep up the performance and it was also advertised on similar models fitted with a manual gearbox—from the 420—without overdrive.

Hardly any non-overdrive XJ6s were made, however: the only reason they were listed was to give a low basic price for advertisements, normal production line cars being fitted with an overdrive at extra cost. These overdrive gearbox cars had a lower (4.55:1) final drive with 3.77 for the 4.2-litre manuals. The initial demand for XJ6s with automatic gearboxes was so high that it was several months before the manual versions went into production.

The Jaguar – or Daimler – name did not appear anywhere on the new cars at first, with only a small badge on the rear bootlid to denote the engine size.

The interior was revamped along existing Jaguar lines with a number of safety features to meet new American legislation: these included reinforced front seat mountings with padding at the back of the seats to protect rear seat passengers thrown forward in an accident. The seat belt anchorages—still at the front only in 1968—were also strengthened and soon after production started, side-intrusion barrier sections were built into the doors of all 4.2-litre cars to meet U.S. safety standards. The same course was not followed with the 2.8-litre cars—which were not exported to North America—because the standards were already high and it was important to keep down the price and weight. The instrument panel of all cars was also fitted with an energy-absorbing surround and rocker-type switches replaced the glorious old toggles. A combined ignition and steering lock nestled behind the steering wheel in place of the earlier exposed key and button. The sun visors were softly padded and the rearview mirror got a snap-off mounting. Wheels replaced catches for quarter light operation with slimline window winders on cars without electric lifts. Hazard lights were also fitted with larger-area side-

The twin fuel tanks were fitted with burst-proof locking caps to combat potential fire damage resulting from rear-end impacts.

lamps and flashers—all showing the new XJ6 to be a far more modern car than the earlier saloons.

Air conditioning was available as an optional extra on de luxe versions of the XJ6 which were, in effect, the standard model. A cheaper basic 2.8-litre car with Ambla, instead of leather, upholstery, a slightly more spartan interior and no power

The rear faces of the front seats were well padded to protect back seat passengers in the event of an accident. Headrests were also fitted to the front seats as an option from August 1969 to combat the whiplash effect of frontal impacts.

Even the knave plates on the standard pressed steel wheels of the XJ6 carried just a Jaguar's head . . . Dunlop's E70VR radial ply tyre was designed specially for the car.

assistance for the steering, was listed but seemed to exist only in advertisements. But a few 4.2-litre cars were produced without power-assisted steering as police patrol cars.

The demand for Jaguar XJ6s continued at such a high level that it would be almost a year before a Daimler variant was offered. But when it made its appearance in August 1969 it was virtually the same car, except for a fluted radiator grille and different badging. In general, these Daimlers incorporated as standard most of the optional extras available for the Jaguars with the exception of air conditioning—and they were not sold in North America. The marque name was hardly known there and Jaguar did not consider it worth the expense of going through extensive duplicate safety tests for what would be few extra sales. In fact, it took the Jaguar a year to pass all the tests, and it was only late in 1970 that the XJ sedan as it was called was exported to the United States—and then only in the more profitable 4.2-litre form.

But once production got under way detail improvements were frequent. The front suspension was stiffened a little later in 1969 in an attempt to stop the tyres grounding on the wheel arches when the steering was locked hard over before new arches gave more clearance from October 1970; optional head rests were offered from August 1969 with inertia reel seat belts. At the same time, all 4.2-litre European cars got a 3.31:1 rear axle ratio and the 2.8 received a 4.09 in readiness for a new

Jaguar and Daimler versions of the XJ6 used the same bodyshell with only minor styling changes, reflecting the policy pursued on the 420 and earlier Sovereign.

Above: It was not until late in 1969 that the name Jaguar appeared on an XJ6, and then only when the new Sovereign was in production, with Daimler being substituted, where appropriate, on the door kickplates.

Borg Warner Model 12 automatic gearbox to be phased in on the European 4.2-litre during the next few months although it would be two years or more before all American cars changed from the old Model 8.

The Model 12 was a much stronger transmission that gave the automatic car acceleration more akin to the manual. New friction materials and a more sophisticated hydraulic system ensured smoother and more accurately-controlled changes. A new gear lever was employed, giving positive manual selection of the two lower ratios, and in

Below: The new four-carburettor overhead inlet manifold 12 cylinder power unit was not so highly tuned as the old straight six, but, naturally, occupied a lot more room underbonnet . . . so much so that the battery, in the bottom right hand corner of the picture, had to have a cooling fan let into the front of its retaining frame.

The wheels of the 12 cylinder cars needed better ventilation for the brakes than those used on the sixes.

addition to the kickdown there was a part-throttle downchange from third gear to second. Instead of a mechanical linkage, the control was now by a vacuum servo, which contained an aneroid for barometric correction at very high altitudes.

Heat shields were also fitted around the exhaust in November 1969 before door locks were improved, vents incorporated in the footwells and reflective brightwork replaced chrome instrument and scuttle vent trimming in the spring. But it would be October—well after the new Sovereign was on sale—before the name Jaguar or Daimler would at last appear on the car, discreetly incorporated in new aluminium door tread plates.

All XK engines received quieter-running camshafts in November 1969, followed by improved engine mountings and the standardisation of US emission manifolds in March 1970. The original camshaft sprocket adjuster then made a comeback after it was found that a new vernier system could strip its lobes. Heavier pistons were also fitted to 2.8-litre engines from June 1970 following a spate of failures in cars used gently for a couple of months and then taken on a long motorway run. This alleviated the problem caused by carbon deposits being heated up sufficiently by exhaust

valves very close to the pistons to burn holes in the crowns—but meant that the engine became more sluggish and from that point the 2.8-litre variant was doomed.

Soon after, a new brake fluid reservoir was fitted to all cars, and an improved crankshaft oil seal to the 2.8 from April 1971. A new three-piece rear bumper appeared at the same time to reduce repair costs, already held down by the use of bolt-on front wings and rear panels.

Sales of lengthened Mercedes saloons were going well, so Jaguar launched their longwheelbase version of the XJ6 in October 1972. This had an extra 4ins let into the rear passenger compartment and was listed as an option for all models, adding more than 100lb to the overall weight. The weight had already been increased considerably over that of the prototype models during production development and improvements were made to the effective power output of European models at the same time although official figures refused to confirm this. The overall impression was that the XK engine's horsepower figures were now a lot more accurate . . . On the road, the result was that, despite the considerable increase in weight, acceleration and top speed were hardly affected!

Facing page: The front bumpers of the series II XJ models (Daimler left, Jaguar right) were raised to meet new American regulations although the rear bumpers remained substantially unchanged.

Handling also felt much the same and the ride had been so good on the short-wheelbase cars that it seemed to make little difference in the new application. It is doubtful, however, whether the long-wheelbase option ever appeared on the 2.8-litre cars as declining sales were about to lead to them going out of production in April 1973.

The XJ12

Although the V12 Jaguar introduced in July 1972 amounted to only a combination of the new engine which had appeared in the E type the year before and a hardly-changed saloon bodyshell, it still caused a sensation because it went so well—proving capable of 145mph in great comfort at a time when few grand touring cars costing three times as much and offering only half the accommodation could match it.

It was a much less highly-tuned unit than the old twin cam six, even having forsaken the emotive hemispherical heads used at one stage of its development because of their weight and bulk. American pollution requirements kept a check on the tuning, too, and the resultant engine achieved a standard of silence and smoothness far ahead of the still-reasonable XK unit. The new engine was not much heavier either because it used an alloy cylinder block with single-cam flat-face heads. Jaguar had experimented with a cast iron block to deaden the sound, but rejected it when it turned out to be 116lb heavier than the alloy block. The water jackets were so large that the sound-absorbing properties of the alloy block were virtually the same as those of the cast iron equivalent. Weight over the front wheels had always been a problem with the XK engine, so the decision to opt for an alloy block was relatively easy, even though it cost more.

The single-cam heads had produced better torque than the twin cam versions below 5,000rpm and had a further great advantage in that the engine was not so wide that it reduced the turning space available for the front wheels. Whereas the XK engine needed inclined valves because it had a relatively long stroke, the new over-square unit had room in its heads for really big valves in a single line which meant that breathing was at least as good. Although these far simpler—and cheaper-to-produce—heads did not produce so much ultimate power as the hemispherical units, Jaguar were not worried: they simply increased the overall capacity to 5,343cc. This was achieved with a 90-mm bore and 70-mm stroke, giving a more than adequate 272bhp at 6,200rpm on a 9:1 compression ratio using the new readings that were the equivalent of 325bhp on the earlier scale. Torque readings of 349lb/ft at 3,800rpm were well able to match any American competitors. Subtle revisions to the compression ratio—running at 8:1 rather than 9:1—and consequent adjustments to the timing and carburettor settings, kept US versions within the American emission regulations, but reduced the overall power output to 241bhp at

A lot of changes were made to the interior of the series II XJ range, which, notably, included a far more advanced heating and ventilation system.

The underbonnet layout of the six-cylinder cars, however, remained virtually the same.

5,750rpm with only 285lb/ft of torque at 3,500rpm. Such was the cost of theoretically-clean air . . .

The cylinder banks were inclined at 60 degrees to each other to keep the engine reasonably narrow with weight and cost further reduced by using a single chain camshaft drive, which had the added advantage of being quieter. Each piston had a shallow depression in its crown, which formed the combustion chamber. The complete unit weighed only 680lb—against 600lb for a 4.2-litre XK—with all its bits and pieces other than the gearbox. The block was very heavily ribbed both internally and externally and the lower face of the block was 4ins below the crankshaft centre line to provide the maximum support and rigidity for the seven main bearings. Cast iron main bearing caps, each located by four bolts, provided great rigidity.

The only real difference between the engine that had been introduced in the E type sports car in 1971 and the one used in the XJ12 a year later could be seen in the sump. On the E type, it was a relatively orthodox unit, but on the saloon it had to be made quite flat to clear the front suspension crossmember, with a separate loop dropping down behind the crossmember. Whereas the sump on the E type was of die-cast aluminium, the XJ12 unit had to use a sandwich piece around the base of the cylinder block with a steel pressing as the main oil reservoir.

Special attention was paid to accessibility, with

the main auxiliaries either on top of the engine or within easy reach either side if they were too bulky. This meant that four of the horizontal Zenith 175CD emission control carburettors had to be placed outside the cylinder blocks because the more efficient downdraught carburettors would have demanded a higher bonnet line. They were located two either side and worked in conjunction with a new Lucas electronic ignition system called OPUS—for oscillating pick-up system. This was linked to a distributor but dispensed with the traditional make and break points, using a revolving disc with 12 sensors to trigger the necessary impulses for correct sparking. The idea was to eliminate problems caused by points wear, an important factor in controlling exhaust emissions.

North American versions of this engine would be fitted with air injection, using a pump driven from the nose of the crankshaft by a belt, with pipes located on top of the vee. Nozzles were located on the manifold side of the exhaust valves to inject air into the gas at the point of its highest temperature, resulting in the best burning characteristics. These provisions were backed up by heat transfer shields and hot air intakes which cut the emissions dramatically when the engine was started in cold air.

Plans were made to produce a 3.5-litre version of this engine to replace the XK unit—which was very heavy at 553lb bare of all fittings other than inlet and exhaust manifolds—in a V8 configuration. This would be achieved by lopping four cylinders off the V12 so that the new engine could be built by the same machines. But this idea was dropped in 1972 after prototypes had confirmed that the added secondary out-of-balance forces required a Lanchester-style balance shaft. Although Porsche were to adopt this line of development on their four-cylinder version of a V8 production engine, it was rejected by Jaguar because it meant that they could not use the same transfer lines. Thoughts had also been concentrated on an in-line six-cylinder version of the V12 using the same

Small leaping cat Jaguar emblems appeared on the sides of the front wings.

production machinery. Initially, they were shelved because the output from a 2.6-litre engine was unlikely to be enough for a Jaguar. Next they looked at the idea of lengthening the stroke from the V12's 70mm to 90mm to give a 'square' six-cylinder engine of 3.4-litres capacity. The disadvantage then was that the height of such a cylinder block would not suit the V12 machinery.

Two further engines were also under consideration: a 48-valve 630 bhp version of the production V12, for racing, which was killed by the British Leyland accountants, and a 24-valve version using an in-line 3.8-litre cylinder block. This was a development version of the original XK unit designed to be lighter and easier to cast. Its performance and economy was good, but other features were considered too old.

Meanwhile the biggest problem with installing the production V12 in the XJ bodyshell was getting rid of the heat produced by such a big engine. A bigger, four-gallon, water radiator was fitted, with an oil cooler for the engine underneath, and the battery—mounted in front of the scuttle—had to have its own cooling fan. The radiator's fan, powered by a viscous coupling which allowed slip above 1,700rpm, was supplemented by an electric fan when temperatures rose in traffic jams. In addition, the steering rack and engine mountings had to be shrouded by stainless steel guards and the

The basic layout of the XJ range is revealed in this cutaway drawing of the new coupe in 12 cylinder carburettor form.

exhaust pipes were double-skinned for better heat and sound insulation.

The extra weight of the engine meant that slightly stiffer front springs had to be fitted. Braking was also improved by the use of ventilated front discs similar to those on the V12 E type and better-vented wheels. This meant that a Kelsey-Hayes balance valve had to be incorporated in the braking system to prevent weight transfer causing the rear wheels to lock up: it distributed the pressure from the brake servo equally between the front and rear circuits at light pedal applications, and increased the frontal pressure under harder braking. The tyres were also uprated with a nylon casing that had been developed for the V12 E type that now incorporated a steel breaker strip.

Not much else changed on the car except for the omission of manual transmission because no

Facing page: The new two-door coupé bodywork was shown at the same time as the series II XJs were launched. Very few 1973-registered models appeared in public, though.

overdrive could be found to cope with so much torque. Eighty-five per cent of all XJ buyers—including even those economy-conscious people who ordered the 2.8-litre model—were opting for automatic transmission, so it made little sense for Jaguar to invest large sums in producing a new five-speed gearbox. It is a sad fact of life that the design and development costs associated with producing a new gearbox can equal those of a new engine—with few of the marketing advantages. Independent producers could just about manage it because they could sell their gearboxes to a wide variety of customers. So Jaguar opted for the Borg-Warner Model 12 gearbox as being well capable of handling the new engine's output, and it was retained, along with the 3.31:1 final drive ratio.

Minor trim changes included a new radiator grille for Jaguar models following substantially the same lines as the XJ6, with the simple substitution

of XJ12 badges where appropriate. Daimlers, however, were called Double-Sixes after a legendary pre-war model. Apart from Sovereign-style armrests for the Jaguar, a black centre console and a 7000-rpm rev counter, the cars looked just like their six-cylinder ancestors.

Certification took a long while in the United States, so North America—including Canada—did not receive the XJ12 until late in 1973. By then European models had been standardised on the long-wheelbase option. It also meant that the capacity of the fuel tanks had to be reduced to little more than 10 gallons each, to move them further away from the action in a rear-end impact. Although this move got the XJ saloons through new American safety regulations it had the unhappy effect of making the range of the new XJ, in particular, distinctly marginal.

A more plushly-trimmed—and expensive—Daimler Double-Six Vanden Plas version of the XJ12, with special hand-finished paint and vinyl roof covering, had been announced using the long-wheelbase bodyshell at the same time as the 12-cylinder car's launch, but did not appear immediately because of labour troubles at Brown's Lane.

The longer wheelbase was so well received that it was standardised on a series 11 variant of the saloon introduced at the Frankfurt Motor Show in September 1973. The most striking difference was in the frontal appearance where a new bumper was raised to 16in from the ground to meet American safety regulations which aimed at forcing all cars to have bumpers at the same height. This was all very well in practice but made little difference to damage bills in reality because it ignored the fact that the nose dives—and the tail rises—under heavy braking, which happens before the majority of accidents. The radiator grilles and lighting also had to be redesigned, and American export cars were fitted with reinforced bumper bars and different sidelights to meet further crash test regulations. The doors of all cars received additional internal bracing to meet American safety legislation.

A lot of changes were also made to the interior. There was still plenty of leather and walnut, but now the instruments were grouped in front of the driver along with the switches. The XJ6 became the first British production car to use fibre-optic lighting cable for the instruments, eliminating bulbs and saving space. Other controls, such as the time-honoured floor-mounted dipswitch, were moved onto steering column stalks.

This all left room in the centre of the facia for a new heating/air conditioning unit. This operated on air-blending principles rather than on the former water valve. It meant that there could be instant changes of temperature, which once obtained could be maintained regardless of outside influences. The heater and air conditioning output were boosted at the same time.

This new unit was a good deal more bulky than the old heater, so the front bulkhead had to be reshaped to accommodate it. This meant that there was room only for a single skin, rather than a double, so heat and sound insulation was restored by asbestos shielding in the engine bay with bitumen, felt and foam in the passenger compartment.

The steering wheel got a padded centre and there was a new central locking system for the doors, with a cut-out switch to stop children playing with the electric windows, which were standardised. A heated rear screen, laminated windscreen, head restraints and inertia reel front seat belts also became standard fittings.

Mechanically, the cars were similar to the earlier XJs. The ventilated front brake discs became standard equipment, and the engines got new air cleaners and an exhaust-heated air intake system, with the six-cylinder's power output revised to 170bhp at 4,500rpm by the new DIN readings. A simpler single tube oil cooler was fitted with extended downpipes replacing the notoriously

The back seat still offered plenty of room, however, in fact far more than would be found in any two-plus-two seater rivals. The rear-seat controls for the electrically-operated side windows were switched to a centre console alongside the compartment's heating and ventilation outlet.

fragile flexible section used before. Again, despite the extra weight, there was no apparent change in performance . . .

At the same time, new two-door coupé bodywork was shown on the short-wheelbase floorpan. The doors were 4ins wider than the normal front doors, fitting in an opening made by removing the central pillar. The rear shutpost was reinforced to make up for some of the lost rigidity, and a wider rear roof pillar fitted. This involved a welded seam in the roof which was masked by vinyl covering! But the removal of the centre post enabled both front and rear windows to be lowered to leave an uninterrupted opening, which was the object of the exercise so far as Sir William Lyons was concerned. It had been hoped to make the new bodyshell sufficiently rigid to pass American crash tests. Jaguar demonstrated a two-door coupé to the press as

early as 1973, and said they anticipated good sales in North America. But, despite intensive development, the new shell could not be made sufficiently strong to withstand U.S-regulation side impacts without major re-engineering. British Leyland had far more pressing problems with investment in rejuvenating its ageing sports car range at the time, so the plans to sell the coupé in the United States were shelved. This decision was taken midway through 1976 after the American magazine *Road & Track* had tested a prototype fitted with reinforced bumpers and failed to stir up enough orders to justify the additional cost of having it crash tested before it could go on sale in the United States.

There were still hopes at Jaguar, however, that the plans could be revived, so the coupé was not abandoned, although it was obvious that there would not be sufficient demand to produce it in large quantities in its present form. In addition,

The coupé led many to dream of another open Jaguar, but experiments in this direction tended to founder on the practical difficulties in stowing the hood with a mechanism that could not be lowered beyond the wheelarches.

Jaguar's development engineers had considerable problems making the rear windows seal well enough to keep wind noise within their tight limits. This was because the window had to tilt to miss the wheel arches as it went down, and was, in turn, easily sucked out by the low pressure area around the roof when it was raised. Eventually a solution was reached using a tensioned pulley arrangement, but with no large orders envisaged, production did not start until early 1975.

Four-door production continued well, although demand for the 12-cylinder cars fell off dramatically after the world's first energy crisis in the winter of 1973–74. It was not worth reviving the 2.8-litre cars, however, especially as the long-wheelbase bodyshell had taken the weight of the 4.2-litre series II cars up to an official 3,914lb—against as little as 3,650lb on prototypes—although road test figures did not always agree with this. On occasions, both need to be quoted because they could be calculated by different criteria.

But the sheer weight meant that it was deemed advisable to introduce a new 3.4-litre economy version of the XK engine for the four-door bodyshell

Jaguar revamped the series II XJ12 with Vanden Plas chromium-plated swageline embellishment and optional new alloy wheels in 1975 *(above)* as they normally reserved the full luxury package for the Daimler variants *(below)* which retained the vinyl roof covering and lacked badges on the sides of the front wings.

in April 1975. This used the 83mm x 100mm bore and stroke made famous by the original XK engine, but had a new block as tooling for the original units had been scrapped. The new engine was similar to the 4.2-litre unit in that it had offset bores and, like that used in the 340, could adopt the same cylinder head to keep down production costs. But in the new form it had additional external ribbing for extra torsional rigidity and redesigned webs which made the crankshaft stiffer and promoted even smoother running. In this form, on SU carburettors and an 8.8:1 compression ratio, it produced 161bhp (DIN) at 5,000rpm with 189lb/ft of torque at 3,500rpm. By then, 8:1 compression ratio pistons were also being used on the 4.2-litre

engines with revised carburettor and ignition settings to help them meet new European emission regulations, notably in Germany.

A 3.54:1 final drive ratio was normally used on either manual, or Borg Warner Model 65 automatic 3.4-litre cars, although automatics were also fitted with 3.31 or 3.07 ratios for economy at the expense of performance. When sold with a manual gearchange, overdrive was a standard fitting, with a lower first—3.328:1—and reverse—3.428—than the otherwise identical gearbox that had been fitted to 4.2-litre cars. In the interest of economy of production, these ratios were then standardised on the 4.2-litre XJ6 at the same time as the 3.4-litre was launched.

Economies were also made in the 3.4-litre car's interior to make it about 8 per cent cheaper than a 4.2 and initially items like electric window lifts

In far more significant vein, the XJ 5.3 litre cars as they were called – any marketing advantages of emphasising a 12 cylinder engine having been lost to a gas-guzzling image – were fitted with fuel injection from 1975.

New cloth interior trim was also featured on the XJ 5.3 litre cars.

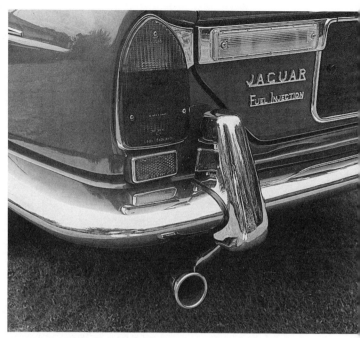

The fuel injection-for-economy (as well as performance) image was discreetly displayed on a rear panel.

could not be ordered on the 3.4-litre XJ6 to encourage people wanting a luxury package to order the more expensive car. The lightweight doors, complete with manual window-winders, from the old 2.8-litre model also helped reduce the weight of the 3.4-litre car to an overall 3,717lb. This was 230lb lighter than quoted for a 4.2-litre at the time although it meant the 3.4-litre could not be exported in that form to the United States. The cloth-trimmed seats—which came with matching door panels—could be specified on the 4.2-litre XJ6, however, to reduce the cost of the more expensive car. Other economy packages included a 4.2-litre version of the Vanden Plas cars which had previously had only the 12-cylinder engine with the 3.07:1 final drive ratio as standard on all 4.2-litre and V12 saloons and coupés.

Fuel injection was also fitted to the 12-cylinder cars at this point to improve the petrol consumption from around 12mpg to 15, and restore power

lost to European emission demands. In its final carburettor form, on US-specification 8:1 compression ratio pistons, the 12-cylinder engine produced only 250bhp at 6,000rpm. The benefit of the fuel injection could be felt immediately in a power output increased to 285bhp at 5,750rpm through electronic management. This D-jetronic system, produced by Lucas, had been originated by Bendix, and developed by Bosch for Europe.

At the same time, handling was further improved by fitting a new steering rack and related suspension parts.

The next major change to the 12-cylinder line was the adoption early in 1977 of the General Motors Hydramatic 400 gearbox used by Rolls-Royce. This three-speed epicyclic unit gave a far more sporting response to the throttle with far less perceptible changes. The 3.31:1 axle ratio was retained, which gave the same gearing in the direct drive top, part of the improved response being achieved by lower intermediate ratios of 1.485:1 and

The new raised roofline of the XJ range was far less noticeable from the front than the rubber beam bumpers, although these were of reasonably elegant design considering the regulations that governed them.

2.485 against the earlier 1.45 and 2.4. Profit levels on the coupé, which still used the by-now obsolete short-wheelbase floorpan, had always been low, because there was never enough money to put it into production for the United States.

Although plans for a completely new Jaguar saloon had been under way since 1972, British Leyland were still not strong enough financially to launch it. So with no new Jaguar in sight, the coupé which would have been one of the most profitable models in the range because it could be sold at a premium with its development costs absorbed by the saloons, went out of production in November 1977.

Only 10,334 had been produced, making them one of the rarer recent Jaguar and Daimler variants.

The fuel injection on the 12-cylinder cars was so successful, however, that it was fitted to the North American 4.2-litre engine from May 1978 to reduce exhaust emissions as well as improve fuel consumption. A three-way catalytic converter was also needed on these cars, which would have reduced power even more. The fuel injection also allowed Jaguar to restore the compression ratio—which had fallen as far as 7.4:1—to 8:1. In conjunction with larger valves, the power output then went back up to 176bhp from 161. A few months later, the injection system, but not the catalytic converter, began to appear on European cars.

They got a new five-speed gearbox in October that had been designed for Rover's SD1 saloon

The fuel-injected version of the six-cylinder engine introduced in the series II during 1978 was carried over to the series III.

rather than the five-speed Jaguar unit that had been designed by Harry Mundy. The reason for preferring the Rover unit was that it would cost less to produce when fitted to both cars. Its operation was a little more fussy because it was lower-geared, but fuel consumption hardly changed.

Massive problems with antiquated plant had led to the last year's serious paint problems with series II cars that resulted in late models being finished only in red, yellow or white. But the long-overdue installation of new spraying facilities in 1979 meant that cars could be ordered in nine colours with every prospect of a first-class acrylic finish which lasted better and needed less maintenance. Rust-proofing was improved at the same

time, the bare bodyshells being dipped and sprayed in phosphates with an anti-corrosive primer, oil sanding and wax-injected box sections. Partly as a result of this kind of investment, costing £15.5 million, British Leyland were still not strong enough to launch a new Jaguar, despite record home sales.

So the series II had to undergo a facelift to keep it competitive—which cost £7 million. This sort of money bought a new raised roofline, more luxurious interior and mechanical changes. It meant, however, that the heavyweight floorpan

(along with the bootlid and bonnet) of the series II had to be retained, in company with the equally-hefty XK engine.

The new roof, designed by the Italian styling house Pininfarina, was less rounded than the old one with more upright pillars giving an additional 3in of forward rake at the front. The rear window was flatter, and the side windows deeper without the old-fashioned quarter lights. The windscreen and rear window were also fitted by thermal adhesion, which increased the bodyshell's rigidity and made it more watertight. Along with the new roofline, the height of which enabled Jaguar to offer a factory-fitted sunroof for the first time since the Mark IX, the drag coefficient had been reduced to 0.412.

American safety dictates led to the adoption of new flush-fitting door handles and massive rubber-covered bumpers. These incorporated the indicator lights at the front and fog warning lights at the back. The lighting system generally was redesigned around quartz halogen headlights, which had the option of washers and wipers. All cars got more sporting wheel trims although alloy wheels remained an option, except on the Vanden

Pleas for the estate car that Jaguar could never afford to make were answered to a certain extent by conversions like this one marketed on a series III base by the Avon coachbuilding firm in 1984. The original car's roof was sawn in half on a line between the doors, and the horizontal surface of the rear deck removed, complete with boot lid. The roof was then extended to meet a tailgate made up from the vertical part of the boot lid and, amazingly, a Renault 5 rear door! New side panels with extra glazing filled the gap between the roof, rear door, wing tops and tailgate. The standard Jaguar bodyshell took little strength from its rear seat bulkhead in any case, so with the substantial new top, the Avon shell was as strong as ever.

Plas Daimlers which had virtually all options as standard. Wider 205/70VR15 Pirelli tyres were now fitted as an option, which improved steering response but had the unfortunate effect of increasing the already substantial 37-ft turning circle to 41ft. They also proved noisier than the Dunlops.

Thick new carpets appeared inside the cars, with concealed inertia reels for the seat belts, a new steering wheel, clearer instruments, a more comprehensive set of warning lights and cruise control and electrically controlled exterior mirrors as options. The front seats were completely revamped to incorporate a wide range of lumbar adjustment with electric height adjustment as a further option. Sound insulation in an already very quiet car was made even better by the use of vacuum-formed rubber and foam covers for the door panels, bulkhead and transmission tunnel. Stalk controls were brought into line with European standards, the right-hand one now looking after windscreen washing, wiping, and—at long last—intermittent operation, plus optional headlamp washing. A speed control button could be incorporated in the left-hand lighting stalk as an option on automatic 4.2-litre and 5.3-litre cars. Central locking was transferred from a switch in the centre console to the door key.

There were also detail mechanical changes to the 4.2-litre engine. Its compression ratio was raised from 7.8:1 to 8.7, the inlet valves enlarged to 1.875ins in diameter and new camshafts fitted which provided earlier inlet timing. In conjunction with

L-jetronic fuel injection as standard, and OPUS electronic ignition, the power output of European versions of the XJ6 was raised to 205bhp at 5,000rpm with 236lb/ft of torque at 3,750rpm—although, in an amazingly-flat torque curve, as much as 231 lb/ft was generated at as low as 1,500 rpm (American cars had 176bhp at 4,750rpm with 219lb/ft of torque at 2,500rpm). It also had an over-run fuel cut-off which cut out when pressure on the accelerator was eased and cut back in at 1,200rpm. Induction roar was reduced by the elimination of the hot-air flap in the air cleaner which had been needed with the carburettors.

The Borg Warner Model 65 automatic gearbox was also considerably modified to improve the quality of its change and response, in fact so much so that it was often called a Model 66. Criticisms that the series II car had been undergeared were countered by returning the final drive ratio of European cars to 3.07:1 now that the engine was

Jaguar's own top-of-the-range Daimler limousine survived until 1991 with every available luxury option, being otherwise updated only when component supplies ran out. This 1988 model has the original S type headlights and cowls with series III XJ-style bumpers.

producing more power and torque. The Rover SD1 transmission used in manual versions had difficulty in coping with the new torque range, so further modifications were made to strengthen the gearbox during 1983.

The steering was also given more weight now that frequent complaints that it was too light had been received from the United States as well as Europe. This was achieved by modifications to the valving and ram actuating torsion bar. At the same time, the steering ratio was increased to 17:1, giving 3.3 turns from lock-to-lock on the XJ6, against the former 15:1 —retained on the 12-cylinder cars, giving 2.9 turns—to make the XJ6 less twitchy on the Pirelli P5 tyres which became a standard fitting with the original Dunlops as an option. The 12-cylinder models, which had more weight over the front wheels, stayed on steel-belted radials.

Although the 3.4-litre cars stayed in production there was still a need for an even cheaper XJ6, so a basic 3.4 was marketed from October 1980 with cloth upholstery as standard and most of the more luxurious cars' options at extra cost.

Far bigger changes were afoot for the 12-cylinder cars which had been withdrawn in the

Some people were never satisfied with even a Daimler and spent large sums on dechroming the brightwork.

United States during 1980 after falling foul of tougher fuel consumption rulings. It was all part of intensive research into making Jaguar's engines more economical, which had started in 1976. The possibility of using revolutionary new cylinder heads designed by the Swiss engineer Michael May provoked the idea that future engines should be in two forms: economy versions with two-valves per-cylinder May heads and high-performance variants with four valve heads.

As a first tangible step in this programme, the 12-cylinder saloons had been fitted during 1980 with an uprated engine used on the 'guinea pig' XJ-S range. This had a new Lucas/Bosch fuel injection system that allowed Jaguar's engineers to take advantage of its improved fuel distribution by raising the compression ratio from 9:1 to 10:1. The revised injection used a vacuum diaphragm arrangement to keep the fuel pressure constant at 36psi, so that the solenoid-operated injector opening time could be digitally controlled to give the right engine performance for all conditions by varying the pulse width according to the usual parameters of engine load, speed, temperature, and throttle movement. Complicated as it sounded, this system was so neat and tidy that it actually simplified the underbonnet lay-out and made access to routine items easier!

These interim developments had been necessary because it was not certain at that point whether British Leyland could afford to put engines with May heads into full-scale production. The fuel consumption of this interim 12-cylinder engine was promptly reduced by 15 per cent with a power increase to 300bhp at 5,400rpm with torque up to 318lb/ft at 3,900rpm.

But by July 1981, sufficient money had been found for Jaguar to be able to fit the new cylinder heads and the revised pistons which went with them, allowing them to re-enter the United States market with 12-cylinder cars. Part of the reason for being able to justify the investment was that it was linked to a new engine that was being developed—and Jaguar sales in America were at their highest level despite having only the six-cylinder saloon on offer.

May's heads had twin combustion chambers with the inlet valve housed in a collecting zone below a bathtub-shaped chamber containing the exhaust valve and sparking plug. As the 12.5:1 compression ratio flat-top piston entered its compression stroke it swirled a very lean low-turbulence mixture around the sparking plug which could then burn it off in a highly-efficient manner, using four-star petrol. This lean and highly-compressed mixture needed special ignition and Jaguar's engineers developed a high performance system using an electronic distributor, an amplifier unit and twin coils to provide the necessary 12 sparks per revolution

and control them up to 7,000rpm. In conjunction with the recently-developed fuel injection these cylinder heads then reduced the petrol consumption of the HE—for high efficiency—model by as much as 20 per cent.

American versions of this engine, which had to run on unleaded fuel, had a 11.5:1 compression ratio pistons, that with other anti-emission modifications led to the same power output being quoted as that of the earlier engine: 262 bhp at 5,000 rpm with peak torque of 290 lb/ft at 3,000 rpm rather than the previous 4,000.

The XJ12 HE was given wider alloy wheels with 215-section Dunlop D7 tyres rather than the old 205 sections, while the Double Six received an even more opulent interior, upgraded further on Vanden Plas versions. At the same time the basic six-cylinder cars got the V12's viscous-coupled fan and an oil cooler as standard. A new GM400 automatic gearbox was fitted at the same time with a redesigned gearchange that no longer restricted

The new XJ6 – nee XJ40 – pictured in basic 2.9 litre form bore a strong resemblance to the earlier cars.

The 3.6 litre car, shown in Daimler trim, had single squared headlights shared with the new Jaguar Sovereign.

The interior of the new XJ range – illustrated in Daimler form – was far more modern than that of the series III cars, although, with the exception of the instruments, it maintained a similar philosophy.

movement between D and 2, but at the same time resisted unintentional movements into neutral or reverse. A safety restriction which prevented first being engaged at too high a speed was retained.

The Daimler name was then dropped for the mainland European market in October 1982 with the Sovereign title adopted by Jaguar for a higher-specification XJ6. Revised interiors on all models included a new centre console and veneer switch panels, and larger areas of wood on the Vanden Plas door panels. The front seats were stiffened at the same time with a new Raschelle material for the 3.4 which was optional on the XJ6 and XJ12. New perforated alloy wheels appeared on the XJ12 HE which became an option on the six-cylinder cars. Daimlers kept their previous spoked wheels and the 3.4 got quartz halogen lamps at last.

A year later the Jaguar Sovereign was offered in Britain with an interior specification midway between the standard car and the Vanden Plas. Only three Daimlers remained, the 4.2, Double Six and limousine, as top of the range models with every available option.

Finally, in September 1985, interior materials were further upgraded with a new herringbone cloth material and extra brightwork as the HE tag was dropped and power reduced to 291 bhp as the

injection was reworked to enable the engine to run on lower-grade fuel. In North America just two models were listed, the XJ6 sedan and the Vanden Plas, which was, in reality, the European Sovereign. The V12-powered versions of the series III car would then stay in production for limited markets such as the United Kingdom and West Germany (with the former U.S. emission control modifications) as a new car replaced the existing six-cylinders in October 1986.

The XJ40

The biggest surprise about Jaguar's first new four-door saloon since the XJ12 was its name: XJ6. The second major surprise was its appearance: it bore a strong resemblance to the old XJ6, although, in reality, the only thing carried over was the herring-bone trim of the previous year.

The bodyshell of the XJ40, as it had been dubbed after its most recent development code, followed existing Jaguar patterns in that it was based around large sills and a braced floorpan. Box sections ran forward from the front bulkhead to support the front suspension mounting beam.

But in detail it was completely different. Years of computerised design and development had reduced the number of panels from 558 to 425, with no loss of rigidity and a considerable saving in weight and manufacturing cost. Resistance to corrosion was substantially improved by the extensive use of zinc-coated steel and advanced new paint-work allied to existing injection of cavities.

The new bodyshell looked a lot like the series III it replaced, but it was better aerodynamically. Improving the aerodynamic efficiency while keeping the traditional Jaguar appearance presented the designers with a considerable challenge. Styling changes were subtle, yet important. The forward slope of the radiator grille was eased, the front end corners given a top-to-bottom radius and the characteristic series III headlamp 'eyebrows' removed. Airflow over the body was improved by the use of a near-flush bonded windscreen while the wake at the back of the car was reduced by tapering in the rear quarters. Other design factors that contributed to a drag co-efficient of 0.38 on European cars included smoothly-rounded A posts, and wing mirrors—now compulsory in most markets—being mounted on a 'cheater' panel. The new XJ6 had a larger frontal area than the series III, but its relevant CDs figure of 0.762 was 0.087 lower. A discreet front air dam with a subtle lip on the trailing edge of the boot lid helped give the car excellent stability and high-speed control. A further subtle aid to aerodynamic efficiency could be seen in the use of a single windscreen wiper blade, with a pivot biased slightly towards the driver. Such was the value of so much detail work in the new car, which was wider at 6ft 6.9ins (including mirrors), a little longer at 16ft 4.4ins, and fractionally higher at 4ft 6.3ins. The wheelbase, 9ft 5ins, and track, 4ft 11ins, were virtually the same although the overall weight was reduced by 150–200lb depending on specification with the bodyshell accounting for 18lb of the saving. Although the overall dimensions of the new XJ6 were little changed, the occupants got more space, with more room for luggage. There was an inch more legroom at the front, with 3ins extra shoulder space, while the volume of the boot was increased by more than 10 per cent to 15.1 cubic feet. This was achieved by replacing the series III fuel tanks in the rear wings with a single 19.5-gallon tank mounted over the rear axle line—which gave it greater protection from impacts.

The rear suspension was much changed, although it retained the principle of linking a lower wishbone with the driveshaft as an upper member from a frame-mounted final drive with limited-slip differential. The big change now was that the wishbones' inner mountings incorporated a unique pendulum set-up which allowed fore-and-aft movement of the lower inner fulcrum, while maintaining a

The Sports Pack option gave Jaguar's 3.2 litre XJ6 a lower and far meaner look that meant it was unlikely to be confused with the 2.9 litre cars which had used similar headlights.

very high lateral stiffness through a tie bar at the back. This meant that the rear wheels could move backwards and forwards with road shock while remaining in the same plane—in effect providing an even more sophisticated ride without the perils of trying to steer the car. The new rear suspension, which incorporated anti-dive and squat geometry, used a single coil spring/damper unit each side with inclined links at the back to control wind-up under acceleration and braking. Self-levelling struts were fitted as standard on the new Sovereign and Daimler models, and as an option on the Jaguar XJ6.

The 10.9-inch disc brakes with Porsche-style integral drums to provide a more efficient handbrake had now been moved outboard to avoid overheating the final drive; 11.6-inch ventilated discs were fitted at the front. A computer-controlled Bosch anti-lock system was fitted as standard on all models except the Jaguar XJ6, where it remained an option.

The front suspension amounted to a refined version of the existing layout. It shared a more highly-developed subframe with the engine mountings and used wishbones and coil springs which now had the pitch control arms raked backwards instead of forwards. In addition, a tie bar braced the inner front wishbone pivot points on the far simpler subframe. An anti-roll bar and rack and pinion steering—with a reduced 2.8 turns from lock to lock—were retained although, for 'belt and braces' safety reasons, the power assistance was now provided by a chain and skew gear from the engine's timing chain.

The 220/65-section 15-inch tyres, jointly developed for European use by Dunlop and Michelin, had relatively soft sidewalls for the most comfortable ride, allied to a flat tread for maximum grip. Special alloy wheels—or cheaper steel ones on the standard XJ6—were used that locked the tyre beads in a groove. In conjunction with an internal gel that became liquid when a deflating tyre ran hotter, they provided protection against blowouts. Narrower Pirelli P5 205/70VR15 in tyres

would be used on American-specification cars that were unlikely to cruise at anything like the speed of a European model. These had the side effect of reducing the drag co-efficient to 0.37.

The new car was powered by either a more refined version of the 3.6-litre twin overhead cam in-line six-cylinder AJ—for advanced Jaguar—engine that had appeared in the XJ-S coupé from 1983, or a single-cam 2.9-litre short-stroke variant using the same cylinder block. These engines—mounted at 15 degrees to the vertical to lower the bonnet line—provided the majority of the overall weight saving, lopping around 120lb off the total for the cast iron-blocked XK.

The four valves per cylinder 3,590-cc engine had a 91mm x 92 bore and stroke because a diesel version had once been slated—and those were the dimensions of the best available at the time from Mercedes. The camshafts' familiar chain drive was retained in the all-alloy unit. Equally familiar was the seven-bearing cast iron crankshaft of similar size to that of the 4.2-litre XK engine. But everything else was new, with the inherently more efficient twin inlet and exhaust valves inclined at 46.5 degrees to each other around a central sparking plug in the 9.6:1 compression ratio pentroof combustion chamber. A simplex chain drove the oil pump below the crankshaft with other engine ancillaries—water pump, alternator and air-conditioning compressor—driven by belt.

Changes since early applications in the XJ-S included stiffened cams with a lift reduced from 0.375ins to 0.36 and gentler profiles to reduce valve acceleration, thinner-wall bucket tappets made from steel rather than cast iron and improved chain tensioners to make the engine smoother and quieter. A great deal of attention went into improving the engine's balance, mostly by tightening tolerances, and partly by improving the torque converter's balance on cars with automatic transmission. Bearing clearances and tolerances were reduced and the connecting rod balance improved. Finally the crankshaft damper, timing ring and pulley were balanced as a unit. A new electronic ignition and fuel injection system developed by Lucas in conjunction with Jaguar gave this engine 221bhp—in place of the original 225—at 5,000rpm with torque up 8 lb/ft on 248 at 4,000. U.S. Federal versions—to the same specification as those exported to West Germany and Japan—produced 185 bhp at 4,750rpm with 221 lb/ft of torque at 3,750rpm.

The harsh manner in which the cut-off re-

introduced fuel as the engine speed dropped to around 1,000rpm on a trailing throttle had been masked during prototype development using an automatic gearbox. Once the engine was linked to a manual gearbox the harshness became obtrusive and the fuel cut-off was then taken off production cars, making them much easier to drive smoothly around a town. It was considered worth the

Daimler's 4 litre XJ6 retained the square headlights, however, along with a coachline and different wheels.

penalty of between 0.5 and 0.75mpg on an urban cycle.

Later, a new programme involved a ramped re-introduction of the fuel on the overrun to eliminate this problem and improve fuel consumption by 3 per cent which meant that maximum power was now developed at 5,300rpm with U.S., West German and Japanese engines now producing 176 bhp 4,750rpm with the same torque as before.

The 2,919-cc unit was completely new, having been designed specifically for the XJ40 saloon. It used the same bore, but a shorter stroke of 74.8mm, which entailed using a new crankshaft of similar construction to the 3.6 unit. Originally it was intended that this engine should be based on half the V12, to save production costs, so it retained the same bore centres with the 12.6:1 compression ratio May heads and the V12 valves and camshaft.

Bosch EZ-F fuel electronic ignition was used with LH Jetronic fuel injection to give 165bhp at 5,600rpm. This was 4bhp more than the series III 3.4-litre engine, although torque was down from 189 lb/ft at 3,500rpm to 176lb/ft of torque at 4,000rpm.

The new engines had been developed from the six-cylinder proposed in 1970 which preserved the 30-degree inclination of the V12, partly because it saved the cost of casting a new sump. The XJ40's engine bay was then designed so that it could not readily accept such a wide engine—in other words a Rover—so that Jaguar would be able to keep its identity in the face of British Leyland cost-cutting. Jaguar's management were especially fearful of such a move because it had been proposed that the cars should be renamed simply Leylands in any case.

Officially, the future of the V12 engine looked bleak, so the 30-degree inclination could be halved to 15 degrees to fit in the new engine bay, while still allowing enough space for long inlet tracts. At the same time, this was around the optimum to accommodate the extra width of a 24-valve twin-cam high-performance head. The V12 had originally been meant to have a gravity die cast head, which was why its heart was more of a shell than a block, with an open top deck and substantial cast iron liners. In the event, it never progressed from conventional casting, and the same layout was inherited by the first AJ6 engine in 1979. But during the following year, Jaguar adopted a normal closed deck in which the liners could be made much thinner and shrunk into cylinders cast as part of the block. This dry-liner construction was lighter and stiffer, which would have been important had they introduced a diesel variant. An experimental V12 was also built using Porsche-style aluminium cylinders etched with silicon. This idea was rejected, however, as being too expensive for the weight saved.

There were other detail changes during the new engine's development. Initially, the camshaft operation was by a toothed belt before it was considered worthwhile to opt for the more efficient, but more expensive, chain drive, which also reduced the overall size of the engine because the pulley could be made smaller.

Both new cars were available with either four-speed automatic, or a five-speed manual gearbox made by the West German Getrag company that was shared with the XJ-S 3.6. The 4HP-22 automatic box also came from a West German firm, ZF. It was, in effect, a three-speed epicyclic transmission with a direct drive third ratio and overdrive top that could be driven like a manual without the clutch. It had been developed from a similar unit used in the BMW 525Eta, but was making its first appearance in the XJ40.

A larger-bore master cylinder was fitted to lighten the clutch action of the manual cars and the automatics features a new selector called the J-gate. This was like a normal selector, with a bend at the back end of the slot, leading across to the left to a shorter parallel slot running forward. The longer part of the gate contained the basic automatic modes park, reverse, neutral and drive—while the shorter slot controlled the second and third gear holds to avoid careless misuse. A GKN-Salisbury limited-slip final drive was fitted as standard on Daimlers and as an option on the Jaguars with a final drive ratio of 3.54:1 for the 3.6-litre cars and 3.77 for the 2.9-litres in Europe and 2.88:1 to reduce fuel consumption—and thus 'gas guzzler' penalty pricing—in the United States.

A vast amount of development went into the electrical system of the new cars. Major features included a new type of ring main wiring system—

Meanwhile the Jaguar XJ6 range in, from the left, Sovereign 3.2, right basic 3.2, and top, 3.2 Sport received uprated engines in October 1990. The new power unit used the same cylinder head as the 24-valve 4.0 litre introduced the year before, developing 35 per cent more power and 32 per cent more torque than the earlier 2.9. The new maximum output figures worked out at 200bhp at 5,250rpm with 220lb/ft of torque at 4,000rpm.

which saved a lot of weight—with numerous on-board computers and the facility for advanced diagnostic connections.

But Jaguar decided that they would have to be more conservative over the use of modern technology in the interior. Research among potential customers—especially in the United States—revealed that one of the prime reasons for buying a Jaguar was the traditional interior.

So as a result, the new XJ6 range had far more wooden veneers and leather than originally intended, with three levels of trim: the standard XJ6 with cloth upholstery in which automatic transmission, anti-lock brakes, alloy wheels and air conditioning were extras, Jaguar Sovereign with lots of leather, the manual gearbox as an option

at no extra cost, and anti-lock brakes as standard, and the Daimler with all the options as standard and a Vanden Plas-style interior. Originally it had been intended to use a futuristic digital display for all instruments, but the customer clinics did not like them. Jaguar's eventual solution was a compromise, using conventional round dials for major instruments like the speedometer and rev counter allied to modern bar graphs for fuel, voltage, oil and water temperature with a computerised vehicle condition monitor to report on vital items like the brakes, radiator, lights and insecure doors. Other thoroughly modern fittings included heated windscreen washer jets, door locks and exterior mirrors plus a central locking system which also closed the sunroof if that had been left open. The heating and ventilation system was upgraded, too, with a humidity control for the air conditioning. But when the new range was launched in the United States the following May, with automatic transmission only, the basic level of trim was not offered and Daimler variants were rebadged as Jaguars to avoid having to put them through another set of Federal tests. But all cars had the twin-headlight system of the XJ6, plus a rear window-mounted central stoplight, to comply with American lighting laws.

Once the new range had been safely launched, intensive development went on to adapt the bodyshell to take the V12 engine for a new flagship, now that the threat of having to use the Rover V8 in a corporate car called a Leyland had been removed. This long-wheelbase version, codenamed XJ41 and subsequently XJ82, followed a similar philosophy to the series II XJ6 developments with an extra 4ins in the floorpan behind the front seats. But now the roofline was raised slightly to give more headroom, rather like the series III cars. Other subtle design changes included a new rear quarterlight which was larger and wider at the top than on the existing car. Complementing the revised styling in this area, the petrol filler cap, previously housed immediately behind the rear screen, was

now placed on the side of the car. At the front, the longer-wheelbase car had the Sovereign's rectangular headlamps, and a larger air intake beneath the bumper for the V12 engine.

Plunging profits linked to the rise in value of the U.S. dollar led to development work on this variant being shelved in February 1989. Demands for a higher-performance limited-edition model were met, however, by starting a JaguarSport offshoot in conjunction with the Tom Walkinshaw organisation which ran Jaguar's competition operation. JaguarSport's XJR 3.6—built in automatic gearbox form only during 1988—used similar suspension modifications to those introduced on the factory-built XJ-S coupé. This featured increased spring rates, with a stiffer front anti-roll bar, modified dampers and new Pirelli 225-55 section tyres on 16-inch Speedline wheels with a 6.5-inch rims. The steering pump was also re-valved to reduce its power assistance by 17 per cent, which, with turns from lock-to-lock reduced to 2.6, allied to stiffer rack mounting bushes, transformed the feel at the wheel—which was a four-spoke affair trimmed in leather to match the more luxurious interior. A colour-keyed bodystyling kit was also fitted that featured a tiny spoiler on the rear lid and the traditional Jaguar-style four round headlights of the standard XJ6 rather than the rectangular lights of the Sovereign and Daimler.

It was at this time that the V12 engine had to be further detuned by using Marelli electronic ignition and reducing the compression ratio to 11.5:1 to enable it to run on unleaded fuel.

Meanwhile the 3.6-litre AJ6 engine continued to be developed at the factory to give it more power and torque along with a revised digital management system that was linked to ZF's latest four-speed automatic gearbox to provide smoother changes. The capacity increase in September 1989—which British Leyland would not countenance at the time the AJ6 engine was being developed—was achieved by the use of a new forged steel crankshaft with a longer stroke, up

10mm to 102mm to give a 3,980-cc capacity. The compression ratio was reduced to 9.5:1 to enable it to run on unleaded fuel and the four-valve cylinder heads fitted with reprofiled camshafts. Compared with the 3.6-litre unit, peak power and torque were then both delivered 250 rpm lower down the rev range. The 4-litre's 235bhp maximum was at 4,750-rpm with the full 285 lbf/ft of torque at 3,750rpm. A low-loss catalytic converter was offered as an extra in Britain.

In company with the units used on BMW and Mercedes cars, the ZF gearbox could be switched from normal settings to more sporting ones in which the kickdown points on part-throttle and the ratio-change points were raised. The surviving fluorescent green bar graph instruments of the XJ40 had attracted much criticism, so they were replaced by four conventional gauges, two either side of a larger speedometer and rev counter. The dot matrix vehicle control monitoring panel gave way to a variety of warning lights. The digital odometer remained with its display operated by a single button. Another change as the result of customer reaction, was back to a normal indicator stalk with detents to hold it up or down. New graphics for the air conditioning controls and changes to the sensor system for faster reaction completed the package. Outwardly all that had changed was an extra strip of chromium plating around the rear lights!

XJ-S for Sporting

Jaguar's grand touring car, the XJ-S, was originally conceived in 1969 as a replacement for the E type sports car which had been such a success during that era. The majority of E types made between 1961 and 1975 were sold in the United States, a trend which Jaguar expected to continue. So the needs of an American market—and especially its proposed safety and environmental legislation—were of paramount importance in shaping the new car.

At the time designers were sketching out the XJ-S, codenamed XJ27, it seemed certain that soon no more open cars would be sold in the United States, because of their great emphasis on roll-over tests. But the people who loved open cars fought back hard and won an historic case in 1974 which held that such legislation was an infringement of their personal liberty. This meant that the open car was reprieved . . . but it was too late for many manufacturers, including Jaguar. Such were the complexities of designing and building a modern car that they had already committed themselves to closed cars.

It was not simply a question of cutting the top off the XJ-S, which by 1974 was close to production. By then it had become far removed from the E type it was about to replace. Once Jaguar had decided that it should be only a fixed head coupé, it became more like their saloon cars. Heating and ventilation had to be of the same standard which meant that the XJ-S would be an expensive car. It would cost more to make than the saloons, because with only limited accommodation in the back it would sell in smaller quantities.

But the opportunity was taken to use it as something of a pioneer at the same time. One of the chief reasons that the E type had to be taken out of production in February 1975 before the XJ-S launch the following September was that its fuel tank, mounted under the luggage boot floor, was in too exposed a position to pass ever more draconian safety tests. Jaguar feared that the XJ6 and XJ12 saloons and coupés might suffer a similar fate with their side-mounted tanks if the tests got tougher. So they re-arranged the rear end of the XJ-S to give it a fuel tank mounted like a saddle across the back axle—as far out of harm's way as possible. This was easier in a coupé like the XJ-S, of course, because only a limited space was needed for the back seats, but it was a pointer to the future in any case.

Apart from the necessities like re-siting the fuel tank, and making the new car look different from the saloons, it was wise to use as many parts from them as possible, to keep down costs. There was nothing much new in that policy: in company with many manufacturers, Jaguar had been doing it for years, in particular with the XK sports car which amounted to short-chassis editions of the big saloons, clothed in different bodies. But once it became apparent that the new XJ-S would have to cost more than the XJ saloons, it was decided to go the whole hog and give it a lot of extra luxury fittings. Air conditioning was fitted as standard, for instance. For the same reason, there was never any question of using the six-cylinder engine, which was expected to become obsolete during the 1970s. Jaguar were happy with it this way in any case, because using only the V12 enabled them to adopt a lower bonnet line. The increasing role played by legislation, rather than stylists, in designing a car was well illustrated by the way in which the bonnet line had to be raised slightly during the XJ27 project's evolution to enable it to comply with

This XJ–S – pre-production model – presented a considerable contrast to its open-topped predecessors, from the left, a series 1 E-type, an XK120 and an XK150.

regulations on crush control and lighting and the shovel nose and disappearing headlights visualised by Sir William Lyons had be abandoned.

But the outer panels still had to be changed quite dramatically so that it did not look like the XJ coupé, intended to sell at a lower price. Jaguar, by now under the control of British Leyland committees rather than the autocratic Sir William, opted for a bland shape related to the new mass-produced cars they planned rather than anything too distinctive which might make them look second-rate. The sheer bulk of the V12 engine, and radiators needed to cool it, ensured, however, that

the new XJ-S did not look like the Austin Princess. All the same, the new bodyshell was highly aerodynamic even if it did not follow British Leyland's new wedge-shaped corporate line. With roll-over regulations of prime importance, flying buttresses were used to support the back of the roof— which came in for criticism after Jaguar's previous slender offerings. Adding a spoiler to the front and an undershield below the engine not only reduced lift by 50 per cent, but also brought down the drag coefficient to 0.37, an improvement not only on the 0.46 of the series II XJ saloon, but the 0.42 of the two-plus-two seater E type.

The interior was even more controversial because it abandoned wooden veneers for the first time in a Jaguar saloon—although they were not a feature of the XK and E type sports cars. Leather was also noticeable by its absence, the seats being upholstered largely in black vinyl like many of Leyland's cheaper cars. No matter that they had leather facings and were designed to give better lateral support; the obvious comparison was that the XJ-S, especially from the inside, looked more like a Leyland saloon than a Jaguar. This impression was heightened by the use of aircraft-style

The XJ–S changed little outwardly during the 1970s, with only minor changes, such as a brighter radiator surround. This example is being raced by Roger Wilkinson in the Lister XJ Challenge at the Jaguar Drivers' Club Donington meeting in September 1985.

rising barrel instruments in place of the traditional dials recording water temperature, oil pressure, fuel contents and condition of the battery. The idea was that when the car was running normally, the vertically-moving needles formed a line across the panel so that the driver could verify the results at a glance. But to many people it all looked too much like a jukebox. One feature that nobody criticised, however, was the specially-designed Cibie headlights which gave a superb range of illumination. Nevertheless, American regulations decreed against single-headlight installations in this case and insisted on a twin layout even if it was much inferior. Happily, the XJ-S kept its Cibie lights in Europe . . .

Under the skin, standard components were used wherever possible. The original XJ chassis platform had its wheelbase shortened to 9ft 6in by moving the back suspension forward under a

Somehow the XJ–S survived the 1970s, and found new life in HE form.

smaller pan for the rear seats. The bulkhead was beefed up, with the flitch plates and screen pillars, to make the whole structure stiffer. Strengthening tubes were also bolted across the engine compartment. With America in mind, massive new bumpers were mounted on Menasco shock-absorbing struts at either end of the chassis. These acted like telescopic dampers, using silicone wax as the hydraulic medium. On impact, a piston forced the wax out of the cylinder, and into small ports within its body. Within 30 seconds of the impact, providing it happened at less than the 5mph prescribed by American safety regulations, the wax flowed back into the cylinder, forcing the piston to return

the bumper to its original position. Partly because of these massive bumpers, the new bodyshell weighed a considerable 710lb, but it was still 110lb less than that of an XJ12, reflecting how much progress had been made in only three years.

Even greater efforts had been made to reduce noise by designing the engine bay so that sound waves were deflected down to the road rather than through the bulkhead and transmission tunnel. Holes which might have admitted noise were eliminated by using multi-pin plugs and sockets for all wiring passing from the interior to the engine bay.

Because there were no plans at the time to use anything other than the V12 engine in the XJ-S, as much weight as possible was moved to the back of the car to counter its weight. The spare wheel was mounted upright between the 20-gallon fuel tank and the vented luggage compartment, with the battery.

The suspension was the same as that in the XJ saloons except that the spring rates were reduced in keeping with the 225lb lower overall weight at 3,892lb. The suspension geometry was also adjusted to suit the shorter wheelbase and new Dunlop SP Super Sport 205/70VR15 radial ply

tyres, with the addition of a 14.2-mm anti-roll bar at the back and substitution of a larger diameter, 0.875-inch bar at the front.

The overall ratio of the Adwest power-assisted steering gear was increased from 16.44:1 to 16 by the use of an eight-tooth pinion, rather than a seven-tooth, to operate the rack.

The engine was the same as that introduced in the fuel injection XJ12, with the option of Jaguar's four-speed manual transmission to the normal automatic box. In either case, a 3.07:1 final drive was used. When the XJ-S was sold in California it needed more comprehensive emission control equipment, which reduced the power to 244bhp at 5,250rpm with torque down to 269lb/ft at 4,500rpm. In these models, a 3.31 rear axle ratio was fitted to improve acceleration as top speed was of lesser importance.

The optional alloy wheels from the XJ12 were fitted as standard, although painted differently, with new Dunlop tyres using steel bracing for a higher speed rating. The braking system was basically the same as that of the XJ12, except that the handbrake lever was moved to a more sporting— and convenient—location on the right-hand side of the floor. It was amusing to note that, as a safety

Discreet display of Jaguar symbols, such as that on the bonnet of the XJ–S and with the V12 slogan on the radiator grille helped confirm its identity.

factor, this equipment was taken directly from one of the Guy trucks that Jaguar made in the 1960s! In this form, the lever fell horizontally to the floor when the car had been parked. It had then to be raised and re-engaged before being released, so that it was not possible to kick the button accidentally when getting in or out of the car and let off the brakes as a result.

Apart from cosmetics, such as brightwork on the radiator grille rather than matt black, the first real changes were early in 1977 when the Hydromatic 400 automatic gearbox was fitted as standard on all Jaguar's 12-cylinder cars. There were sufficient supplies of Jaguar's four-speed gearbox to meet the small demand for manual editions of the XJ-S until 1979, after which they all became automatics. This was partly due to the plunging sales of the XJ-S — capable of only 11mpg in strangulated Californian form – and a poor reliability record for Jaguars generally. By the 1980 model year, fuel consumption regulations made it no longer worth exporting the V12 engine to North America, until it had been made more economical. So XJ-S production stopped for several months, until it was decided to use the model as a guinea pig because relatively few were being ordered.

The meant that the XJ-S was able to get the Lucas/Bosch electronic injection later in 1980 ahead of its introduction on the May-headed V12s the following year. The transformation was startling; this interim XJ-S with uprated 10:1 compression ratio pistons needed 15 per cent less fuel despite a rise in power to 300bhp at 5,400rpm and torque to 318lb/ft at 3,900rpm.

Similar moves, with the substitution of a three-way catalytic converter in the United States, relieved the V12's breathing to such an extent that it produced 262bhp. This allowed the final drive ratio to be raised to 3.07, in turn improving fuel consumption to 14mpg.

When the May heads could be fitted in July 1981, the extra power they liberated enabled Jaguar

New wheels were also fitted to the XJ–S HE.

to increase the final drive ratio to 2.88:1, which, in turn, further improved fuel consumption on European cars to around 16mpg. The XJ-S HE, as this model was known, also looked different, with wider 6.5-inch rims and bright-coloured bumper cappings like the series III saloons, but even more significantly, had a much-changed interior. Wood veneer appeared all round, with leather seats and trim, and a full range of electronic gadgets taking it up to the top XJ saloon standards.

Two years later, in September 1983, the XJ-S was back to being a guinea pig. It became the first Jaguar to receive the new 3.6-litre engine and remained in relatively short supply because of problems with refining its running. The modifications needed to improve the engine were phased in as they were developed in time for the XJ40 saloon's launch in 1986.

At the same time as the 3.6-litre XJ-S was introduced, Jaguar experimented with public reaction to having a manual gearbox again—the Getrag five-speed which would appear on the new XJ6—by fitting it as standard after prototype engines linked to the existing Borg Warner automatic transmission had proved that that was not strong enough. Jaguar did not want to use the

As Jaguar were launching their cabriolet at the 1983 London Motorfair exhibition, Lynx Engineering – who had produced D-type replicas since the mid-1970s and an estate car version of the XJ-S called the Eventer – were showing their completely open XJ-S Spyder convertible. This conversion sold reasonably well until Jaguar introduced its own edition in 1988.

General Motors transmission adopted for the 12-cylinder cars because it was too heavy.

Softer front springs were fitted to all versions of the XJ-S to compensate for the lighter engine and transmission with a slightly-thinner 0.811-inch anti-roll bar. The rear anti-roll bar was also deleted now that the front end was lighter. Apart from badging there were a few clues to the car's new identity outside, other than for a more-pronounced bulge in the bonnet to clear the taller AJ6 engine and the less-exclusive drilled alloy wheels used on the XJ6 saloons. Costs were partly contained, however, by replacing the leather seat facings with Ambla like that used on the old 240 saloons.

As a further test of market reaction, there was also the option of a return to open-air motoring. There could be seen to be a demand: various specialist firms were taking advantage of the XJ-

S's inherently-strong construction to produce small numbers of convertible models. These did not have to pass the same sort of safety tests that faced a major manufacturer, so Jaguar had to tread carefully. They took a leak out of Porsche's book by fitting their new open car with a substantial built-in roll cage which replaced the strength lost by cutting off the roof. The trim was re-arranged around this hoop so that by removing two roof panels, and storing them in the boot, the occupants could enjoy most of the attractions of open-air motoring. Jaguar had offered this sort of thing before, on the XK chassis, calling it a drophead convertible. But this was not quite the same, so it was called a cabriolet, after the roll-back tops that were popular on pre-war limousines. The restricted rear seats of the normal two-plus-two XJ-S were replaced by a parcel shelf, hiding two lockers. Ever safety conscious, Jaguar were afraid that rear seat occupants, who did not have to wear seat belts in many countries, including Britain, might be thrown out in an accident. At the same time, their marketing men watched with considerable interest to see if sales would really be affected by the loss of the rear seats

The demand for more individual versions of the XJ–S was further met by the first Lister conversion in 1984, produced initially under the auspices of machine tool salesman Iain Exeter and Jaguar race patron John Lewis. The name Lister was derived with the approval of Cambridge engineer Brian Lister who had built highly-successful sports racing cars in the 1950s, often fitted with Jaguar engines. Early versions of the Lister Jaguars sold in the 1980s – the car pictured is the first one to be demonstrated near Exeter's base in Birmingham – featured colour-coded body kits and the option of a variety of engine conversions by Ron Beaty's Foward Engineering.

which Porsche had always said were vital on their rival 911. They had also proclaimed long and loud that their Targa-topped variant—with a cabriolet style roll bar—had increased overall sales of the 911 by a substantial amount.

As the Jaguar cabriolet was essentially only an exercise to test public opinion, much of the production of this specialist bodyshell went to outside contractors while they worked on a fully-open variant like the one Porsche had belatedly introduced in 1983. Obviously such a Jaguar would command a prestige price, so it shared the HE's star type alloy wheels and full leather upholstery—again to see if the public really wanted it.

This sort of manufacturing exercise enabled the factory to concentrate on fulfilling an ever-increasing demand for XJ saloons. As a result, XJ-S bodyshells, minus the roof, tonneau and boot-lid, were taken across Coventry to the Park Sheet Metal works, which strengthened the floorpan and installed the roll cage—an exercise which added more than 100lb to the overall weight. It was then returned to Leyland's Castle Bromwich plant for painting, before going on to Brown's Lane for assembly, and continuing to Aston Martin Tickford for trimming. Cabriolets then had to return to Brown's Lane for quality checks before dispatch . . . hardly a mainline production job although matters were streamlined later with more work being done at Brown's Lane.

Next on the list was another guinea pig: a V12 cabriolet introduced in July 1985 as a result of a strong demand from West Germany, although enthusiastic reactions were expected in the United States when it had passed Federal safety checks. Again supplies were limited, not only by the production problems, but because Jaguar was checking future public demand for the more glamorous engine. There had not been a great demand for the series III V12 saloon now that the new six-cylinder XJ cars were available and already

Lister conversion production was switched later to WP Engineering in Surrey, run by Laurence Pearce, son of former E-type racer Warren Pearce. The conversions featured a wide range of engine modifications and found favour in British club racing as well as on the road. Exeter's younger brother, Tim, is pictured here with a 'works' Lister XJ-S competing in an Intermarque championship round at Mallory Park in May 1985.

Motor sport enthusiast Simon Taylor, deputy chairman of Haymarket Publishing who normally drove an XJ–S on the road, took time off to compete in the 1986 Brighton Speed Trials with another Lister conversion.

they were wondering whether it was really worthwhile tooling up for a longer-wheelbase V12 version in the new range. Such were the costs involved, that it seemed that whatever money was available might be better spent on further improvements for the six-cylinder saloons, leaving the XJ-S range as the 12-cylinder flagship.

Eighteen months later, in February 1987, an automatic gearbox—the ZF four-speed linked to a 3.54:1 final drive—was again listed as an option for the XJ-S in either form to gauge the demand for manual boxes. It is hard for the layman to credit, but major manufacturers were already complaining that it cost too much to develop a new gearbox. This was the prime reason for Jaguar's continuing reliance on gearboxes from outside

sources, while undertaking the relatively expensive course of market research on the XJ-S to see if it was worth making transmissions in-house. Soon after, the six-cylinder cabriolet was phased out, followed by the 12-cylinder by the end of year. Demand for what was seen as only semi-open topped motoring had not been high enough to justify the complex production methods.

New ideas for improving the XJ saloons continued to appear on the XJ-S coupé at the same time. Increased spring rates, 43 per cent up at the front and 34 per cent higher at the back, with a

Other attempts by agents such as Guy Salmon to customise the XJ–S – pictured here during 1985 on demonstration at Silverstone in Jaguar form in the first picture, and as a 'Daimler' in the second – were less than successful, although the twin headlight treatment heralded what would become a factory trend.

stiffer front anti-roll bar and the return of the rear anti-roll bar, along with modified Boge dampers and new Pirelli 225-60VR15 tyres on 6.5-inch rims, reduced body roll and improved the handling. Following 20 years of complaints from sporting drivers, the steering pump was also re-valved to reduce its power assistance by 17 per cent, which, with turns from lock-to-lock reduced to 2.6, allied to stiffer rack mounting bushes, transformed the feel at the wheel — which had a thicker, more sporting, rim. Reshaped, more body-hugging, seats were fitted with optional electric lumbar adjustment and heating.

The stiffer suspension was not fitted to the cabriolet—and rejected for Jaguar's projected convertible version of the XJ-S—because it was feared that it would induce bad vibrations unless the bodyshell was re-engineered to such an extent that it would then become impossibly heavy. But anti-lock brakes were introduced across the XJ-S range in February 1988 following a demand by potential customers. Jaguar opted for a system developed by the Albert Teves company following a joint engineering programme. It used the existing Girling discs with a hydraulic power boost operated from an electric pump mounted in the body. One of the major benefits was the system's ability to provide significantly more assisted stops in the event of a booster failure than with a conventional vacuum servo. Each wheel incorporated a separate sensor

Jaguar retained the original headlighting as the V12 version of the XJ-S coupé entered the 1990s.

There were also few outward features to distinguish the 3.6 litre XJ–S other than the removal of the supplementary driving lights.

which fed information to a central electronic control unit. This controlled the brakes through three channels, one for each front wheel and one for the rear wheels, according to which area of contact was most likely to lock. In company with XJ6's anti-lock brakes, the Teves system had a yaw control. This allowed the control unit to differentiate between differing road surfaces under the near and offside wheels.

The range then reached a logical conclusion with the introduction of the first completely open Jaguar since the E type. With a fine sense of occasion, the XJ-S convertible was launched at the Geneva Motor Show in March 1988, 27 years after the E type made its debut at the same venue. As a top-of-the-range model, initially it was available only in V12 form, using a bodyshell modified for production at Brown's Lane. The big difference between the two-seater convertible—apart from its lack of a roll hoop—and the cabrio was that its chassis strengthening was built in from the start, rather than added afterwards.

More than 100 new panels were needed, with tooling by Karmann and another 50 modified ones from the Rover Group's body plant in Swindon. Between them, they represented about one third of the bodyshell's panel count. Karmann also supplied the body shell assembly tooling and designed the hood.

Jaguar were particularly pleased with the hood. It had a conventional fabric envelope linked to a rigid glass rear window complete with heating element. The whole lot, tinted glazing included,

The factory convertible became a popular option, however, as the only open Jaguar.

A twin headlight system was adopted for the Le Mans commemorative edition of the XJ-S V12 in 1991.

sank into an area forward of the boot at the press of a switch. It was a very substantial unit which put their last, skimpy, effort of the E type to shame. The new hood was filled with sound-deadening material and fully lined. All that was needed to lower it was the release of two securing catches on the leading edge of its frame, followed by pressure on a rocker switch. This operated an electro-hydraulic mechanism which took 12 seconds to lower the hood. Raising it was just as easy, the immensely-rigid frame locating the securing lugs in the windscreen rail automatically. The only real penalty, apart from the rear seats which had been lost on the cabriolet without any undue drama on the sales front, was that the bulky operating

mechanism meant that the fuel tank capacity had to be reduced to 18 gallons. It was Jaguar's opinion, however, that the people who brought an XJ-S convertible would have been less concerned with a minor reduction in range than those who opted for the higher-performance coupé, drove harder, and used more fuel, relatively speaking.

To ensure longevity, Jaguar had put the hood and its mechanism through rigorous tests which included raising and lowering the hood 8,000 times—the equivalent of once a day for 22 years. Unlike the E type, however, in which the far more simple single-skin hood could be lowered while it was stationary in a traffic jam, the new power-operated roof could only be operated, for safety reasons, while the gear selector was in park and the handbrake on—discouraging poseurs!

Jaguar entered the 1990s with a comprehensive variety of XJ–S models.

Jaguar had chosen Karmann to work on the conversion because of the German firm's vast experience in engineering open cars. The changes to the skin panels were fairly obvious: frameless doors, revised rear wings with a redesigned 'saddle panel' between the bootlid and interior. But a double-skinned floor was also necessary with steel post reinforcement for the inner sills and front door-hanging posts, allied to strengthening around the transmission tunnel to combat scuttle shake. The result was an overall weight increase over the coupé of 220lb, with a marginal worsening of the drag coefficient to 0.39.

But the weight increase could have been a lot more, which is what put Jaguar off producing a convertible for so long. Early experiments with top-less XJ-S bodyshells involved the use of the heavy 'harmonic' bumpers that appeared on the convertible version of Triumph's fixed-head TR7 sports car produced by British Leyland in 1980. The idea was that these massive bumpers would act as low-frequency vibration dampers to combat scuttle

Along with Lister, Tom Walkinshaw had been one of the pioneers of expensive aftermarket customisation kits, and it was no surprise when JaguarSport introduced the XJR-S 6.0 in 1989.

shake. It was effective on the TR7 and more-powerful TR8 but looked ugly because such massive beams were needed on the already very heavy XJ-S.

Detail changes to the mounting rubbers for the engine, front and rear subframes and suspension arms were part of the development that resulted in the spring and damper rates being softened by 5 per cent over those employed on the standard, non-sporting, XJ-S and cabriolet. The lighter steering was retained with automatic transmission as standard because it was anticipated that customers would want a car that was more of a boulevard cruiser than a road burner like the new 3.6-litre XJ-S coupé. There was no intention to produce a 3.6-litre version of the convertible, however, because it was felt that there would only be a minimal demand for an economy variant of such a lush, and more expensive, model.

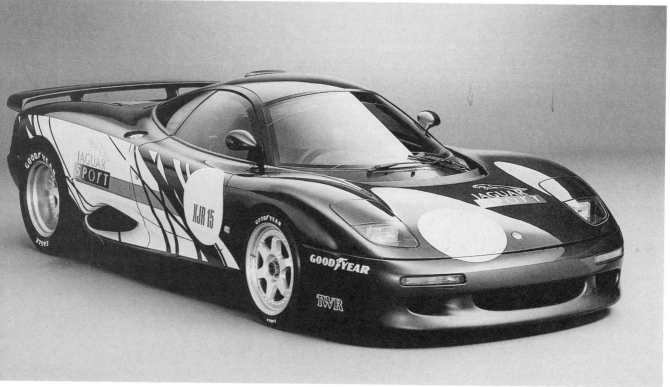

Facing page, top: Jaguar also floated the idea of cashing in on the exlusive market for short production runs of exotic sports cars that had been highly successful in publicising marques like Ferrari, with the F40, and Porsche, with the 959. As a result they produced a prototype called the XJ220, using a version of the V12 engine from the XJ–S that had been adapted for their Le Mans-winning sports racing cars.

Facing page, bottom: JaguarSport then put the car into very limited production as the XJR–15, although its top speed – mooted at more than 200mph – meant that environmental lobbies had to be placated by the proclamation that it was only for racing. Little work was needed, however, to convert it for road use.

But the fatter and more modern steering wheel from the sporting version became a standard fitting with the better-gripping Pirelli P600s running on 6.5-inch rims. In this form, the XJ-S convertible seemed assured of a far longer life than the cabriolet which had tested the water and met a less-than-rapturous reception in the United States, where road-testers pleaded for a proper open car.

The JaguarSport operation, which had been marketing bodystyling and suspension kits for the XJ-S as well as a more sporting limited-edition XJ6, then followed a similar line with the big coupé. The XJR-S launched in August 1989 had its engine capacity increased to 5,993cc by lengthening the stroke to 78.5mm from 70, which meant fitting new pistons, liners and crankshaft. In this form the power was increased to 381bhp from the 286 to which it had fallen as a result of modifications to run on unleaded fuel that paralleled those in the XJ12 saloons. Torque was much increased to 362lb/ft at 3,750rpm—with more than 300lb/ft all the way up from 2,000rpm. The GM400 automatic transmission was recalibrated at the same time to give a more responsive kickdown.

Chassis developments were similar to those on the 3.6-litre coupé, with stiffer springs and anti-roll bars linked to Bilstein gas-filled dampers and increased negative camber at the rear wheels. The 16-inch Speedline alloy wheels featured on the XJR 3.6 saloon conversion also found their way onto the XJR-S with wider Dunlop tyres of 225/50 section at the front and 245/55 at the back. Extensive colour-coded bodykit modifications—including a prominent spoiler on the rear deck—and a full leather interior completed the package aimed at restoring the performance of the original HE that had been lost on the altar of unleaded fuel.

Jaguar's Competition Saloons

Although the saloon cars prepared by Jaguar for competition in the early years were highly successful, it was more a result of the sheer horsepower and torque provided by their XK engines than by the extreme modifications that characterised later years.

The Mark VII saloons were the first to benefit from such attention as they provided an ideal mount for the Monte Carlo Rally, which received enormous publicity in the 1950s. This was because of regulations that favoured saloon cars and the fact that the Mark VII, which weighed more than two tons with full rally equipment and crew, was uncommonly good at ploughing through the Alpine snowdrifts typical of this mid-winter event.

Engine work reflected parallel development on the C type sports racing car and the XK120, which was dominating other rallies favouring sports cars. As a result, the early Mark VII competition saloons were only likely to have the compression ratio increased to 8:1 and high-lift cams in a carefully-assembled, fully-balanced engine producing around 180bhp. It was considered pointless to use a more highly-tuned power unit because of the difficulty in obtaining supplies of high-octane fuel in remote parts of France.

They were also fitted with a 4.55:1 final drive ratio, rather than 4.3:1, which gave them broadly similar acceleration when fully laden with a rally crew of two or three, two spare wheels, extra jacking equipment, snow chains, long-range fuel tanks, luggage and spares, as they would have enjoyed with only the driver on board. An additional advantage was that the 4.55 ratio improved ploughing power on snowy rallies like the Monte Carlo. This ratio was originally used as standard on the 2.5-litre Mark V saloon that preceded the Mark

VII and was listed as an option for the XK120 sports car. Higher ratio steering, using 3.75 turns from lock-to-lock, rather than 4.75, was also fitted to improve manoeuvrability at speed, along with stiffer torsion bars, stronger rear springs and uprated dampers. The Mark VII rally cars also had extra instruments, high-sided bucket seats at the front that closely resembled those that would be used as standard on the E type sports car between 1961 and 1964, stick-on windscreen demisters and flexible pipes from the heater which could be directed at individual parts of the interior. In common with the other rally cars, they also had additional windscreen wipers on top of the windscreen to complement the standard equipment operating from the scuttle. Any further special preparation tended to concentrate on meticulous assembly, and the use of wire or cotter pins on bolts to make sure that nothing came loose.

Basically-similar mechanical specifications were used for touring car races which switched from sports to saloons around 1952. The works cars built for the chief race, at Silverstone, used full C type engines however, and sports racing tyres. Running on twin 2-inch SU carburettors, they produced around 200bhp by dint of a 9:1 compression ratio which could be used because top-quality fuel was available. Lightened flywheels and the closer ratio gearbox and steering gear from the XK120 were fitted because they would be racing with only the driver and without the weighty additional equipment carried in the rally cars. The same stiffer torsion bars were fitted to reduce some of the body roll—rather than simply support extra weight—along with an extra leaf in the back springs. The driver also had the competition bucket seat, which was reckoned to be worth a second a lap because it provided far better location, apart from saving weight.

The 4.55:1 final drive ratio was favoured in all competitions because top speed was never a problem with a Jaguar. It was just as vital on the race track as in rallying: the majority of circuits were too tight for such big cars to spend much time flat out, so it became more important for them to reach a high speed quickly.

Rally cars remained little altered, apart from a general move towards studded tyres—which did nothing for dry-road handling—in the Monte Carlo. Cars run in the RAC Rally could use normal rubber because it was held in the spring, rather than the winter which has become so popular.

The racing Mark VIIs received more attention as the Silverstone event—supporting the British Grand Prix—became very important for publicity. Chassis were lightened and stiffened and superfluous panels, such as splash guards, omitted from the bodywork. At the same time, the power was increased, in company with C type developments, to 210bhp, although Weber carburettors—which gave more top-end power—were considered too extreme a modification. High-pressure fuel pumps were definitely in, however.

Fully laden, and with a crew of three – Ronnie Adams, Derek Johnson and Frank Biggar – works Mark VII Jaguar rally cars weighed in at more than two tons. This car, which had already started in one Monte Carlo Rally as well as the Silverstone production car race, proved more than a match for the snow-covered roads in the 1956 Monte, finishing first despite a handicap system that ensured that no other car of more than 2,500cc finished in the first 38!

Adams, left, surveys the scene as snow chains are fitted to the rear wheels of the Mark VII saloon during the 1955 Monte Carlo Rally. Soon studded tyres would become the order of the day.

Rally machinery benefited from these modification because often the cars were the same, although they were more likely to have softer engines and a wide-ratio transmission.

By 1954, the competition looked like being so intense at Silverstone that Jaguar had several sets of magnesium panels made up to replace the far heavier steel items on the factory Mark VIIs. This was in response to strong rumours that the rival Armstrong-Siddeleys were likely to resort to similar weight-saving measures. Then the rumours became so widespread that the race organisers clamped down and standard body materials were retained by all parties. Nevertheless, the Jaguars got alloy radiators, which not only saved weight but proved more efficient.

Still the rally cars remained basically standard as some of the alloy panels—such as floor skins—appeared on the racing cars for Silverstone in 1955. Lap speeds rose as the weight fell, but soon the Mark VII's days in front-line competition would be numbered as Jaguar introduced the smaller and lighter Mark I saloon.

Heavy snow—and brilliant driving—gave the Mark VII its greatest success the following year, however, as it won the Monte Carlo Rally and still had a big enough power advantage over the 2.4-litre Mark I to finish first at Silverstone. This was despite the tuning kits listed by the works that could take the power output up to 150bhp with a close-ratio gearbox, stiffer dampers and anti-roll bar and higher-ratio steering.

It soon became evident that the Mark I chassis needed reinforcement, though, as Panhard rod mountings began to tear out on the racing versions.

To a certain extent, these modifications were reflected in changes to the production cars, although the bodyshell reinforcement was taken further on the competition cars. Extensive—and expensive—seam welding was common to stiffen the shell with aluminium for non-stressed panels, such as the doors, bonnet and bootlid, to reduce weight. The rather clumsy rear wheel spats were invariably discarded. The back springs were stiffened with an extra leaf and special competition shock absorbers used. Heavy anti-roll bars were fitted front and rear with a Powr-Lok limited-slip differential. Stronger competition clutches were fitted with close-ratio gearboxes.

Almost as soon as the 3.4-litre Mark I was introduced, it got disc brakes. Negative camber front suspension became popular with as much weight as possible shifted to the back to improve traction. This included re-locating the battery in the boot. Full C type engines were retained, running on twin 2-inch SU carburettors, rather than the later Webers, or D type sports racing car unit, to comply with contemporary touring car regulations. Rally cars were prepared to similar standards, with other additions like extra lights and long-range fuel tanks. Eventually, the 3.4-litre Mark Is ran with 10:1 compression ratio engine and triple 2-inch SU carburettors to take the power output up to around 250bhp (by contemporary power ratings). The bodyshells were lightened wherever possible with panels like the flitch plates cutaway—which was also necessary to provide room for triple carburettors. Twin-plate competition clutches were fitted with a 3.77:1 final drive and overdrive close-ratio gearbox.

Stirling Moss leads the sprinters for the three Mark VII Jaguars that set fastest times in practice for the 1954 Silverstone production car race. Alongside him are rallyman Ian Appleyard and Le Mans winner Tony Rolt. Moss's car, which finished third behind those of Appleyard and Rolt, had already seen service with the BBC's Raymond Baxter and Gordon Wilkins in the Monte Carlo Rally and won the Silverstone race in 1952 and 1953.

Racing subjected the early Mark I Jaguars to unexpected stresses, especially around the rear axle, where the Panhard rod mounting proved to be the weakest link. Some idea of the forces involved is well illustrated by the negative camber angles adopted by the inside front wheel of Tommy Sopwith's 3.4 litre car at Silverstone with the following rear wheel close to positive camber as the tail slides out. Hard as Sopwith drove, with considerable success that year, he had to give best to world champion Mike Hawthorn in the even faster 3.4 litre Mark 1 holding a tighter line around Woodcote in the 1958 International Trophy meeting.

Suspension modifications were limited to high-rate coil springs, 0.8125-inch anti-roll bar, revised mounting blocks to lower the roll centre, and more positive castor at the front, along with uprated rear springs and Koni shock absorbers all round. The battery was sited in the boot to improve weight distribution and traction.

Early 3.8-litre Mark II saloons received similar modifications as wire wheels became compulsory wear to aid brake cooling. By 1961 they had full-race E type engines producing around 300bhp with lightened flywheels, close-ratio gearboxes, overdrive, stiffer competition shock absorbers and springs, seam welding, alloy suspension uprights, thicker Mark IX brake discs, alloy calipers, alloy body panels, and wire wheels wide enough to take 6.40 x 15 racing tyres.

Eventually these Jaguars were defeated by as much as 400bhp in American V8 saloons and carried on with all sorts of modifications in club racing. It would be more than a decade before more front-line Jaguar saloons would emerge, initially in the United States as a logical extension of a highly-successful E type production sports car racing programme. The American Group 44 organisation concentrated on the XJ-S in Transam racing, their equivalent of the European touring car events, to replace the E type—which had become obsolete in 1976—because it was the lightest production Jaguar using potentially the most powerful engine, the V12. In Britain, Leyland made a fatal mistake when they opted for the heavier XJ

By the time the Mark II appeared on the competition scene, special parts were being made for Jaguars, such as the cut-down front coil springs, stiffer dampers, reinforced tie rods, extended front anti-roll bar and modified spring plates that gave the front suspension negative camber on cars with Coombs conversions.

The bodyshell of the Mark I Jaguar proved so strong that some examples seemed indestructible despite a lurid career in competition. One of the best-known was registered VYM924, pictured first in a Jaguar Drivers' Club meeting at Silverstone in September 1961, some three years after it was first raced, then at Castle Coombe in October 1971.

An early road-going saloon raced initially by Albert Betts in the mid-1960s – it is shown here at the Bombhole in Snetterton during 1967 – was later restored and driven by the editor of *Classic Cars*, Tony Dron at Donington at a Jaguar Drivers' Club meeting in August 1986.

coupé in Group Two touring car races. The thinking behind this decision was that the coupé might still be re-engineered to sell at a premium in the United States, so it was worth giving it a high-performance image, while saving the XJ-S for a new silhouette Group Five which could achieve their greatest dream: victory at the Le Mans sports car race in which the C type and D types had done so much to boost Jaguar's fortunes between 1951 and 1957.

The V12 engine had already been well developed for Sports Car Club of America racing when Group 44 began work on the XJ-S in 1976. Power was taken up to 475bhp at 7,600rpm by careful assembly, 11:1 compression ratio pistons and six Weber 441DF carburettors on special manifolds. Reliability was enhanced by the use of dry-sump lubrication and stronger driveshafts although the standard manual transmission—with an aluminium flywheel and competition clutch—was retained. Suspension, steering and brakes were uprated, but retained the standard lay-out in a bodyshell lightened as far as possible by stripping out the interior, lighting and replacing glass panes with plastic.

As SCCA regulations changed to allow bigger weight reductions and improved aerodynamics in 1977, the British effort was just getting underway. The European Group Two regulations were a lot more liberal than those in the Transam category one which attracted Group 44. They allowed extensive modifications within a basically-standard bodyshell. This meant that Ralph Broad, who ran the Broadspeed organisation which had 'sold' the project to British Leyland, had to opt for maximum power, rather than increasing performance by extensive lightening.

At one point it seemed as though they had much of the British motor industry supporting them. Armstrong made special shock absorbers, Lucas produced a new engine management system, AP developed a clutch that could handle 600bhp, SKF made wheel bearings that would withstand such outputs and Lockheed developed eight-pot brakes. Such operations cost a fortune, of course;

Classic Mark I and II cars, along with any other Jaguar or Daimler saloons of the appropriate period, continue to be raced with relatively few modifications in the Pre-1968 Jaguar Challenge. Brian Shepherd's 3.8 litre-engined Mark I is seen leading the bunch at Oulton Park in April 1990.

Rally cars sprouted a variety of extra lights to cope with the all-night events popular during the 1950s and 1960s. This Mark II, driven by Bobby Parkes in the 1960 Tulip Rally, featured not only the standard headlamps and spotlights, but spotlights on the front overriders and a swivelling navigator's light on the roof – which is now illegal because it is moveable.

the CSI governing body accordingly became alarmed that the spectacle of Group Two racing would deteriorate as only two manufacturers, BMW and Jaguar, could afford to carry on competing. So they tried to contain power outputs by banning dry-sump lubrication.

Broadspeed tried to get around this handicap with a complex wet sump system using numerous baffles, but it proved inadequate for a car producing as much as 550bhp which could generate enormous cornering and braking forces on massive wheels shod with wide, slick, racing tyres. The stresses involved with putting down so much power in such a heavy vehicle played havoc with the drive shafts, too. Jaguar—rather than British Leyland—had considered the project ill-advised from the start and were loath to devote valuable engineering time to producing new parts—so the awe-inspiring Broadspeed XJ coupés soon gained a reputation for unreliability despite numerous changes of specification from one event to the next. Even when the CSI relented and allowed dry-sump lubrication in an attempt to present some sort of a spectacle, the Jaguars fell by the wayside frequently after outrunning the BMWs in practice.

In stark contrast, the lighter Group 44 XJ-S was highly successful, partly because the Americans were able to make stronger hubs, driveshafts and gear ratios and move as much weight as possible to the back of the car to aid traction. They also improved the braking with far better aerodynamic ducting, and found ways to keep the drivers reasonably cool as they worked hard with these heavy cars in very hot conditions. Often driver fatigue had played a large part in the problems experienced with the XJ coupés.

In addition, ever-changing regulations gave the American XJ-S a new lease of life in 1981. The basic bodyshell no longer had to be retained, so long as the car still looked like an XJ-S. So Group 44 built a far-lighter tubular frame around which were hung lightweight panels—rather like the silhouette XJ-S that had been visualised for Group Five racing five years earlier. A 525bhp version of the V12 was also mounted 7.5 inches further back to improve weight distribution with power conveyed by a Franklin quick-change final drive like

The American Group 44 racing team took over Jaguar's semi-official competition role in 1976 as British Leyland's marketing department in Coventry deemed that maximum promotional effort should be put behind the Triumph TR7 in the lower sporting price brackets and the Jaguar XJ-S in the higher. With Quaker State oil sponsorship, Group 44 – which had been highly-successful with the V12 E-type – proved more than competent with the heavier coupé in Transam events, their XJ-S pictured here leading typical Chevrolet Corvette opposition.

It was the beginning of the end of the Jaguar 3.8's dominance in British saloon car racing as three massive Ford Galaxies, each of 7 litres engine capacity were imported from the United States. These machines also had top-flight drivers, with world champion-to-be Jim Clark pictured leading Sears at Brands Hatch in August 1963. The current world champion, Graham Hill, is hanging on with Coombs's car, but he could take only second place to Clark after Sears pitted with a tyre burst by the heavyweight Ford's frantic cornering, with Salvadori third in the Atkins 3.8.

the units used in America's NASCAR saloon car racing. The resultant effort was sufficiently successful for Group 44 to take the project further into the new Group C sports racing car category which formed the basis for Jaguar's current world championship wins.

At the same time as the old Groups One to Six international sports and touring categories were revised as Group A (semi-modified production), Group B (highly-modified production), Group C (all-out racing) and group N (near-standard), with strict limits on minimum weight, the XJ-S once again became an attractive proposition. The only real problem to making an XJ-S competitive was that the new regulations were framed towards economy as well as performance.

Not long before, this would have ruled the XJ-S out of such competition. But with the advent of ever more sophisticated computerised engine management systems, there was hope of extracting enough horsepower without having to use an

In Britain, Leyland made the mistake of opting for the even-heavier XJ coupé, in the vain hope that the lighter XJ-S could be adapted for the potentially-higher market rewards of a win in the Le Mans 24-hour race. When it came to the crunch, every obstacle imaginable defeated the Jaguars – other than the BMW seen trailing one of the coupés on the racetrack. BMW had already won their battle to assume a high-performance image and simply needed the Jaguars to prove that – in the absence of Porsche, and the long-gone Ford – they were supreme. So they stayed behind the Jaguars until they exhausted themselves, and then won the races with apologies, saying they had defeated stern opposition. At this point, Jaguar really were lagging behind the times . . .

impossible amount of fuel; weight saving would also be critical in this respect.

The equation as worked out by the Tom Walkinshaw racing organisation was that the XJ-S ought to be competitive in the new Group A if 400bhp could be extracted at no less than 5.5mpg in a car with its weight reduced from 1,750kg to near the class minimum of 1,400kg. Extensive engine modifications were allowed, although there were restrictions on valve lift. As a result, the engine was completely reworked with special 12:1 compression ratio pistons, new camshafts and a re-programmed Lucas injection system to give around

300bhp at 5,000rpm on the way to 400 at 7,000 early in 1982. Three years of development—chiefly to the wet sump engine's management system—improved these figures to more than 450bhp at 6,750rpm with 390lb/ft of torque at 4,900rpm on the way to 7,500rpm maximum.

Early examples of the Group A XJ-S raced on the original four-speed gearbox before Getrag's five-speed transmission was homologated in July

Much of the British motor industry was behind Jaguar in their attempt to show the Germans what they could do. The engineering, such as that seen in the fuel injection system of the XJ coupés, was fantastic.

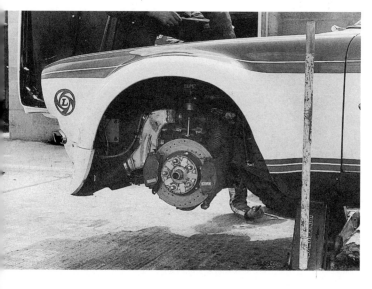

1983. Final drive ratios varied between 3.77:1 and 3.07. Although the suspension remained basically the same as standard—production line mounting points had to be retained—the components were all special fabrications to take the enormous strain of cornering and stopping such a heavy car at speeds up to 150mph and provide adjustment for geometry and ride height. Rubber was replaced with metal wherever possible for improved strength and response, and spring rates were sky high at up to 1,800lb front and 450–475lb at the back, Bilstein shock absorbers replacing the Armstrongs

Above: Ventilated disc brakes were capable of stopping these cars competively, despite the bodyshell's great weight.

Below: Everything about the Broadspeed XJ coupés was beautifully made – notably the rear air dam, and fuel fillers.

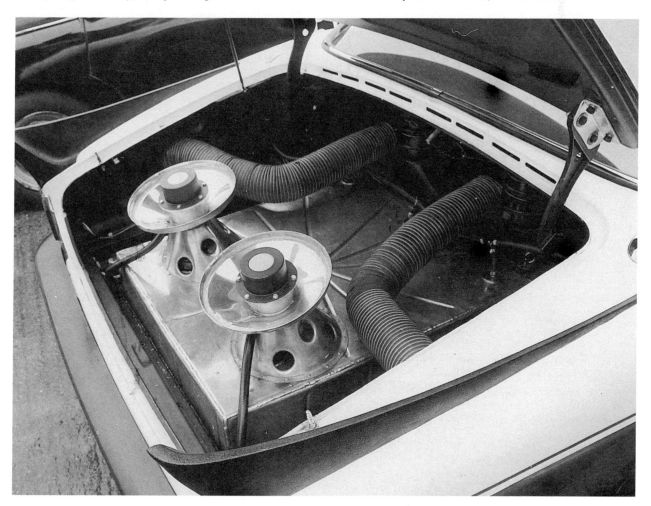

Eventually the equally-seasoned Walkinshaw team calculated that the XJ-S could be made competitive in the European Touring Car Championship. The proprietor himself is seen here at the wheel in the Tourist Trophy race at Silverstone in 1982 in a car he shared with fellow businessman and former Classic Saloon Car racer Chuck Nicholson.

used on the XJC. There were no restriction on brakes under the Group A regulations which was a great help to Walkinshaw. From the start the rear discs were moved outboard to relieve strain on the driveshafts and, even more important, not to subject the final drive to undue heat.

Initially an oil cooler was fitted to this vital component, with an aerodynamic fairing under the rear skirt during 1983. In 1984, Walkinshaw switched from 13-inch wide, 16-inch diameter, BBS racing wheels to 17-inch rims by Speedline to increase the diameter of the ventilated discs, served by four-pot calipers, from 13ins to 14.

This saved the weight of as much as six gallons of water needed to cool the earlier discs, although braking ability was always marginal on these big cars.

With the exception of the period when the rear 'under wing' was used in 1983—and incited numer-

ous protests—the bodywork remained basically as standard except that it was lightened wherever possible, especially by the removal of all undersealing and sound-deadening material. Full roll cages were compulsory, and the time saved during pit stops by an on-board compressed air jacking system was considered well worth its weight.

In this form, the last of the 'works' Jaguar racing saloons was almost as far removed as it was possible to conceive from the early rally cars without radical changes to the appearance . . .

For a time, the Walkinshaw XJ–S front-runners had to resort to inter-cooler's mounted under the rear bodywork, almost concealed by spray on the example driven by Walkinshaw and Nicholson at Donington in 1983.

Walkinshaw's XJ–S team held the top three positions in Britain's oldest race, the Tourist Trophy, at Silverstone in 1984. Then a massive rainstorm resulted in a multiple crash, and the necessity to use a pace car while the wreckage was cleared cost Walkinshaw's car the lead to BMW. Never mind, by then Jaguar had a moral victory, not only on the racetrack, but for the XJ–S in world markets.

The Glorious Saloons

Jaguar's sports racing cars hogged the headlines in the early years of the marque and the exploits of the saloons provided an ideal back-up. The impact of the C type and D type winning five Le Mans races would have been far less had the production cars not performed so well in their own competitions. When a Mark VII saloon won the Monte Carlo Rally in 1956, the resultant publicity boosted sales almost as much as victory at Le Mans in the same year. And when the Mark I and Mark II saloons began to dominate touring car races, they took over where the D types had left off. Such victories established Jaguar with a reputation for high-performance that would last more than a decade until British Leyland felt it necessary to generate more publicity by ranging XJ coupés against BMWs in Europe. Sadly, this effort proved ill-advised, and was only forgotten when the XJ-S proved a far more capable racing car on both sides of the Atlantic . . .

The Mark VII's predecessor, the pushrod-engined Mark V, had already proved the value of such a strong heavy car in deep snow when Cecil Vard from Dublin took third place in the 1951 Monte Carlo Rally. The snow was worse in 1952, but could not stop the Mark VIIs of French crews Cotton/Didier and Heurtaux/Crespin from taking fourth and sixth places in this winter spectacle. Ford fared even better, however, as leading special builder Sydney Allard won with their V8 engine in a saloon of his own construction. Allard sports cars had provided tough opposition for the Jaguar XK120 on the track, but the Monte Carlo saloon could not match Stirling Moss's works Mark VII when the Silverstone production car race switched to saloons that year. Moss won this British Grand Prix-supporting event from Ken Wharton's Healey.

Ford hit back in the 1953 Monte Carlo Rally when Dutch ace Maurice Gartonides won with a works Zephyr from Ian Appleyard's Mark VII, shared with his wife, Pat, daughter of Jaguar chief William Lyons. Three months later Denis Scott won his class in the RAC Rally with a completely standard Mark VII borrowed from his father before Moss again outran the field to win the Silverstone production car race with the same Mark VII, registered LWK343. This time Harold Grace was second in a Riley 2.5-litre saloon.

Louis Chiron was the 1954 Monte Carlo Rally in a Lancia Aurelia GT—although some of the glitter was dulled by the odds stacked in his favour: the weather was good, his highly-tuned car was ideally suited to circuit racing, and nobody knew the ground for the final test on which the rally result hinged better than Chiron: the veteran Monegasque Formula One driver was completely at home on the Monaco Grand Prix circuit. Nevertheless rally leaders Adams and Desmond Titterington captured the crowd's hearts by losing only three seconds to Chiron on the last lap with their unwieldy Mark VII while taking sixth place.

Moss broke the lap record with LRW343 at Silverstone later that year, but could manage only third place behind the Mark VIIs of Appleyard and Le Mans winner Tony Rolt after his starter jammed on the line. Mike Hawthorn raised the record lap speed from 77.48mph to 81.06 with LRW343 in 1955 as more weight was pared off the Mark VII, Ian Stewart and Titterington taking second and third places with similar cars. Adams, who had led the winning team in the Monte Carlo Rally with his eighth-placed Mark VII was further down the field with his private entry at Silverstone.

By 1956, Jaguars were facing daunting odds

The French crew of Rene Cotton and Louis Didier are pictured starting the climb out of Monaco on the final loop of the 1952 Monte
Carlo Rally in which the British driver Sydney Allard ploughed
through appalling snowdrifts to win with his Ford V8-powered car.
Cotton and Didier were fourth, however, with compatriots Heurtaux
and Crespin sixth in another Mark VII.

in international rallies which were now being run
to rules that heavily handicapped large-capacity
cars. Then Adams, in company with Derek John-
stone and Frank Biggar, shocked everybody by
winning the Monte Carlo Rally. The extent of his
achievement could be seen when it was realised that
his Mark VII was the only car of more than 2,500cc
to finish in the first 38!

Initially, it looked as though the 2.4-litre Mark

Treacherous conditions like those which eliminated Briton J. W.
Banks's Bristol in a collision with a bridge during the 1955 event
helped boost the chances of the numerous Continental entries in Mark
VII Jaguars.

Adams *(centre)* with Johnson and Biggar is pictured receiving their award for eighth place in the 1955 event before going on to win the following year in the same Mark VII Jaguar.

I—boosted by optional high-performance equipment—might be good enough to hold its own against Ford Zephyrs and Austin A90s in the medium-capacity classes. Frank Grounds won the under 2,700-cc category and finished fourth overall in the 1956 RAC Rally on the 2.4's competition debut, and Paul Frère used one in the same year to win the production car race at Spa, in Belgium, where nimble good handling was of paramount importance. The higher-powered Mark VII was still quicker on most circuits, however, especially in lightweight form. So Jaguar hedged their bets for the Silverstone production car race. Hawthorn and 1953 Le Mans winner Duncan Hamilton were entered in Mark Is, with Frère and Ivor

Bueb in Mark VIIs. It was just as well . . . Hawthorn howled into the lead, only to blow up his engine, letting Bueb through to win from Wharton's works Austin A90 with Hamilton third and Frère fourth.

But when Jaguar answered American pleas in 1957 for a 3.4-litre Mark I, they found a guaranteed race-winner. Hawthorn, Bueb and Hamilton in works disc-braked cars were split at Silverstone only by Lister-Jaguar star Archie Scott-Brown in a private Mark I on drums until his brakes faded.

Although the engine capacity of the 3.4-litre Mark I militated against it in international rallies, there was one such event in which it could shine: the Tour de France. This was because it was made up of a series of circuit races and hill climbs, linked by closely-timed road sections. Originally this event had favoured sports cars, but the categories were

revised in 1957 to provide two winners, one in a GT car and the other in a tourer. This meant that the front-running Ferraris did not come into direct conflict with touring cars like the 3.4-litre Mark I. Jaguars driven by Hernando da Silva Ramos, Bernard Consten and Sir Gawaine Baillie proved competitive, but ran into trouble in 1957, before Baillie took third place with Peter Jopp the following year. Then da Silva Ramos found reliability in 1959 for the first of a series of Jaguar touring car wins.

Baillie, meantime, was one of the leading exponents of the Mark I in the newly-established British saloon car championship. His team leader, Tommy Sopwith, won numerous events in 1957 and 1958, with the chief opposition coming from a fac-

Ivor Bueb, pictured in the Ecurie Endeavour 3.4 litre Mark I bearing the distinctive registration number IVA400, did most of the winning for Tommy Sopwith in saloon car racing during 1959. In the first picture, he is leading close rival Sir Gawaine Baillie, in a similar car, at Castle Combe, and, in the second picture, inching out the even more formidable Roy Salvadori in John Coombs's Mark I, registered BUY1.

tory development car entered by Surrey Jaguar dealer John Coombes. This also had the benefit of works drivers such as Hamilton and Ron Flockhart, with a guest appearance by Walt Hansgen, who drove factory-backed Jaguars in the United States for Briggs Cunningham. The divergence of drivers in the unofficial works car left Sopwith tying for the championship with Jack Sears in Wharton's old Austin A90 . . . and Sears won the title in a race-off in BMC-loaned Riley 1.5s. Sopwith then retired from driving but carried on as an entrant with Jaguars under his Equipe Endeavour banner.

The occasional good results also came Jaguar's

way in top-line rallies. Farming twins Don and Erle Morley began a great career by winning their class in the 1958 RAC Rally with a 2.4-litre Mark I before Bobby Parkes and George Howarth won their class in the 1959 Monte Carlo Rally, taking eighth place overall, in a 3.4-litre Mark I. They made up the winning team with fellow Jaguar drivers, Phil Walton and Michael Martin, Eric Brinkman and John Cuff. The Morleys then bought a new 3.4-litre Mark I and created a sensation by winning the Tulip Rally, a top European event in which only five cars survived appalling weather without penalty.

Bueb took over as Sopwith's team leader to raise lap records slightly and maintain Jaguar's hold on the Silverstone production car race by winning from Roy Salvadori in the Coombes car. Baillie, Dick Protheroe and Tommy Dickson took

Jack Spears joined Mike Parkes in the Ecurie Endeavour team's 3.8 litre saloons in 1961. He is seen here leading Parkes before both ran out of petrol on the last lap during the Lombank Trophy meeting at Snetterton in 1961 – leaving Baillie to win in his Mark II.

World champion-to-be Graham Hill became the leading Jaguar Mark II driver in 1962 with Coombs's 3.8 litre car registered BUY12. In the first picture he is seen winning at Silverstone and in the second team mate Roy Salvadori leads Charles Kelsey's Chevrolet Chevvy II at Crystal Palace. It was the start of an American invasion that was to relegate the Mark II Jaguars to also-ran status the following year. Sears's Mark II is on Kelsey's tail, followed by Baillie. Sears got past Kelsey, who was subsequently disqualified for having an illegal exhaust system, but it was the beginning of a new era in production saloon car racing.

Facing page: Keen amateur John Sparrow bought an ex-works 3.8 litre Mark II saloon registered 1628VC which had been campaigned by Salvadori to race in 1963. He is seen in the first picture in the *Motor* Six-Hour at Brands Hatch, sharing with Neil Dangerfield, and leading the semi-works MG1100 of Alan Foster and Andrew Hedges, and the HF Squadra Corse Lancia Flavia of Patria and Rossi. Salvadori and Denny Hulme won the event in another 3.8 litre Mark II. In the second picture, Sparrow is seen chasing the 'Ford Consul Cortina SS' of Doc Merfield – in reality one of the first Lotus Cortinas – at Mallory Park later in the year when they finished fourth and sixth in an event won by Mike Salmon's Mark II. Lighter cars such as the Cortina would soon outrun the Jaguars, however, along with the more powerful American saloons.

third, fourth and fifth places in 3.4-litre cars with Peter Blond finishing sixth in a 2.4. The smaller class, however, normally fell to Jeff Uren's Zephyr—and such was the rivalry between the Coombes and Sopwith cars that he won the saloon car championship.

But Jaguar's string of outright wins continued unabated with the competition debut of the Mark II in 1960, David MacKay starring in the Australian Tasman series with Salvadori doing most of the winning in Britain although Jaguar competitions chief Lofty England gave the car to Lotus constructor Colin Chapman for the Silverstone race. Chapman repaid him by winning from Sears in Sopwith's car!

As part of the RAC Rally's progression to true international status, its spring date was switched to November with more forestry track stages to attract star European drivers as a grand finale to their season. Such rough surfaces militated against the Mark II, so Jaguar concentrated on the Tour de France. It needed only the fanatical preparation of the top French crew, Consten and Jack Renal, to carry off four wins between 1960 and 1963. Jose Behra and Rene Richard also won the touring class on the 1960 Alpine Rally's fast roads with their 3.8-litre Mark II from another crewed by Bobby Parkes and Geoff Howarth.

A third professional team, Peter Berry Racing, bought two 3.8-litre Mark IIs for Grand Prix star Bruce McLaren and Dennis Taylor in 1961—with world champion-to-be John Surtees standing in for McLaren on occasions. But Salvadori, in the

Coombes car, did most of the winning from other Jaguars driven by Mike Parkes and Graham Hill, due to become world champion the following year. In the smaller classes, Ferrari 250GT driver Chris Kerrison had some success with a 2.4-litre Mark II.

But the writing was on the wall for Jaguar's racing saloons. Dan Gurney led them all at Silverstone in a massive Chevrolet Impala that owed a lot to America's NASCAR saloon car racing until a wheel collapsed. Meanwhile, however, Bob Jane won numerous races in Australia in a 4.2-litre version of the Mark II before Hill joined Salvadori in a second Coombes car for 1962. Parkes carried on with an Equipe Endeavour car with David Hobbs leading other Jaguar drivers. Again, Salvadori did most of the winning, although he was beaten once by Charles Kelsey in a Chevrolet Chevvy 2. Sopwith had some satisfaction, however: his Mark II, driven by Parkes and Jimmy Blumer, won *The Motor* six-hour race at Brands Hatch from German Jaguar drivers Peter Lindner and Peter Nocker. Nocker went on to win the first European Touring Car Championship from Mer-

Jaguar saloons still made good mounts in club racing during the late 1960s, including this 3.8 litre S-type saloon in caravan racing at Snetterton during 1967!

In the first picture, Britain's Derek Bell is seen powering away on the first lap of the 1976 Tourist Trophy race at Silverstone with his Broadspeed 'Leyland' XJ coupé, leading Gunnar Nilsson's BMW Batmobile. The lead swopped several times before one of the Jaguar's rear tyres burst, costing five laps by the time the car had reached the pits for new rubber *(right)*. The Nilsson suffered a similar fate and Bell set a 107.15mph lap record before losing a wheel and victory to Nilsson's team mates, Jean Xhenceval, Pierre Dieudonne and Hughes de Fierlant.

cedes in a works-prepared 3.8-litre Mark II in 1963.

Salvadori in publisher Tommy Atkins's Mark II and Hill in the Coombes car started 1963 as they had left off the previous year until 7-litre Ford Galaxies entered by Uren and Baillie proved too powerful. It was left to the Atkins car driven by Salvadori and yet another world champion-to-be, Denny Hulme, to give the Jaguar 3.8-litre Mark II its last great win in the Brands Hatch six-hour race at the end of the season before the big Fords took over.

Jaguar's saloons continued with the odd success, chiefly in club racing, until their fortunes were restored by Group 44 taking pole position in the SCCA championship finals at Road Atlanta in 1976. Once teething troubles had been eliminated, the XJ-S came into its own in 1977, winning five races out of 10, including the Mosport six-hour in Canada for regular driver Bob Tullius with preparation expert Brian Fuerstenau. This effort was good enough not only to beat the rival Chevrolet Corvettes but take the overall SCCA title from John Bauer's well-developed Porsche Carrera RSR.

Meanwhile the Broadspeed's XJ coupé had been launched with much patriotic enthusiasm in Britain only to be hindered by basic weaknesses in the driveline, lubrication and the sheer weight of the chassis. Further complications arose from the fact that they were racing on top European circuits which now had tight chicanes to slow Grand Prix cars. Heavy braking for these chicanes compounded Broadspeed's problems, with the result that they frequently promised much by setting fastest lap in practice then failing during the long-distance races that made up the European Touring Car challenge. Despite a close second to Dietar Quester's BMW at the Nurburgring, it was obvious by the end of the season that the XJ coupés had too many problems ever to be really competitive . . . so Leyland cried enough.

All that British Jaguar fans were left to cheer was the ever-spectacular sight of ancient Jaguars in the new Classic Saloon car races which had been started in 1975. Initially, these events were only for cars built before 1957 so that they would not be dominated by the 3.4-litre Mark I and the Mark II Jaguars. As it was, the chief opposition to cars like the Mark VII of Graig Hinton came from 2.4-litre Mark Is driven by journalist Gordon Bruce, Bob Meacham, and Bill Pinkney, Borgward

Isabella exponent Miles Marshall, Mike Hawes in an MG Magnette, and Ford Zephyrs driven by Peter Kitchen and Chuck Nicholson.

In the United States, however, the XJ-S went from strength to strength. Tullius won five of the 10 Transam category one professional races entered despite tough opposition from the Corvettes—vital to British Leyland because they competed in the same marketplace—and the Porsches, which were less important because they were normally regarded as pure sports cars. It was enough to keep Jaguar competitive in the vital North American car sales market and more than made up for their home ground defeat.

Porsche won the overall Transam title in 1978 with Ludwig Heimrath's 935, but this mattered little to Jaguar. The 935 looked a far more extreme racing car than the XJ-S and was linked in the public mind with sports racing cars like the D type of old. These feelings were supported by the way the 935—loosely based on Porsche's Turbo road cars—made mincemeat of the opposition in long-distance races like Le Mans. The XJ-S, and the Corvettes, were much more readily identifiable with everyday machinery, so Leyland were more than happy when Tullius took the SCCA category one championship with the bonus of beating Chevrolet for the all-important 'makes'—or marques—title.

Classic Saloon Car racing soon became a preserve of the Jaguar Mark I, initially run to a Pre-1957 format to stop 3.4 litre and 3.8 litre Jaguars from winning everything. In the events, which started in 1975, only Graig Hinton's Mark VII Jaguar was able to stay on the 2.4 litre Mark I cars' pace, Bob Meacham seen here leading Hinton at Brands Hatch in July 1976.

Bill Pinckney, pictured here at Silverstone in 1977, also emerged as one of the front runners in Classic Saloon Car racing with his 2.4 litre Mark I.

However, Triumph was in greater trouble than Jaguar, and Group 44 had to concentrate their efforts on this British Leyland marque in 1979 and 1980, which meant that the XJ-S coupés had to go into cold storage. By 1981, however, Jaguar were well on the way to recovery, so Leyland again could provide the finance to make the XJ-S competitive in Transam racing. The result was Group 44's spaceframe coupé which went on to provide Eppie Wietz's Corvette with a close run for the 1981 championship. The big difference this time, apart from a far lower basic weight, was that because of John Egan it had carried the name Jaguar rather than Leyland . . . and Tullius had won more races overall than either the Corvette or Porsche rivals.

No matter how important Class One wins had been, it meant more in the marketplace to have an overall winner, so Jaguar were happy.

The American Jaguar operation then progressed into sports racing with Le Mans as the prime objective, leaving a vacuum in production car events. The chief problem here was that with the increasing sophistication of all forms of racing car, it was likely to cost as much to compete with a production-based machine as the potentially more glamorous sports racers. It was into this gap that stepped a natural successor to Ralph Broad, sometime BMW racer Tom Walkinshaw. He not only spotted the potential of the XJ-S in 1982's Group A but raised most of the finance to compete through the French Motul oil company and later, the Japanese Akai audio concern. All Jaguar had to do was to provide the hardware—Walkinshaw, with his foreign finance, would provide a sufficiently different car to gain good publicity. Ironically, one of the firms that wished him well was BMW. Their continuing winning ways in the European Touring Car championship were seeming hollow without significant opposition from a non-German manufacturer.

It was also significant to note what a small world Walkinshaw was operating in. His co-driver in the XJ-S would be the well-heeled, and competent, Chuck Nicholson, anxious to move up from Ford Zephyrs in Classic Saloon car racing to Jaguars in the international events. Walkinshaw's first season with the XJ-S saw only four wins—and highlighted the problems that had defeated Broad in moving into modern competition. But they were enough for second place in the title race to BMW. Second place had to be good enough for

Walkinshaw again in 1983 as BMW and Quester put up stern opposition, but sheer determination, as much as technical prowess, landed the 1984 drivers' championship for Walkinshaw—by now irrevocably associated with the name Jaguar. It remained only for the Walkinshaw XJ-Ss, clothed in John Player Special tobacco livery, to win at Macau in 1984, followed by the James Hardie 1,000-km race at Bathurst in Australia, with long-time Jaguar enthusiast John Goss and works driver Armin Hahne at the wheel. By winning both the European Touring Car challenge and the Australias' top race, Walkinshaw had taken Jaguar saloons back to the top.

Pinckney is pictured here at Brands Hatch in October 1977 splitting the similar 2.4 litre Mark I of Peter Trent and the Wolseley 15/50 of Hugh Hutton.

A wider range of Jaguars were eligible for one-make club racing with Roger Wilkinson's Marx X pictured having a great battle with John Young's 3.8 litre Mark II at Woodcote in the Pre-1968 Challenge race at the Jaguar Drivers' Club meeting in April 1982.

Jack Sears's son, David, is pictured behind the wheel of the leading Jaguar XJ–S in the 1984 TT race at Silverstone as Walkinshaw won both the European drivers' championship and the overall title race.

Tony Moore became one of the leading drivers in Classic Saloon Car racing in 1983 with his 2.4 litre Mark I pictured here at Oulton Park in the Jaguar Drivers' Club Cheshire Car meeting.

Meanwhile Jim Lowrey's 3.8 litre Mark II was starring in the Jaguar Drivers' Club's first Mark I and II Challenge race at Thruxton in March 1983.

Geoff Maycock does his best to hold up the opposition by making his 3.8 as wide as possible in the Jaguar Drivers' Club's Mark I and II Challenge at Brands Hatch in August 1984.

Appearances can be deceptive . . . Laurence Sayers-Gillan managed to get an entry with this mixture of Jaguar and Daimler XJ6 parts at an international meeting – in the Intermarque Challenge during the Aston Martin Owners' Club's FIA meeting at Brands Hatch in April 1984.

Rarer-than-rare sight . . . an impromptu participation by the Mayor of Brighton, Councillor John Blackman, in his chauffeur-driven Daimler limousine at the seaside town's 1984 speed trials.

Iain Exeter and Roger Mac found more racing for their Lister–Jaguar XJ-S – in Thundersaloons race at Oulton Park in July 1985.

Iain Exeter also drove in the Pre-1965 Classic Saloon Car series with a 3.8 litre Mark I, seen here leading a gaggle at Brands Hatch in May 1985.

Peter Litchfield powers his Lister XJ–S round Donington in the Jaguar Drivers' Club production car challenge in August 1986.

Rob Newall's 3.8 litre Mark II leads the Jaguar Production Car Challenge during the Cheshire Cats meeting at Oulton Park in April 1987.

Above: Tony Hildebrand and Peter Jopp climb the 10,000 twisting feet of the Stelvio in their 3.4 litre Mark I as part of the 1990 Classic Marathon.

Facing page: The 2.4 litre Mark II of Martin Hughes, Paul Brown and Stephen Fagioli is pictured being cheered on at the Site du Claps in Provence during the 1990 Monte Carlo Challenge.

Right: Father-and-son team of Laurence and Gordon Grainger pit their 3.8 litre Mark II against one of the last of the loose road Alpine descents – the Gavia – during the 1990 Classic Marathon.

Traditional night rallies are making a comeback in Britain . . . notably the Targa Rustincana on the back roads of central Wales. The 3.8 litre Mark II of Paul Hinkley and Simon Linley is pictured here at the dead of night near the Brecon Beacons.

Jaguar saloons continue to make effective classic competition cars all over the world, as the Mexican-registered 3.4 litre Mark I of Martin Turado and Javier Rivau demonstrated at 10,000ft during the 1990 Carrera Panamericana.

What the Road Testers Said

The sheer performance, comfort and value for money offered by Jaguar's saloons and coupés has always led to glowing reports from road testers in specialist magazines. But they were not always so dewy-eyed. From the start there was a hint of criticism that the steering was too low-geared, or too light, for European tastes, although, in the early days, there were no complaints from the American market which dictated it. The drum brakes on early cars suffered under heavy usage, but came in for little criticism because they were still good by comparison with those fitted to other cars—in fact the Americans thought they were just great! But overall the impression was of cars offering a unique blend of high performance, comfort and refinement at a very low price.

The Mark VII

Gordon Wilkins, a journalist employed by *The Autocar*, provided what amounted to the first full road test of a Jaguar Mark VII. It was the works development car registered LWK343 which would later become famous on the racetrack in the hands of Stirling Moss. Although Wilkins took over the car only late in 1951, it was one of the first seen in Britain, a strike having delayed initial production after which most cars went for export. Part of the plan was for Wilkins to share the car with Raymond Baxter of the BBC in the 1952 Monte Carlo Rally, so it had the lowest, 4.55:1, final drive, high-lift cams and fully rally equipment including higher-geared steering. Wilkins went as far as to point out that he preferred the higher ratio, although he realised that American buyers wanted at least five turns from lock-to-lock as they were used to 'twirling' the steering wheel while parking.

As if in compensation, the rival British weekly, *The Motor*, managed to get in the first specialist road test with a Mark VII, in April 1952, covering more than 2,000 miles in a car registered LRW173. Judged on a basis of value for money and all-round merit, they reckoned it was one of the best cars tested since the Second World War. Practically everybody on the staff seems to have joined in the jaunt through England, France, Belgium and Switzerland, the Mark VII carrying five in complete comfort for more than 300 miles a day when motorways were in their infancy. And as for the luggage boot, 'it can only be said that the amount of space provided, far exceeds any reasonable European expectation, the normal baggage and overcoats of five people representing considerably less than a full load.'

The performance—101mph maximum, 13.7-second 0–60mph, 19.3-second standing quarter mile and 18mpg—was described as 'American plus a little'. But the little bit extra, allied with excellent handling, made so much difference than 'on fast roads, the Jaguar has the legs of any production saloon car its owner is likely to meet'. Like Wilkins, however, they found the steering rather low-geared and noted that the roadholding could be improved by increasing the recommended tyre pressures at little expense to the ride. The brakes could be made to fade, but no more so than on other fast and heavy saloon cars. The engine was so smooth and refined that it highlighted the ponderous nature of the long-throw gearchange and the need for 'slightly more powerful synchromesh'.

Within a week, *The Autocar* hit back with another test in LRW173, although the mileage had to be confined to only 1,000. But the extra time behind the wheel seemed to have loosened the car as it returned 102mph with a 13.4-second 0–60mph time, 19.3secs for the standing quarter mile and 19mpg. Otherwise, *The Autocar*'s findings were similar to those of *The Motor*.

Jaguar's problems in getting the Mark VII into production were illustrated by references to a 'few bugs' that had been apparent in the finish of early cars, when the American magazine *Road & Track* tested one in October 1952. They wrote these bugs off as a 'certain roughness which often plagues a manufacturer during a car's early production stages' and were glad to report that they had been almost completely ironed out. American tastes were reflected in approval for softer rear springs 'which unquestionably give you a smoother ride, although our standing start acceleration was somewhat hampered by this softness. Enough firmness is retained, however, to prevent "apple-bobbing" at stops and "motor-boating" in quick take-offs . . . but if it's a case of wheel judder as opposed to smooth, high-speed, travel, you'll probably choose the latter.'

On one long trip, the Mark VII 'proved time and again that the American stock sedan "just didn't have it" . . . particularly when any curves were involved. The Jaguar would get through winding, hilly, country without backing off from its 60–70mph cruising speed, whereas all the other traffic instinctively slowed to 45mph or less.'

It was notable, however, that the brakes were adjudged to be 'really wonderful'—obviously those on contemporary American cars left a lot to be desired—and there was no criticism of the steering. All that really upset *Road & Track* on the way to 104mph, a 12.6-second 0–60mph time, and a 19.1-second standing quarter of a mile by dint of a dual exhaust system was the projecting horn button 'which caused me to honk while parking', and the long throw gearchange.

Road & Track listed only steady-speed fuel consumption figures, with 17mpg at 50mph as the most typical. But *The Autocar* found that the addition of an overdrive (along with the 4.55:1 final drive ratio) on a Mark VII, registered OVC771,

tested in September 1954, made quite a difference: 'When averaging 35mph on an easy main road, 24.8mpg was obtained with the overdrive in use as against 22.8mpg in direct top gear. On the other hand, on another test run when the car was driven comparatively hard, the consumption was increased to 17mpg with the overdrive compared with 19.7mpg in direct top gear. The reduction on this occasion . . . may be accounted for by the reduction in the amount of gearchanging that was necessary.'

Obviously the heavy Mark VII used a lot of fuel moving off the mark . . .

The build-quality was also good now that the big saloon had been in production for the best part of four years. *The Autocar* reported: 'The general smooth running and overall silence of the Mark VII tend to give both driver and passengers the impression that they are travelling much more slowly than in fact applies . . . the body is well insulated from the mechanical components and there is very little road-excited body noise, although a regular "thump, thump" can be heard if the car is driven over regularly-spaced objects such as cat's eyes reflectors.'

The Motor then tested an overdrive Mark VIIM, registered RHP440, in September, 1955, which they felt was a considerable improvement on the early model although their performance figures did not really support that view. Top speed was slightly higher at 104mph, but the 0–60mph time was only 14.1secs and the standing quarter mile took 19.5secs. Fuel consumption remained unchanged at 19mpg overall although it was estimated that there was a 10 per cent improvement during average driving. Hard new brake linings could be made to smell during tortuous tests, but did not fade.

Technical editor John Bolster then wound up the series of specialist magazine tests on manual versions of the Mark VII with an inspiring write-up of what it was like to drive the 1956 Monte Carlo Rally-winning car in the British weekly,

Autosport, in March:

'During really wintry weather, all normal road testing must come to a stop. The figures for a standing quarter mile on ice are not of much interest, and nor is the timed both ways maximum speed over, or through, snow drifts. However, the recent temporary hiatus provided an opportunity to try a rally car in conditions far worse than were experienced this year on the way to Monte Carlo . . .'

Bolster took the car, registered PWK700 and still bearing its competition number 164, straight from the relatively snow-free showrooms of London Jaguar agents, Henlys, and headed off for his home on a farm in frozen Kent. Bolster reported:

'My entry into the snow belt was somewhat dramatic, for I had inadvertently chosen a road home that had been closed for some hours. As the drifts got larger and larger, I felt that there was no hope of turning back, and I pressed on hard in second gear, while the screaming wind covered my tracks almost as soon as I had passed. The sheer weight of the car, once it was really in motion, carried it through drifts that would have stopped even some four-wheel-drive vehicles.

'Frequently all the lamps and the screen became completely obscured, and I had to brake to a stop in a panic to clear them. Eventually, miles from anywhere in the early hours of the morning, I suddenly saw before me a drift much higher than the roof of the car, which stretched as far as the eye could see. To drive head first into that would guarantee a cold wait till the snow plough arrived in the indefinite future!

'There was only one solution, which was a long drive in reverse, but the blizzard was making drifts behind me. Speed was vital, so I flung myself on my back on the ground, wildly fitting tyre chains with fingers that were soon almost insensible. That did the trick and, more by luck than judgement, I managed to race backwards through the drifts until I found a slightly less impossible road. Naturally, the eventual completion of this foolhardy journey gave me an extremely high regard for the Jaguar.

'My road tests invariably include a dice round a racing circuit, and I had always had a secret longing to lap Brands Hatch when covered with bags of *neige*. Plunging through the snow-filled tunnel from the paddock, I was soon zooming uphill to Druids ("wheelspin all the way in third, old man"). The corners could be taken surprisingly fast, and the Jaguar could be slid quite considerably without loss of control. Above all, one could drive continuously right on the limit without any conspicuous effort, which is the greatest virtue of the Mark VII as a winter rally car. When braking for Paddock Bend, I found no tendency for the tail to sway or for the wheels to lock unexpectedly.'

Road & Track's VIIM, tested in the sunny climes of Southern California in November 1955, returned far more impressive figures than earlier road test cars, despite being fitted with automatic transmission. A maximum speed of 106mph was recorded with an 11.6-sec 0–60mph time and 18.45 secs for the standing quarter mile. Fuel consumption was down to between 15 and 17mpg, however, doubtless due to the power losses associated with automatic transmission. *Road & Track* commented: 'Half the fun of driving our 1952 test car was its brilliant performance in second and third gears, but make no mistake, the automatic box is no "slush pump". In 1952, it took four cars and a dual exhaust system to break the timed 100-mph barrier. This car benefited, however, in that it had done 9,250 miles . . .'

With one eye on ever more extreme annual styling changes to American cars, they added: 'In these lush days of forced obsolescence and high-pressure selling, the Jaguar sedan is something of a novelty, and its adherence to simple styling in the face of flamboyance and sheer bad taste is one of its strongest selling points.'

Mark VIII

The Autocar had its own comments in this vein when it produced the only full road test of a Mark VIII in January 1957. The relative lack of publicity for the new model was related to its short production run and intense media interest in the

The Mark VII saloon registered LWK343 enjoyed a long career at the top, being pictured here at Stowe winning the 1955 Silverstone production car race for Mike Hawthorn by lapping as fast as the contemporary formula three racing cars!

several years, so that it is fully proved . . .' Happily, *The Autocar*'s Mark VIII, an automatic model registered SKV946, came near to being the answer to both viewpoints.

Its maximum speed was up to 106mph, and the standing quarter mile time reduced to 18.4secs, with an even more dramatic 11.6-sec 0–60mph figure. Fuel consumption suffered, readings as low as 15mpg being recorded, although 18mpg was considered quite realistic on average. At the same time, the engine modifications that improved the performance so much did not detract from the Mark VIII's refined manners.

The Autocar's testers had mixed feelings, however, about the new one-piece windscreen. They realised that it improved visibility, but wished that the windscreen pillars were not so thick and found that, now the seats had been repositioned, the

contemporary new Mark I saloons, but *The Autocar* commented: 'On more than one occasion we have noted a strange contradiction of thought—a motorist will criticize one new model for not being entirely different from its predecessor and, almost in the same breath, praise another for being the outcome of painstaking detail development over

Despite its dowager image following the introduction of the Mark I saloon, the Mark VIII Jaguar was still capable of a fair turn of speed and pleased the *Autocar*'s road testers with the results of painstaking detail development. This car, driven by Dick Bradley, is pictured competing in the Pre-1965 Classic Saloon Car race at the Jaguar Drivers' Club meeting at Silverstone in April 1983.

interior mirror could form a blind spot. Smoking was considered far more social than anti-social at the time. Jaguar were praised for providing no less than three outsize cigarette lighters, two in the back and one centrally-mounted in the front, although the ashtrays left a lot to be desired.

The front ones were sited in such a way in the doors that it was not possible to operate the window winders when the trays were in use; at the same time it was all too easy to miss the trays altogether and accidentally fill the map pockets below with ash . . .

Mark IX

The Mark IX, with power steering and disc brakes, as well as automatic transmission, came in for a lot of praise from *The Motor* in October 1958, even if its fuel consumption had increased to a regular 15mpg. Of that aspect, they said: 'As the difference between 15 and 18mpg is only some 10s a week on a 10,000-mile year, this is not a matter which is likely to deter possible buyers of this class of car from enjoying the extraordinary combination of comfort, performance and value for money.' Fuel consumption mattered even less in the United States at the time, of course, with the average gallon costing only a few cents.

The Motor's Mark IX, registered WRW536, had a far higher (114-mph) maximum speed than the Mark VIII, but the considerable weight and relative newness of its mechanical components kept its acceleration times in the same bracket: 11.3secs for the 0–60mph and an 18.1-sec standing quarter mile. The new disc brakes made up for all that, however: 'Should the driver wish to pass any other road user travelling at 100mph he can do so with a margin of some 15mph and should he wish to get down from 100mph to 30mph he can do so *infallibly* within 15 car lengths on a dry road.' Obviously, meeting a Mark IX on the road could be formidable, especially if *The Motor*'s comments were taken literally: 'The brakes can be used all

the time up to the limit set by human endurance, which is about 0.6g . . .'

The Autocar managed only 113mph with the same car two months later, in December 1958, but obtained better acceleration: 11secs for 0–60mph with a 17.8-sec standing quarter mile. Fuel consumption was even heavier, at 14.4mpg, and they said of the steering: 'There were divided opinions among the staff . . . the raised ratio results in more load and feel than is the custom with transatlantic products. The boon of power steering in low-speed manoeuvring is universally agreed; it is questionable, however, whether it is so sensitive as an unassisted gear at high speeds, particularly on moderately straight roads where small deviations are necessary. Over some of the steeply cambered roads of Northern France the driver was less at ease than his passenger; but on straight roads with little camber, the Jaguar pursued its course with complete stability and a minimum of attention. A feature of this installation, in contrast with many others tried, is that self-centring action is strong and quick.'

Mark I 2.4-litre

The Autocar's new technical editor, former Coventry Climax development engineer Harry Mundy, who would later move to Jaguar Cars, was the first journalist to describe what it was like to drive the anxiously-awaited 2.4-litre saloon. His report in November 1955 was highly favourable, finding the new engine as smooth as the old one. Fears that its unitary body construction might lead to drumming and rumbling were unfounded and the brakes and suspension felt well balanced. Visibility was good despite what seemed to be thick screen pillars even in those days.

During a full road test of a 2.4-litre saloon registered SWK986 in September 1956, other members of *The Autocar*'s staff were in broad agreement, although they found the transmission 'a mite disappointing', with a problematical gearchange. Touching their forelocks to Jaguar, they explained at length that the near-horizontal position of the gearlever in second or top was useful when the driver wanted to slide across the front seats to exit or enter at the kerbside—but an advantage at no other time. The up-and-down movement needed to change gear was not helped by a sticky operation.

On the other hand, they found the suspension, steering and brakes were excellent. Handling was improved, however, by raising the tyre pressures by as much as 25 per cent: 'Liberties could then be taken without upsetting control . . . there is no appreciable under-or oversteer. At very high speed when the car is forced deliberately to slide a little, there is no trace of vice.' Oddly, though, no brake fade was reported during sustained hard driving to achieve performance figures of a 102-mph top speed, 15.8-sec 0–60mph and a 20.5-sec standing quarter mile with 23mpg from this overdrive model.

Meanwhile *The Motor* had returned 101mph, 14.4secs and 19.6mpg with a similar car registered SWK803 in July, commenting: 'On indifferent pave, passengers may ride at any speed in comfort equivalent to that given by cars with independent rear suspension. The real achievement of this suspension is that it combines such suppleness with damping which quickly gets rid of the effects of hump-backs or trenches, and allows the car to roll slightly, but not wallow, in a fast corner . . . As more of these cars come on the road, it is pertinent to explain that when the Jaguar is being cornered in a really enterprising manner the rear wheels, as seen from a following vehicle, present a rather alarming spectacle, of which no trace is felt from the driving seat.'

Road & Track returned better acceleration figures—13.1secs for the 0–60 and 19secs for the standing quarter mile—in August despite their car having covered less than 2,000 miles. They also felt that it was one of the few cars justifying the popular sports-saloon tag, and commented on its appearance: 'A first visual impression of the 2.4 is

quite favourable, especially from the front end which is nicely styled. The bulbous sides and rear end are not universally acclaimed but this treatment is responsible for a roomy interior and a low drag factor.'

They joined in the general criticism of the gearchange but found everything else very much to their liking.

By the time Bolster tested SWK986 for *Autosport* in December 1956, it had loosened up a bit to record 104mph, but he still could not quite match the *Road & Track* acceleration times. He was puzzled by the gearchange at first, but soon became used to it and ended up preferring it to that of the larger Jaguars. He summed up its salient points as having a 'sensational lack of road noise,' a very soft ride with exceptionally good handling, especially in the wet, and performance figures which made it a little faster than any rivals while being at least their equal on fuel consumption. All told, he said, it was the best car ever tested by *Autosport*.

Mark I 3.4-litre

He also waxed lyrical following his first brief run in a 3.4-litre Mark I—an overdrive model—during a visit to America in April 1957. Performance figures taken on the road indicated a 10-sec 0–60mph time with a top speed of around 120mph. But even more impressive was the way in which the power was delivered—in almost complete smoothness and with hardly any sound!

Motor had managed the first comprehensive test of a 3.4-litre car a week earlier, but, ironically, had to be content with a left-hand-drive example, registered TRW316, with the automatic transmission fitted to most cars bound for America . . .

They noted that American manufacturers had responded to Jaguar's challenge by beginning to market cars with 'specially-tuned V8 engines aimed at extracting the last ounce of performance.' But this car, which proved capable of 120mph with an

11.2-sec 0–60mph time and 18secs for the standing quarter mile proved more than a match for transatlantic rivals. Other features that were particularly appreciated included being able to hold the middle ratio up to 80mph while overtaking and the anti-creep device that made the handbrake redundant in traffic. But already the drum brakes were proving inadequate, one emergency stop from 100mph being enough to start them juddering and the car switching direction. *The Motor* said: 'A braking system able to withstand harder usage without protest would greatly widen the appeal of this car.'

Road & Track were equally impressed with their overdrive car tested in June 1957. They produced similar performance figures without revving the engine to the limit because it was still relatively new. Fuel consumption averaging 20mpg was

The *Autocar*'s road testers had mixed feelings about the Mark VII's one-piece windscreen – as opposed to the split screen of the Mark VII – although Bradley seems to be encountering fewer problems in the Jaguar Drivers' Club production car race at Silverstone in April 1984.

considered remarkably good. The hard use of first gear had a sensational effect, leaving long black rubber marks from spinning wheels while second-gear take-offs became the norm on wet roads. The only let-down was the Laycock overdrive, considered rough and noisy by American standards.

Handling remained excellent, although alternating between a 2.4-litre car and the 3.4-litre confirmed that the extra weight of the larger-capacity engine made the steering a little heavier. World champion racing driver-to-be Phil Hill took the new car for a 'hot lap' around a very rough winding road at Playa del Rey and came back gasping: 'Imagine trying to do this in an American sedan!'

Surprisingly, however, the drum brakes worked perfectly and displayed neither sign, nor smell, of fading linings following several stops from more than 100mph. Presumably American drivers were kinder to their brakes than the Europeans . . .

The Autocar were quite happy, however, with the disc brakes on the 3.4-litre, registered VRW974, tested in June 1958. They said 'Judgement can be made fairly only in relation to the demands which the brakes have to meet in a car of this nature; the speed is much higher than that of most other models, and the driver unconsciously makes much greater demands in the 3.4. Silent and quite light in operation, the brakes are outstandingly good and come into their own particularly at high speeds . . . it would be a false economy to specify a 3.4 Jaguar without disc brakes.' Happily, drum-braked models were now as much a part of the past as cars without heaters, although Jaguar continued to list such items as optional extras to maintain an artificially-low basic price in advertising.

Although *The Autocar*, like every other journal to test a Jaguar, appreciated the exceptional overall value for money, they considered the standard of the manual gearbox fell behind that of the rest of the car. Not only was the synchromesh weak, but the lower gears were noisy and the gearlever had too long a throw for average-sized drivers. Surprising, for European testers, *The Autocar*'s staff suggested that the optional lower-geared steering might be better than the existing mechanism using four turns from lock to lock. They pointed out that the car could be placed accurately even at exceptionally high speeds on indifferent surfaces, but added: 'Even at medium speeds, appreciable effort is required at the wheel when sharp turns are made, and some fatigue may be caused on long runs at relatively high speed on winding roads.'

Despite the obvious appeal of the 3.4-litre's 120mph, 9.1-sec 0–60mph, 17.2-sec standing quarter mile and 16-mpg performance, magazines were becoming more critical. *The Autocar* said of the heating and ventilation: 'Its efficiency could not be properly judged in the temperate weather which accompanied the test. On the assumption that it is better to keep the windows closed to reduce wind noise and buffeting, the ventilation system did not prove adequate, even when the manually-operated ventilator intake at the base of the windscreen was open. An appreciable amount of engine heat is transmitted to the interior, and in warm weather the occupants may become undesirably hot.'

They summed up, however: 'In spite of some minor criticisms, the Jaguar 3.4 emerges as a totally outstanding car. The provision at relatively low cost of this standard of performance, coupled with town carriage docility when required, and of such quality and comfort, is a remarkable achievement.'

Bolster then managed to extract 125mph from VRW974 in overdrive with 118mph in direct top gear, but only 10.2secs for the 0–60mph dash and 17.6secs for the standing quarter mile when testing it for *Autosport* in August 1958. He was happy to cover a lot of ground flat out early one morning and said, with the true 'Gung-ho' approach, that he had 'been able to maintain that velocity through some appreciable bends. I also applied the disc brakes hard at maximum speed, bringing the car to a standstill with howling tyres in a dead straight line. I deliberately drove on the brakes, but they remained powerful and progressive throughout . . .

'Overtaking may be carried out in the shortest possible distance, and only a momentary visit need be paid to the wrong side of the road. I am sure that many people may buy the car for this one reason, without any intention of driving it at over two miles a minute. Indeed, I hope that this is so, for it needs practice if one is to have infallible judgment at such speeds. Nevertheless, with so much power at his disposal, coupled with disc brakes, the driver of this Jaguar should be able to avoid the consequences of other people's mistakes. That is a real contribution to road safety.'

Bolster's colleagues, Paddy McNally, then managed a quick test in one of the ultimate 3.4-litre

Mark I racing Jaguars, the former Coombes and Peter Sargent-owned car being raced by A.C. le Fort at the time of the test in May 1962. No power output was revealed for this lightweight machine, but its performance was exceptional: 144mph top speed in overdrive, 6.9-sec 0–60mph acceleration and 15-sec dead for the standing quarter mile. What's more, it proved capable of 0–100mph and back to 0 in exactly 23secs. McNally reported in *Autosport*: 'The back axle is extremely well located and the rear suspension so well set up that it doesn't take a real expert to achieve really quick getaways. However, careless use of the throttle will cause snaking and excessive wheelspin.' McNally found the car practical to drive in heavy traffic with a 12.5mpg fuel consumption as the only penalty for such performance.

Mark II 3.8-litre

It was hardly surprising that the Mark II saloon received such a rapturous reception because it eliminated many of the minor shortcomings in the earlier saloons. But tests were chiefly of the 3.8-litre variant as Jaguar, quite naturally, wanted to publicise their top medium-range model. Only one 3.4-litre car escaped officially, and nobody had the opportunity to test a new 2.4-litre Mark II because its top speed—around 95mph—seemed inadequate in the face of glowing tributes to the 3.8.

The Autocar led the way with an introduction to their road test of February 1960: 'Very few cars indeed set out to offer so much as the 3.8-litre Mark II Jaguar, and none can match it in terms of value for money. In one compact car, an owner has *Gran Turismo* performance, town carriage manners and luxurious family appointments . . . The changes made for 1960 without doubt represent together the greatest improvement so far achieved between a Jaguar model and its predecessor—short of a wholly new design.'

The wider rear track was one of the most noticeable changes: it not only increased roll resistance, but improved stability. The heavier 3.8-litre engine was a help in this area, too, and showed that it had lost none of the sweetness nor flexibility of the 3.4-litre unit. The other advantages of the capacity increase in this overdrive car, registered YHP790, were obvious—a top speed of 125mph, with a 8.5-sec 0–60mph and 16.3-sec standing quarter mile times. Fuel consumption was up to 16mpg, however, which highlighted the limited capacity of the 12-gallon tank. But thinking back to the sheer performance, *The Autocar* added: 'This occasional five-seater saloon will also glide silently in heavy traffic, snatch-free in top gear, down to 14mph. But the aspects of the performance which our drivers most appreciated were the smooth, silent, cruising up to 100mph in overdrive top on autoroutes at home and on the Continent, and the splendid acceleration for quick, safe, overtaking in direct top or third.'

The standard fitting of a limited-slip differential was also credited with eliminating the axle hop and tramping that could be induced on earlier models. But on a cautionary note, *The Autocar* said: 'Since there is sufficient power to spin the rear wheels quite readily in third gear on wet roads, and because the weight distribution is markedly in favour of the front, care has to be taken to use only light throttle when coming out of bends or away from corners; experienced drivers likely to be attracted by the 3.8 will adopt this technique instinctively . . .

'Should the back end of the car slide, lifting the accelerator foot is usually enough to check it at once. Here, however, the low-geared steering—five turns from lock to lock with rather slow response around the mid-sector—is at a disadvantage, and it is difficult to apply quickly enough opposite helm to correct a skid at once.'

Enlarging on this nose-heavy understeering tendency, *The Autocar* said: 'The wide slip angle on the front tyres is clearly seen by an observer. The steering is better suited to the low and moderate speed sections of the car's wide range . . . As speeds rise over about 50mph there is increasing need to take bends early and to hold the car tight into them, otherwise it may swing wider than intended. There is quite powerful self-centring and this, no doubt, is in part responsible for the good line that the car holds on straight roads at all speeds. Up to about 100mph, side winds have little effect on the car; above this speed (and strong side winds were experienced at times during the testing) quick and delicate corrections were needed to hold course.'

The greatly improved visibility was much appreciated, although *The Autocar* noted a slight body shake over rough roads. This phenomenon was also mentioned in at least one later road test, but never seemed to be apparent otherwise, leading to the thought that the early road test cars were pre-production models that were not necessarily so stiff as the normal products.

Like all the rest of the European road test cars, this Mark II was fitted with the normal steel disc wheels, rather than the optional wires, which cost more. Nevertheless, there were no criticisms of the braking efficiency, and Jaguar could see an advantage in that it kept down the published price of the car being tested. The top-line model had a slightly different image in the United States, however. *Road & Track* reported in August 1960 that: 'In just 12 years the British Jaguar has become virtually synonymous with the term "expensive foreign car" in the minds of the American public for, if you ask people you meet at random to name one or more imported cars, Jaguar always comes out on top of the list.' So, in keeping with this image, the 3.8-litre Mark II tested by *Road & Track* had options such as power steering—not yet available in Europe—and snazzy wire wheels with whitewall tyres.

Initial reactions were similar to those of *The Autocar*, and, in deference to the newness of their test car, *Road & Track* did not try too hard with the performance figures. But they said of the new power steering:

'It is one of the few we have tried that we liked. While the average man driving the previous models felt no need for power steering, many women did object to a slight heaviness, which increased to a considerable force during parking. The new system eliminates this objection, and its particular virtue is that it is absolutely impossible to detect when the power comes on. Thus, the oft-encountered lumpiness at either side of straight ahead is not present and, as a matter of interest, several people drove the car without suspecting that it had power steering.'

And so far as the new-fangled radial ply tyres (typified by Michelin's X as opposed to the time-honoured Dunlop cross-plies normally fitted by Jaguar at the time) were concerned, *Road & Track* said: 'The "old" cars handled very well for sedans, this feature being particularly appreciated by a driver used to a standard American car. On the other hand, a driver used to any of the more popular sports cars would, generally, dislike the feel of the 3.4 models, particularly the very pronounced understeer when cornering hard and fast. Michelin X tyres [radial plies] would completely transform the general feel of the 3.4 but, unfortunately, parking effort went even higher and the car's normally excellent high speed stability decreased. The 3.8 has new suspension geometry . . . Power steering makes it difficult to evaluate this change because rim pull in a high speed bend is now very light. Nevertheless, the car definitely handles better than before and body roll appears to be less, as it should be on theoretical grounds. The new model also turns in an appreciably smaller circle than before. Our only criticism of the steering would be that, with power, it could have been made closer to four turns lock to lock rather than five.'

Road & Traffic's 1957 3.4-litre test car had the

Facing page: So far as *The Motor* was concerned, the Mark IX Jaguar presented an extraordinary combination of comfort, performance and value for money. Doubtless Marco Marioni and Anthony Vorley would agree as they cross the border from Austria into Italy, sunroof open on a snowy pass, during the 1989 Classic Marathon.

Plate 1 Grace, space and pace the ultimate Mark VII – Jaguar produced enough magnesium panels to build a lightweight version for racing in 1954.

Plate 2 Jaguar's big saloons progressed to the Mark IX, which still had enough pace to provide Mario Marconi and Anthony Vorley with an effective mount for the 1989 Classic Marathon on the Moistrocca hill climb in Yugoslavia.

Plate 3 When Jaguar progressed to a 3.4 litre version of the Mark I they found themselves on to a winner – like Tony Hildebrand and Peter Jopp at Modave, Belgium, in the 1990 Classic Marathon.

Plate 4 Jaguar's promise was fulfilled when they produced the Mark II saloon, offering a combination of superb performance with comfort, quality and value.

Plate 5 The heart of any Jaguar is the engine, as typified by the XK unit in this S-type saloon.

Plate 6 Jaguar made a valiant attempt to capture the American market with the Mark X saloon, which went on to herald their greatest cars.

Plate 7 The 420 was developed from a combination of the best attributes of the S-type and the Mark II saloon.

Plate 8 The highly-popular Mark II range eventually developed into the lithe 240.

Plate 9, above left: Walnut and leather in abundance were an integral part of the traditional Jaguar and Daimler interior.

Plate 11, above right: Part of the package Jaguar inherited from Daimler included an uncommonly smooth small V8 engine.

Plate 10, below: Jaguar's enforced takeover of the old-established Daimler company resulted in neat saloons like the V8–250.

Plate 13 Every Jaguar can tell a tale . . . especially the XJ6 prototype that became the first XJ12 and spent the last years of its life as a fire engine at the Silverstone circuit in Britain.

Plate 14 Jaguar's XJ12 saloon offered performance in the realms of the fantastic . . . at a high price in fuel.

Plate 12, previous page The qualities of the XJ6 were so beyond those of rivals that it became Jaguar's greatest car.

Plate 16 Sir William Lyons's last car . . . the enigmatic Jaguar XJ coupe, fitted, in this case, with the ultimate V12 engine.

Plate 15, previous page Market pressures forced styling changes to the XJ range that resulted in a series II – pictured in Daimler form – from 1973.

Plate 17 Broadspeed's full-race version of the XJ coupe offered a stunning performance even if the venture was ill-conceived.

Plate 18 Jaguar's XJ-S was the cat they could not kill, enjoying an extraordinarily long life.

Plate 19 Eventually the XJ range proved so well designed it was able to run to a series III that saved Jaguar Cars.

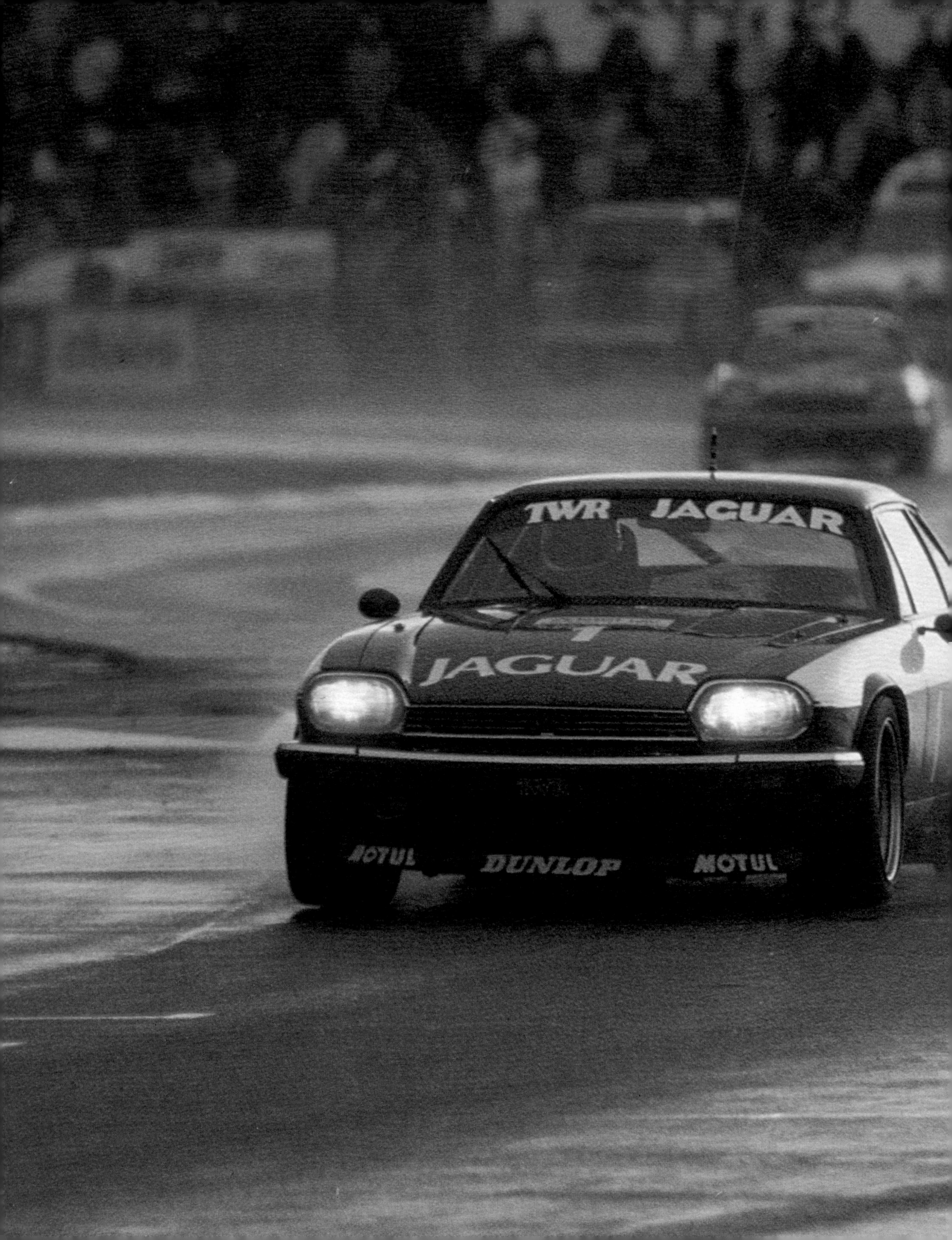
TWR JAGUAR
JAGUAR
MOTUL
DUNLOP
MOTUL

Plate 21 Jaguar tested public opinion on a return to open cars with a cabriolet variant of the XJ-S.

Plate 20, previous page Long-time saloon car racer Tom Walkinshaw extracted enough performance from the XJ-S coupe – pictured here in his hands in the 1984 Tourist Trophy race – to become a world-beater.

Plate 22 Jaguar bonnets became very full with the advent of the fuel-injected version of the V12 engine.

Plate 23 Ultimately, Jaguar developed the XJ6 into a fourth series, using a new lightweight construction.

Plate 24, below left The XJ–S continued to be marketed into the 1990s in both open and closed forms.

Plate 25, below right Jaguars became ever more sporting with the 4 litre XJR saloon.

Plate 25 Grace, space and pace . . . the mainstay of Jaguar's range remains the Sovereign 4.0 saloon.

C-type close ratio manual gearbox which they considered near perfect. The 3.8, however, had the wider-ratio gearbox which reverted to the earlier 'creeper' first gear. In the opinion of *Road & Track*, the only advantage was that the synchronised second gear could be used for starting: 'The provision of five speeds forward (via overdrive) seems superfluous . . . However, the four-speed with overdrive model is primarily for the enthusiast and most of the cars coming over are equipped with the three-speed plus converter type of automatic transmission. While this item takes all the fun out of driving a car such as this, we must admit that the performance is still fantastic and a driver used to, say, a four-passenger [Ford] Thunderbird will find the Jaguar a tremendous advance in terms of roominess, accuracy of steering and ability to cruise safely and comfortably at very high speed.'

Road & Track went on to say that readers might think the fuel consumption of a $5,000 car unimportant, but could not help noting that the 3.8's 17mpg was little heavier than a home-market compact with 130bhp less. The automatic was capable of 21–22mpg driven sensibly, which was identical to the best figure obtained from the compact with manual transmission. It was obvious where their sympathies lay . . .

Road & Track also used their road test to summarise complaints most often levelled against Jaguar's products by readers and the measures taken to alleviate problems. The most consistent troubles related to speedometer and rev counter failure, brake servo leaks, electrical ailments, defunct automatic choke, engine oil leaks, timing chain rattles, fast-wearing carpets, fading and blistering paint. They were pleased to note that the speedometer's oil seal had been redesigned, the new electric rev counter solved that problem along with the tachometer drive—the most common source of engine oil leaks—rerouting the servo's manifold vacuum feed kept out petrol deposits, the new hinge-down dashboard panel made electronic troubleshooting easier, Jaguar owners were best advised to counter sand and dirt intrusion in the automatic choke by having a manual over-ride fitted while external adjustment usually cured the timing chain rattle. But so far as the paint and carpets were concerned, that was a quality control problem . . .

Editor Gregor Grant tested a 3.8-litre overdrive Mark II for *Autosport* in January 1961 and was much impressed with virtually everything except the gearbox. On this score, he pleaded for an all-synchromesh unit 'of the type found on certain Continental cars . . .'

Later that year, in August, *The Motor* managed to test what was becoming another popular option on the Mark II theme, a 3.4-litre (registered 6834HP) fitted with power steering and automatic transmission. They rated it as 'one of the best all-round cars for motoring on civilised roads yet seen anywhere in the world,' and devoted many words to describing how much they liked the interior. *The Motor* found the transmission 'very satisfactory' despite not being the smoothest they had sampled and suggested that the second gear hold might be included in the selector quadrant for more logical operation. And although the steering ratio had been raised to four turns from lock to lock, they felt it might well be increased even further. Performance figures, although more sedate than those of the manual 3.8, were still outstandingly good on 119mph: 11.9secs for 0–60mph and 19.1 for the standing quarter mile, allied to 16mpg.

As was only to be expected, a 3.8-litre version, registered 7392RW, tested by *Autocar* (which had abandoned *The* from its title for trendy reasons), proved a lot more lively on test in April 1963. Maximum speed was little affected at 120mph, but the extra torque made all the difference to acceleration, with a 9.8-sec 0–60mph time and 17.2secs for the standing quarter mile. It also lifted the fuel consumption to 17mpg . . .

Autocar also found that such a car could be driven with considerable enthusiasm, reporting: 'Full throttle kickdown allows the intermediate range to be held up to the governed point at 5,000rpm (74mph) when direct drive re-engages. Intermediate hold control, within fingertip reach of the steering wheel, enables the change-down to be made on part-throttle. With intermediate hold switched in, there is limited engine braking on the overrun. In either the intermediate hold or the low position on the selector, the driver can override the normal full-throttle change-up points. At the maximum recommended engine speed of 5,500rpm, 50mph is reached in low—this ratio gives overrun braking—and 80mph in intermediate. In full-throttle take-off from rest with drive selected, intermediate comes in at 43mph.'

Motor—which by now had also dropped *The* from its title—had last tested a 2.4-litre Jaguar in 1956; it was nevertheless quickly off the mark with a road test of the new 240, registered LHP240F, in January 1968, commenting:

'It is a pity that the praises of the 2.4/240 have been a trifle neglected in the past because the car has so much to offer. If this is Jaguar's economy package, it manages to be both jumbo-sized and lavish. It has the usual elegant and well-placed set of instruments, rows of impressive-looking switches, bags of walnut (which some of us don't like very much), and a toolkit which has more tools in it than are to be found in some complete households. More important, the 240 is surprisingly wieldy on twisting roads, has excellent handling and adhesion, and will carry four people in comfort and quietness at high speeds over long distances. Always providing that the filler stations are not too far apart—the overall fuel consumption of 17.1mpg is one of the few drawbacks. Another is heavy steering at parking speeds [this economy model did not have power-assistance]. These faults are to some extent offset by the patriotic feeling (experienced by more than one of our testers) engendered by looking down that long bonnet from the driver's seat at the Jaguar mascot, and by the sensation of being encased in a great deal of solidly-constructed motor car.'

With those words, *Motor* celebrated by extracting 98mph from the 240 on the rev coun-ter's red line of 5,500rpm. although it proved possible to see 105mph with a few seconds' over-revving. Acceleration times on the standard 4.27:1 final drive were considered reasonable at 11.7secs for 0–60mph and 18.4secs for the standing quarter mile.

Autocar, which tested an overdrive 240 registered LDU852F in the same month, were able to take it up to 106mph (with an overall 18mpg), although the acceleration times were disappointing considering that it has a 4.55:1 final drive: 12.5secs for 0–60mph with a standing quarter mile in 18.7secs, leading to the comment: 'What were once very brisk acceleration times and a high top speed can now be matched by several cars of under two litres. Nevertheless, from behind the wheel there is never a moment's doubt that this is a full-blooded Jaguar with all the virtues of a thoroughbred.'

The non-assisted steering came in for criticism, but *Autocar* considered the new all-synchromesh gearbox a great improvement, finding it 'hard to fault on any score. The lever, with its large knob, is ideally placed and moves sweetly between all ratios.'

Bolster found the 340 overdrive model, registered LDU835F, far faster, recording a 124-mph maximum for *Autosport* in February 1968 with an 8.8-sec 0–60mph time and 17.2 secs for the standing quarter mile—times that paralleled the fabled 3.8-litre Mark II by dint of its lower weight with a superior 18mpg. Bolster said: 'The engine is the latest version of the immortal twin-cam 3.4 litre . . . This is a very sensible size to choose, for it is notably more economical than the 3.8 and 4.2-litre versions, while still offering most of their performance. The gearbox is the greatest improvement over earlier Jaguars. It has excellent synchromesh on all four gears and, although the ratios are little wider, this evidently suits the characteristics of the engine for the acceleration figures are better than ever [for a 3.4-litre car].

'When I first took over the car, I disliked the

steering. It seemed too low geared, yet it was also heavy at parking speeds. The manufacturers [who had only just started recommending the use of radial ply tyres] advised me to inflate the optional Dunlop SP41 radials to 35lb pressure for high-speed work—which transformed the steering. Not only did it become far lighter, but the improved responsiveness made it seem higher geared. Personally, I also preferred the ride with the harder tyres although for really fast driving I would have liked more damping . . .'

Daimler 2 litre V8

The installation of Daimler's small V8 in the Mark II Jaguar bodyshell was welcomed by the specialised Press, even if the Borg Warner transmission had some shortcomings and the car seemed too low-geared in its initial form. *The Motor* commented on power-steered variant registered 4545VC in April 1963:

'It is a very quiet, smooth and comfortably sprung car. The lines are attractive, visibility is good and the interior trim and furnishing have an air of quality and good taste.

'Measured performance figures [110mph maximum, 13.5sec. 0–60mph, 19.8sec standing quarter mile and 17mpg] surprised us; the turbine smoothness of the engine and the deceptive relationship between speed and engine rpm with a torque converter transmission conspired to make acceleration feel less impressive than it really is. Nevertheless, although the power is available when needed, the Daimler has clearly been designed for less hurried motorists; low final gearing helps top gear performance but gives only 16.6mph/1,000rpm in top gear so that at high cruising speeds the Daimler lacks the effortless feeling that high gearing confers. Automatic gearchanges which are barely perceptible in gentle driving become distinctly jerky at large throttle openings and when baulked by slow traffic or climbing very steep hills one feels the lack of a more readily available bottom gear. The combination of low gearing and automatic transmission makes it a fairly thirsty car, but

fuel consumption is probably not a dominant factor for buyers in this class.'

A clue as to how well a V8 with manual steering handled was given by *Autocar* when they tested 4545VC in May 1963. A flexible pipe between the steering pump and gearbox failed 'enabling us to experience the quite acceptable lightness of the mechanism without assistance.'

Acceleration figures were much the same as those recorded by *The Motor*, and a 112-mph maximum achieved by going through the rev counter's red line to 6,800. The engine did not object, but the transmission caused some problems. The most notable came when the car was parked pointing up a 1-in-4 slope, with the transmission lock selected. As soon as the handbrake was released it rolled back a fraction, jamming the transmission pawl. A Land-Rover had to be called to tow the Daimler a few inches up the hill before the transmission lock could be released. The other fundamental shortcoming with the early Borg Warner model 35 became apparent when it was discovered that you could not kick down into low gear or select it manually from intermediate at above 5mph. *Autocar* found this a serious nuisance in hilly country.

John Bolster was particularly looking forward to testing the car because of its engine. In fact, he told *Autosport* readers in August 1963: 'I doubt whether I have ever sat behind a better power unit than the 2.5-litre Daimler V8,' but he added that: 'Fundamentally, a superb sports engine like the Daimler is less well suited to automatic transmission than a "slogging" type of unit . . . if ever an engine deserved a five-speed, all-synchromesh gearbox, this is it.'

Bolster also discovered: 'Owing to its revised weight distribution, the Daimler handles particularly well and can out-corner a Jaguar. The power-assisted steering has no vices and must be very highly praised because it gives light operation while preserving the "feel". The car imparts a great sense of confidence to the driver, the good roadholding and accurate steering rendering fast driving a pleasure.' Quite extraordinarily, Bolster managed to record virtually identical performance figures with 4545VC to those quoted in *The Motor* and *Autocar*!

The higher final drive ratio made a considerable difference to the Daimler, registered FWK480D, tested by *Autocar* in May 1966. Not only was the car faster, recording a 115mph maximum at only 6,300rpm, but the fuel consumption improved dramatically to 19mpg. Acceleration times were not a lot slower, by around 1sec on average, up to 80mph, after which the higher ratio really took its toll. But as *Autocar*, which recorded 19.9secs for the standing quarter mile, pointed out: 'Many owners may feel happier to drive the Daimler at 90mph than they would have been before, as it now requires only 5,000rpm . . .

'Since our previous test, the D1/D2 version of the Borg Warner automatic gearbox has been adopted, offering gentler starts in intermediate using position D2 on the selector. In D2, also, there is a positive control to prevent the car from running backwards on hills even with the engine idling. Acceleration in D2 is, of course, appreciably slower than in D1, adding nearly 4secs to the 14.7sec rest-to-60mph time [obtained in D1], but it is mainly for town use and can help economy as well. On full throttle, upward changes in D1 occur at 5,100rpm, but with the lock-up these limits can be

The *Autocar*'s technical editor, Harry Mundy – who later worked for Jaguar Cars – was always happy to help out with tests, such as those involving this Mark I in the water splash at the Motor Industry Research Association's track near Nuneaton. As a result, he became the first journalist to drive the new saloon . . . with this prototype still showing some indecision in exactly how to handle the styling of the sidelights.

overridden, offering a small improvement for ultimate performance, and maxima of 44 and 75mph in low and intermediate respectively, at 6,500rpm, can be used.'

A repeat test of the transmission lock on a 1-in-4 hill still resulted, however, in difficulty getting the lever out of its parking position.

Close to the end of its production run, *Motor* managed a test in a car registered LRW800F, one of the rare manual gearbox V8 250s. This was based on the Jaguar 240, rather than the earlier model, and had the lower, 4.55:1, final drive because it was fitted with an overdrive.

Although the recently-introduced 240 had an uprated engine, the new Daimler still presented a logical alternative with its superior trim and totally different engine. *Motor* said: 'In most respects, the performance [108mph maximum, 11.1-sec 0–60mph, 18.5-sec standing quarter mile and 18mpg] was virtually identical to that of our road test 240, except that overdrive allowed a much higher maximum speed.

'But it was at very high rpm that the V8 really came into its own, especially during the hilly parts of our Continental trip when it became possible to keep the engine at 5,000–6,000rpm for long periods with little sense of strain. For the hard driver, the V8 engine is a good choice.'

Bolster's prayers were answered when he tested the same car for *Autosport* in October 1968—in the same issue in which the XJ6 was announced! He managed to extract 112mph from the V8 with similar acceleration and fuel consumption figures to *Motor* which suited him well, along with the handling, of which he said: 'It is a little better than that of the equivalent Jaguar due to the shorter and lighter engine. Now that the V8 is available with a manual gearbox, the owner can enjoy the sporting side of its character without prejudice to its more stately virtues.'

Mark X

Teething troubles, especially involving the cooling system, made Jaguar less than happy to put the Mark X on general release for road tests immediately after its introduction in 1961. But *Motor*'s Midland editor, Harold Hastings, who could be relied upon to remain reasonably discreet, landed a short drive in one example, registered 6100RW, in October 1961. He reported:

'Undoubtedly the biggest surprise which this new Jaguar gives on taking the wheel for the first time concerns the matter of size. Its beautiful sweeping lines seen from the outside, and its spacious and luxurious interior sampled from within, both suggest the large car that it really is . . . yet it does not *feel* a large car to drive. The finger-light controls, the good forward vision and, above all, the taut 'oneness' about the whole car all combine to place a driver immediately at ease.

'The ride struck me as outstanding, being soft without undue movement and good in both front and rear. With the back seats occupied, both ride and handing were, if anything, even better than with only driver and passenger. My one criticism (which was not shared by all passengers) was that I would have liked something to support my toes when sitting in the back with legs fully stretched and feet under the front squab recesses.

'On corners, the Mark X reaches a very high standard indeed, and one goes round fast with no perceptible roll and a feeling that all four wheels are doing their full share of the work—and doing it silently and efficiently. The power-assisted steering is light and, as a personal preference, I think I would sacrifice a little of the assistance for a little more feel, although neither that quality nor self-centring action are lacking. It is all a matter of degree and long acquaintance might well change my view.'

There were similar problems with road tests in the United States. As a result, in May 1962, *Road & Track* were outpaced by their rival, the monthly *Car and Driver*, for the first transatlantic driving impressions. *Car and Driver*'s first impressions of this brave new car, equipped with the contemporary cross-ply tyres, were similar to those of *Motor*. It is significant, however, that they commented, in an era when American cars used exceptionally soft suspension:

'The suspension is fairly soft, especially the front end, which dips under braking. There is some body lean on cornering, and we would have preferred a stronger anti-roll bar.

'The rear suspension is a highly advanced design for which we had great expectations and tried to be as critical as possible. Traction remained practically unimpeded on a variety of surfaces in all kinds of weather, including rain, snow, ice and dry roads; on turnpikes, back roads, city streets and Vineland race track. The Powr-Lok limited slip differential assures remarkable road grip in the wet or on ice, and the independent suspension keeps both rear wheels on the ground at all times. The tail will naturally drift out to some extent on tight bends, but the car remains completely controllable, and can be brought back in line by merely lifting the throttle foot.

'The front suspension is softer than the rear, and small bumps that are not absorbed by the tyres can be heard but they are hardly ever felt. On long stretches of rough road surface steering corrections may become necessary, but passenger comfort remains undiminished. On smooth surfaces the car will track perfectly, but it is curiously sensitive to variations in road camber. In directional stability and resistance to side winds, the Mark X is an improvement on the 3.4-litre and 3.8-litre sedans, but at high speed a strong lateral gust of wind can still bring the car off course. At normal speeds, however, side winds have little effect.'

Car and Driver then compared the Mark X to the recently-introduced E type sports car and said they both enjoyed a capacity for fast travel 'in almost complete silence'. This was all the more remarkable because of the absence of sound-deadening material under the bonnet.

It was not until November 1962 that *Autocar* were able to publish the first full road test of a Mark X in a car that had been registered 8172RW little more than a month after the example used by Hastings. *Autocar* explained:

'Just over a year has now passed since the Mark X Jaguar was the belle of the 1961 London Motor show, and our readers' natural desire, so often expressed, to see a full road test of this striking car has certainly been matched by the test staff's eagerness to try it. At last the makers have submitted one for this purpose, and the experience has been worth the long wait . . .'

The car in question, an automatic model with the standard UK compression ratio of 8:1, had been comprehensively shaken down, with 13,000 miles on the clock, but still developed a radiator leak towards the end of the test. Nevertheless, *Autocar* commented that it was otherwise 'in near-perfect condition with neither body creak nor rattle'.

Naturally, after such a long wait for a full road test, the performance figures were of prime importance, and, happily, were far from disappointing: a 120mph maximum speed with a 0–60mph acceleration time of 12.1secs and standing quarter mile in 18.5secs. 'One cannot expect to carry so many people so fast without paying a substantial fuel bill,' said *Autocar* about a car with the widest back seat of any British product. They found an overall 14mpg 'very reasonable, all things considered'.

The interior left them with mixed feelings. 'Very wide individual front seats are, indeed, as comfortable as easy chairs in a library while the car is travelling in a straight line,' said *Autocar*. 'The back rests are adjustable and can be lowered almost to the horizontal. However, the free width between the doors and the small folding arms in each back-rest, together with the absence of any shaping to bolster one against cornering forces, are real drawbacks. Wearing a safety harness (as provided in the test car) counteracts this to some extent, but from the driver's viewpoint the need for conscious muscular effort to hold himself upright on the slippery trim reduces his control over the steering. In the back, too, this seat is basically very soft and comfortable, but a wider centre armrest would be welcomed.'

Nevertheless, the overall impression was of a superb luxury car endowed with 'a very soft and "expensive" ride, together with almost sports car stability through fast bends and over rough road

The Motor decided that the real achievement of the Mark I's revised suspension was that it 'allowed the car to roll slightly, but not wallow, in a fast corner.' Anthony Lake is pictured showing just that ability with his 2.4 litre car in the Pre-1957 Classic Saloon Car race at Cadwell Park in April 1989.

surfaces, thoroughly justifying the complexity of a superb independent rear suspension. As befits a car in which many a business executive will be driven by his chauffeur, one can write easily and legibly in the back while being whisked along at high speeds.'

Road & Track were less than happy about having to wait until October 1962 to test a Mark X. Even then it was not a factory car, but a demonstrator loaned by British Motor Cars Inc in San Francisco. It was with a sense of wonder then that they reported: 'Despite our earlier suspicions, the car turned out to be one of the most pleasing luxury sedans we've ever driven.' So far as they were concerned, its only direct competition came from the 3.8-litre Mark II! *Road and Track* added:

'Our first impression of the car, fostered somewhat by its body design, which bears a strong family resemblance to both the present 3.8 and the discontinued Mark IX (and, as someone pointed out, the 1951 Hudson), was one of fairly large bulk. This is not entirely true, as the specifications will bear out, but whether by design or

accident, the car looks big. But actually, at 486cu ft, the Mark X is substantially identical in box volume to our "standard" size Ford or Chevrolet and its overall length is shorter, being identical to the 1962 Plymouth and Dodge.'

The only major complaint about the interior was: 'We suspect that older people and those who lack athletic ability will notice the huge box section body sills which, though responsible for exceptional sturdiness, are definitely obtrusive and somewhat of a nuisance when getting into the rear seat from the sidewalk. However, we have always argued that it's better to be safe, once under way, than to have easy entrance and exit.'

In contrast to the experiences of *Car and Driver*, they found that the Mark X handled exceptionally well in a cross wind although it displayed some understeer on tight winding roads: 'The precise, easy steering and the good handling characteristics resulting from the suspension design make the driver want to drive with more abandon than is really prudent with a car of this size and weight . . . In trying to analyse the motives of the designers and manufacturers, we feel that the ultimate goal was creature comfort. In this realm they have succeeded admirably where American designers still have room for improvement.'

Although this 9:1 compression ratio automatic model was faster than *Autocar*'s British edition at 120mph, it had better acceleration: 10.6secs for the 0–60mph dash, and 18secs for the standing quarter mile.

Not even former racing driver John Bolster could get the 8:1 compression ratio British road test Mark X 8172RW below an 11-sec 0–60mph for *Autosport* in March 1963, although he managed a 17.9-sec standing quarter mile with the by-now well-established 120mph maximum speed.

It was hardly surprising that *Autocar* concentrated on the performance figures when they tested a 4.2-litre Mark X, registered AWK134B and fitted with the optional 9:1 compression ratio engine, in October 1964. They said of this automatic model:

The *Autocar* found that the 3.4 litre Mark I could be placed accurately even at exceptionally high speed, thanks to its low-geared steering. Derek Goodacre is seen driving one of the fastest examples in Historic Saloon Car racing at Brands Hatch in August 1989.

John Bolster explained in *Autosport* that he had been able to drive his 3.4 litre Mark I flat out 'through some appreciable bends.' Chris Wood pursues the same line in Pre-1965 Classic Saloon Car racing at Mallory Park in August 1985.

Bolster found the 3.4 litre Mark I's overtaking ability a real contribution to road safety, as David Conod relished at Mallory Park in August 1985.

Sir Gawaine Baillie demonstrates the amount of power available from a Mark I by leading a 3.8 litre Mark II at Silverstone in 1959.

'An increase in engine size does not necessarily mean heavier petrol consumption. Often the reverse is the case, as more torque is obtained with less throttle . . . the new car performs better than the 3.8-litre Mark X and yet uses slightly less fuel. Many other changes, particularly to the power steering, have made it more controllable and rewarding to drive; and good though the 3.8 is, the 4.2 is so much better.

'One result [of the increased torque] is a great improvement in the middle speed ranges of top gear acceleration, so that there is more punch in hand after a change-up from intermediate to top, for instance. The 4.2 model can accelerate from 60 to 100mph in the same time (within half a second) that the 3.8 version took to go from 30 to 70mph. From rest to 110mph it is a full eight seconds quicker—at 36.5secs instead of 44.9.

'Maximum speed has gone up marginally from 119.5mph to 121.5; but at this speed the engine is revving hard, with the tachometer needle beyond the 5,500rpm limit on the scale. Only at such rapid speeds does the final drive gearing seem a little low; but a higher ratio certainly would spoil the excellent top gear performance.

'On the road, the improvements are really appreciated, and the car covers the ground in the forceful, tireless manner of the smaller Mark II models. Overtaking distances are shortened by a hard tread on the accelerator, which gives kick-down to intermediate if speed is below 58mph, or to first if under 21mph. These lower gears can be held to 5,000rpm and then the transmission changes up to intermediate (at 43mph) and top at 69mph.

'Except for starts and low-speed work the transmission stays in top gear for most of the time, but with the extra torque there is never any lumpiness to make the driver feel that it should have changed down.'

Final performance figures worked out at 9.9secs for the 0–60 with 17secs for the standing quarter mile and marginally-better fuel consumption of 14.5mpg. *Motor*'s 9:1 compression ratio Mark X automatic, registered CLB526B, was not quite so quick on test in July 1965, but just as impressive. *Motor* reported:

'Classic cars, like the best wines, improve with the pas-

sage of time. The special position of Jaguar, selling high-quality cars in relatively small numbers at a price which can only be achieved by volume production over a number of years, has made the axiom true of every post-war model. It is certainly true of the Mark X . . . which has developed into an extremely good car.

'The Mark X has always been virtually without a rival in Britain, offering size and performance on an American scale at a price matched only by a few imported American cars of barely equal comfort and inferior roadworthiness. When we tested the original 3.8-litre model two years ago, we were impressed by the car as a whole yet found a number of details to criticise. In almost every respect the maturing process has done its work. The 4.2-litre Mark X has a better transmission, far better steering, a more efficient and controllable heating system, and, in the main, excellent finish. It remains a large, powerful, roadworthy and luxurious car, able to transport five people and their luggage in great comfort over long distances. Most of all it is at home in countries where rough or wavy roads have too often in the past made high-speed travel a matter for strong stomachs. Independently sprung all-round, it has very few competitors for its combination of ride and handing—probably none of the same size at less than twice the price.

'For the British customer size may well be a deciding factor, for the car is not economical of space. Five people may sit in it very comfortably and take plenty of luggage with them, but the deliberately long, low and wide envelope of a body is a good deal longer and wider than is either strictly necessary or convenient for parking. It is fair to add that the 4.2-litre saloon bears the hallmark of all good big cars in feeling smaller on the move than it is.'

Surprisingly, *Autocar* could not match the automatic Mark X's acceleration figures with a manual version despite its use of a 3.77:1 rear axle ratio rather than the 3.54:1 used in conjunction with the torque converter. Top speed on this overdrive model, registered AWK986B, was up to 122.5mph and fuel consumption improved to 16mpg, but the 0–60mph time was only 10.4secs with a 17.4-sec standing start quarter mile.

Autocar explained that they tried to improve

Paddy McNally managed a memorable road test for *Autosport* in the ex-John Coombs 3.4 litre Mark I registered 287JPK – pictured with Roy Salvadori leading Sir Gawaine Baillie's similar car at Silverstone in May 1959.

the figures several times, before adding that the latest all-synchromesh gearbox was a great improvement over the old Moss box: 'Movements between gears are quite long, but the gate is well-defined, and the synchromesh quite unbeatable . . . Many another engine producing around the Jaguar's 63bhp per litre is much more "peaky" and must be urged along with the gear lever, whereas the Jaguar is docile to a degree. It can potter down to a mere 20mph or so in overdrive top, although this may be a little unkind to the transmission.

'Such is the combination of well-bred power, nicely-matched ratios, and an easy gearchange that even the most timid driver would find himself pushing the Mark X along very quickly on almost any sort of road, yet at city speeds it is restrained and quiet.'

Of the new Dunlop SP41 radial-ply tyres and

Markes Varamatic steering, they said:

'At any speed the car runs arrow-straight without steering correction, and changes of direction call for negligible effort, even though the overall (but varying) steering ratio is fairly high. Ride comfort is outstanding, and on good surfaces the car remains stable and level.

'Rapid cornering, though awe-inspiring to watch from the roadside, produces only limited body roll. Quite a lot of wheel-twirling is needed to hustle the car along winding roads due to the consistent understeering characteristics, and the formidable adhesion of the rear tyres.'

It was left for Bolster to really put AWK986B through its paces on test for *Autosport* in August 1965. He related with some satisfaction:

'Naturally, you and I, as enthusiasts, are keen to get the last drop of speed out of a car. For us, the manual gearbox and overdrive are ideal. We are aware that this model will normally be sold in automatic form, and that a small gain in maximum speed is of no interest to the average owner. If he can touch 120mph he will be happy, and why not? The manual change car does better than this, partly because the drag of the planetary box is removed, but principally as a result of the very high gear that the overdrive gives. At the timed maximum speed of 128.5mph, the engine was running below its peak.'

Acceleration times were equally impressive at 10 secs for the 0–60 and 16.2 for the standing quarter mile.

S type

Midland editor Edward Eves had the first opportunity to try the new Jaguar S type for *Autocar*, delivering a 3.8-litre overdrive model, registered 2300KV, to the Turin Show. It was surprising that Jaguar released this car for road impressions because it was still fitted with the soon-to-be-superseded Moss gearbox. Tactfully, Eves did not comment on that. The overall performance, however, surprised him, a cruising speed of 110mph on the pre-70mph limit M1 motorway reducing an anticipated three-hour cross-country journey time to 2hrs 10mins. But a heavy thirst for fuel—at 33.5p per gallon!—left him wondering whether he could afford to eat well en route. Happily the trip to Italy turned into a gastronomic tour, described at some length, with odd bursts of high-speed motoring, which led Eves to comment in December 1963: 'To be able to make a transcontinental journey taking in great plains and a couple of mountain ranges is the only true way to assess a car such as the S type. On this journey the point-to-point ability of the car made it possible to spend much time in interesting places, yet driving 934 miles in three days left me feeling a good deal fitter than when I started.'

Some time later, in June 1964, *Car & Driver* were able to carry out a full road test on 2300KV. Their comments gave credence to reports that some Moss gearboxes—presumably those set up very carefully—were better than others. At any rate, *Car and Driver* said:

'The current fashion for decrying the Jaguar gearbox is only partly justified. The gearbox on the test car was actually pretty good, if the clutch pedal was fully depressed with each shift. It's strange how they vary—the transmission of the last E type that we drove was just terrible. The box is reassuringly stout, and if it is slow, it is so only relatively to what we have come to expect from modern transmissions.'

After praising the rear suspension, *Car and Driver* commented on handling with the Dunlop RS5 cross-ply tyres and the new power-assisted steering:

'Directional stability, handling and braking are all fully in keeping with the S type's performance . . . If the road suddenly becomes wet, the driver is instantly warned of the fact through the lightened feel of the steering, despite the power assist. This Burman unit is quite satisfactory at all times and a particular boon during parking as well as full-bore cornering.'

Performance figures were exceptionally good, 2300KV recording a 126mph maximum with a 10.2-sec 0–60mph time and 17.6secs for the standing start quarter mile. Extensive use of the overdrive resulted in fuel consumption around 16mpg.

Road & Track then managed to test a 3.8-litre automatic S type in the United States, reporting in October 1964: 'We weren't wholly convinced that the proportions of the car are improved by the longer rear end and increased overhang—we always admire the taut, compact, look of the 2.4 sedan that came out in 1956 [in America] but certainly the changes that result from the alterations more than make up for it . . . The upholstery is fine English hide, the carpeting is sensually deep and all facia and window trim is in that perfectly finished walnut veneer that no one has yet been able to duplicate in plastic—and, as a matter of sour grapes, requires meticulous care if it is to be kept in its original condition. Lots of wax and elbow grease will do it, though.'

Despite, or perhaps because of 'an awful lot of gearshifting going on under your foot', this Borg-Warner-equipped car could manage only 116mph, with an 11.5-sec 0–60mph time and 18.9-sec standing quarter mile. Fuel consumption fell between 14 and 17mpg.

Back in Blighty, *Motor* were full of praise for their 3.8-litre automatic S type, registered 2233KV, commenting in December 1964:

'It is now over a year since the S type Jaguars were introduced to supplement but not to replace the Mark II saloon . . . The two models share many common mechanical components and a basic similarity of shape and size. Some of the differences are obvious . . . There are numerous other improvements of this sort, all of them valuable, but all relatively insignificant by comparison with the conversion to independent rear suspension which has altered the whole character of the car. At the end of an unusually long road test which included 2,000 miles abroad, we came to the conclusion that this design change is easily worth the £200 price difference between the models [the S type, as tested, costing £1,885].

'The S type is one of the most comfortably sprung cars in the world and it will maintain its extremely high cruising speeds with the utmost safety and stability over road surfaces which demand a considerable reduction in speed from most cars. Dunlop SP41 [radial-ply] tyres are now standard and with these and the optional power steering fitted to the test car, the handling inspires a similar degree of confidence. The S type weighs some 3cwt more than the Mark II, so that in terms of performance figures it is not quite so impressive.'

Motor's figures were similar to those of *Road & Track*, and not even the redoubtable Bolster had been able to improve on them with the same car for *Autosport* in August 1964. But some of his comments were significant:

'As regards the performance of the S type, this can be

Facing page: Jaguar Mark II saloons proved popular mounts for European road tests. The 3.8 litre example of Richard Elvin and Colin Anderson is pictured near Rheims during the 1990 Monte Carlo Challenge.

defined as slower than the Mark II in figures, but faster across country. The more luxurious car is naturally heavier than its smaller brother, but its independent rear suspension allows it to corner faster. Furthermore, the rear passengers receive a much less hectic ride, which again encourages the driver to press on. The better roadholding is obvious on a racing circuit, but its benefits are even more apparent on the road, where one cannot risk hanging out the tail . . . The theoretical advantage of the [rear suspension] system have actually been achieved with the assistance of the Dunlop SP41 tyres.'

And then with the side-long glance at Rolls-Royce, he added:

'Until recently, it has been argued that the virtues of independent rear suspension were not appreciable for large, heavy, cars. Now Jaguar have proved that for roadholding, safety and riding comfort, a good independent rear end cannot be equalled. This car will cause a lot of rethinking among the manufacturers of luxury vehicles.'

The relatively-restrained performance figures of the 3.8-litre S type, of which automatic models made up the bulk of production, worried Jaguar to such an extent that they encouraged a second round of road tests in a car registered EDU482C fitted with the new all-synchromesh gearbox. Amazingly, *Autocar*, *Motor* and *Autosport* all returned near-identical times of 121–122mph maximum speed, 10.2–10.4-sec 0–60mph, and 17.1–17.5secs for the standing quarter mile. Fuel consumption varied wildly, however, *Autocar* achieving only 12.8mpg overall, *Motor* 15.4mpg and *Autosport* somewhere between 13 and 18mpg.

Autocar reported first, in March 1965, that 'in these days when we are surrounded by plastics and shiny metal, it is pleasant to slip back to the days of gracious living and a rich atmosphere of polished woods, leather and deep carpets.'

Of the gearbox, they commented:

'It is a vast improvement over the former unit and ensures quieter changes. The movement between gear positions has been increased slightly . . . [the] movements are a little heavy, and there is some baulking when reverse is selected. The synchromesh is very effective and cannot be beaten, no matter how fast the gear lever is moved.'

And of the SP41 tyres:

'They give excellent grip. Their radial ply construction does make them transmit small jars and bumps to the chassis, but not to an annoying degree.'

Motor then followed up in August 1965 by saying:

'Our previous S type road test car was fitted with automatic transmission and at the time we felt that the manual version with its overdrive and still with power-assisted steering, would provide an almost ideal sporting saloon. Time and the subject of this test have proved the point. The car does not set out to be a four-seater E type, and indeed it is not so fast as the lighter 3.8 Mark II, but the extra weight has been well distributed in sound damping and general insulation from the outside world, and the overall feel of the car is that it would probably lose nothing to either on any non-motorway journey and be completely untiring whatever the distance. It is only when travelling at over 100mph that wind and some engine noise begins to rise above an unobtrusive rush. The only point which might deter the 3.8S owner from maximum indulgence is a petrol consumption which can drain the 14-gallon tankage in under 200 miles—15.4mpg at our overall rate; astute use of the overdrive might raise this to nearer 18mpg—the consumption at a steady 90mph.'

Their comments on the new gearbox were similar to those of *Autocar* although they added that 'for the smoothest changes, it is still necessary to concentrate, as one tends to allow the revs to drop too much while using the whole of the long clutch travel, which is only necessary to engage reverse. Fast changes with quick foot and handwork, or slow changes with the throttle eased rather than released, produce the smoothest results. The clutch, without the diaphragm fitted to the 4.2-litre units, is noticeably heavy only in creeping traffic.'

Following vehement comments about cars still fitted with live rear axles, Bolster added to the general praise for the S type in *Autosport* in May 1965 before commenting, with large American cars in mind:

'To me the pleasure of driving is greatly increased when a plentiful array of dials tells me what is going on. I am never at ease if I have only those beastly little lights to warn me that the oil pressure has dropped or that the water has boiled away. In cheap cars, I always fear that the filaments of all the bulbs have gone and spend my time sniffing for hot metal or burning rubber. In a Jaguar, I can put my nose in neutral and relax, for all the proper dials are there, bringing me cheerful messages.'

Jaguar 420

Road tests involving the Jaguar 420 tended to be confined to the overdrive version, although a solitary test of the one equipped with an automatic gearbox revealed little difference in performance. Perhaps Jaguar were being over-cautious by releasing only manual cars to testers, although outright performance was deemed to be of paramount importance when *Autocar* tested a 420 registered GKV67D in March 1967. They reported:

'Against the S type, the savings of half a second and three seconds respectively in acceleration through the gears to 60 and 100mph may appear trivial, but the big difference is that the much greater torque enables the car to do this more effortlessly. The extra power also shows up better at the top end of the scale. Above 100mph, where the S type's performance is beginning to tail off, the 420 still has acceleration in hand, and takes only 11sec to go from 100 to 110mph. The ideal cruising speed seems to be just over 100mph. Top speed, with a one-way maximum of 126mph and 123mph mean, is much the same as that of the 3.8 Mark II, but faster than the other big Jaguars. Fuel consumption has to be related to the fast travel provided. Test consump-

tion varied between 12mpg in London traffic crawling, 15mpg in motorway work and generally fast driving on the open road, and 17mpg with more gentle use of the performance.'

John Bolster then set marginally quicker figures with the same car for *Autosport* in May 1967—125mph and a 9.5-sec 0–60mph with the 16.4secs for the standing quarter mile—before remarking:

'The car displays remarkable stability. Previous Jaguars have sometimes tended to twitch in a sidewind, but the 420 seems to ignore the rudest blasts. The power-assisted steering is extremely light, but it succeeds in transmitting the message from the road, which is rare. I would place this steering in the very top class, and

Wire wheels – like those fitted to Adrian Frey's 3.8 litre Mark II racing in the Pre-1965 Classic Saloon Car championship at Silverstone in March 1990 – were typically fitted to the higher-priced American road test cars.

though I would personally prefer higher gearing, the ratio chosen is just about ideal for the average driver. Understeer there is, but there is enough power to alter that and the balance of the car is beyond criticism.

'Curiously enough, the springing feels rather too soft at low speeds and the car rolls noticeably on sharp bends, in spite of its wide track and low build. At higher speeds, it becomes taut and responsive, the standard of riding comfort on all surfaces being exceptional. The cornering power is very high, especially on wet roads, and the handling of the car breeds confidence which is never misplaced.

162

'The stability during heavy braking is also impressive, the reluctance of the wheels to lock being praiseworthy. Hard driving heats up the inboard rear brakes but fading is not experienced. In praising the power of the brakes, I must also shed a tear over the parking device. The handbrake is feeble indeed and the right-hand lever is so placed that one is almost bound to kick it on leaving the car. I did just that, releasing the parking brake and starting the Jaguar off driverless down a hill. By breaking the world's record for the long jump, I was able to regain my seat, just in time to prevent the car from crashing through a level crossing gate! As I have said before, a simple guard over the button would prevent the ratchet from being released accidentally.'

It was hardly surprising that after 12 years' production using substantially-similar lines that the 420 was beginning to look dated. But *Road & Track* still liked their wire-wheeled version, commenting in December 1967:

'In our opinion it is the most aesthetically successful of the whole series of Jaguar compact sedans, as well as looking considerably better than the 420G! But it is not a modern look that the 420 possesses; rather it is a classical one, and the age of the basic structure shows through in such matters as the comparatively small glass area and the layout of controls and instruments. Still, the entire effect is most pleasant and one feels surrounded by opulence, grace and dignity; to many, these things are far more important than having the latest in styling.'

Some of their other comments were distinctly prophetic, although it is doubtful whether anybody outside the realms of Jaguar engineering realised it. Still harping on the theme of old and new, *Road & Track* said that the very heavy engine must be hideously expensive to produce in comparison with American V8s of comparable power and considered a change overdue—if only to reduce the front-end weight bias. On the other hand, the brakes and suspension were well up to the minute . . . and so far as the general package was concerned it was adjudged excellent, despite some misgivings about

the lack of grip from its Dunlop Road Speed crossply tyres, fitted as standard for the American market because radials were not available at the time with white sidewalls. Radial-ply tyres with conventional black sidewalls could be ordered as an option, however!

Although the car was fitted with air conditioning, the heating and ventilation still came in for criticism, chiefly because its lack of through-put. It was interesting to note the difference in performance, however, this overdrive version returning a 120mph maximum speed, with an 11-sec 0–60mph time and 17.1secs for the standing quarter mile. Fuel consumption was much the same at 12–17.5mpg, eventually working out at 16.4mpg during a 20,000-mile extended test during which the air conditioning was used for much of the time.

Motor then managed to test an automatic 420, registered GKV66D, in May 1967, finding that although the top speed was much reduced at 115mph, it lacked nothing in acceleration: 9.4secs for the 0–60mph and 17.5secs for the standing quarter mile. Fuel consumption was also directly comparable at 15.4mpg overall.

Of the automatic Jaguar saloons they had tested recently, *Motor* commented:

'The 420 has a useful edge over the 3.8 S type in the middle speed ranges and is just about level-pegging with the more powerful (but much heavier) Mark X. It is interesting to see that the least powerful of our quartet, the 210bhp 3.4 Mark II, is still the fastest we have tested, suggesting: (a) that aerodynamically (and aesthetically, too, perhaps) the Mark II has the best body shape and (b) that the 3.8 Mark II is probably still the fastest Jaguar saloon made. Perhaps we should add that Jaguar were disappointed with the top speed we recorded for the 420; they were expecting more.'

Possibly *Road & Track* had taken a lead from *Motor* when they commented about the XK engine, as the British magazine noted that it was no longer so impressive, so far as performance and smoothness at high revs were concerned, as rival American V8s. In the same way the Borg Warner Model 8 transmission also felt fussy at speed and was noticeably jerky when subject to changes at more than 3,500rpm. Their 420 also displayed what was to become a common tendency for the front end to ground itself on badly-rutted roads or hump-back bumps. But despite the softness of the suspension, the handling was excellent:

'Wide-section SP41 tyres give tremendous adhesion: even in the wet it is often possible to use full throttle out of sharp corners without breaking the tail away or lifting the inside wheel. Normally there is mild, stable, understeer but the rather sudden degree of modest body roll announces that the back wheels are on the threshold of a slide. Significantly, not even our fastest drivers can recall actually breaking adhesion, deliberately or not, to the extent that opposite lock correction was needed.'

Although *Motor*'s braking tests indicated little fade, they soon provoked a lot of juddering which led the magazine to suggest that the composition of the lining materials were biased towards long life and that alternatives ought to be offered.

The four-headlight system using to large lamps on the outside was adjudged excellent, 'showing a clear advantage over rival systems using four small headlights.'

Daimler Sovereign

Motor also managed to test a Daimler version of the 420 in November 1967, returning similar performance figures despite the fact that it had a manual gearchange. This car, registered JWK811E, must have been a real disappointment to the Jaguar engineers, because it reached only 117mph, with 9.2secs for the 0–60mph time and 17secs for the standing quarter mile, even the fuel consumption working out at almost the same: 15.6mpg!

Nevertheless, the character was different, even if the change of radiator grille and badging was considered to be purely a marketing ploy:

Autocar considered the 240 to be a 'full-blooded Jaguar with all the virtues of a thoroughbred'.

'Of the 420 automatic, we said that despite its performance and E type pedigree, which shows up as outstanding roadholding even on very poor surfaces, this is not a car with any strong sporting pretensions, as the wide, slippery, seats will reveal on a twisty road. Likewise, the steering was considered more notable for its lightness and stability than for its feel when cornering near the limit. None the less, the terms GT and sports occurred fairly regularly in the verbal and written comments of staff members who drove the manual car. One remarked that it was more sporting than many sports cars and certainly grander than almost any other GT proclaiming the distinction. No doubt much of this sporting flair stems from the availability of five ratios instead of three and the freedom from restrictions imposed on the automatic by its rather jerky kick-down and very limited range of manual control.'

Jaguar XJ6

Seldom has a new car received so much adulation as Jaguar's XJ6. Not only did road-testers fall over themselves to heap praise on it, but waiting lists ran into years as the word got around that this really was a superlative car. Often the only way to jump the queue was to pay a premium as high as 50 per cent over list price at a time when exports had not even begun to the biggest market, the United States. *Motor*, which had a growing reputation for extracting the best performance figures of the specialist motor trade weeklies, were more than happy to run the first full test in May 1969, although the new British monthly, *CAR*, and *Autosport* carried driving impressions using factory performance figures (and pictures of 2.8-litre cars rather than the 4.2-litre models on which they were commenting). These 'tests' featured factory-supplied figures based on a 127-mph maximum one-way speed rather than the average of two-way tests aimed at eliminating the effects of either head, or

tail, winds. And naturally, the factory were not at all keen for anybody to publish test figures on the 2.8-litre car, which was in full production, but much slower than the 4.2-litre model. At any rate, *Motor* commented in May 1969 on a 4.2-litre overdrive prototype, registered MWK22G:

'Like many hopeful customers, we have had to wait a long time to get our hands on an XJ6 for a full road test: the only qualms we have now about publishing the report is that it is going to make the waiting list even longer and Jaguar's problems of supply and demand even more acute. Not only is the XJ6 far and away the best saloon that Jaguar have ever made—and their standards have always been high—but we believe that in its behaviour it gets closer to overall perfection than any other luxury car we have tested, regardless of price. If not faultless, it is impossible to charge it with any sig-

John Bolster found the 340 overdrive model far faster than the 240 during an *Autosport* road test. Benjamin Sill's example is pictured here leading Tony Moore's 3.4 litre Mark I in the Jaguar Drivers' Club Pre-1968 Challenge at Mallory Park in May 1989.

nificant criticisms, even when judged by absolute standards, and its tally of top marks make impressive reading.'

The areas in which *Motor* judged that the XJ6 excelled were comfort, roadholding, handling, quietness and performance. Even items that had been traditional Jaguar weaknesses, heating, ventilation, fuel capacity and seat design, were now much improved. Jaguar had made no secret that they intended to install their new V12 engine, when it had been fully developed, in the XJ6, but *Motor* considered the time-honoured XK unit perfectly adequate, returning performance figures of 124mph flat out, 8.8secs for 0–60mph acceleration with a 16.5-sec standing quarter mile. They added, however:

'What impressed us even more than the stopwatch figures was the effortless way in which they were recorded. There is an object lesson here, we suspect, in engine isolation for the XJ6 seems altogether smoother, quieter and mechanically more refined than previous Jaguars.

'That the car can do 124mph with the same power that gives, say, the Daimler Sovereign a top speed of 117mpg, suggests that the body is more than just a pretty suit of clothes; it must be aerodynamically quite efficient, too. This is also reflected by the fuel consumption which, though still fairly heavy at 15.3mpg overall, is no worse than that of the lighter Sovereign and really quite creditable considering the performance that goes with it. With gentle driving, you could probably get 20mpg, though 17 would be a more realistic average.'

Needless to say, the new, increased, range of more than 400 miles received *Motor*'s complete approval.

They found the new steering responsive and accurate, although a shade too light, preferring the more heavily-weighted systems used on the NSU Ro80 and Aston Martin DBS. And so far as the handling was concerned:

'The car just floats round corners with such enormous reserves of adhesion that the driver's nerve will invari-

ably be lost before the grip. We had to try much harder and faster than usual to discover that the initial mild understeer doesn't, as you might expect, build up to a total front-end slide at the limit—at least, not on a dry road—but that the tail drifts gently out. This seems to apply both under power and on the overrun if you lift off in mid-corner.

'While the enormous SP Sport radial tyres will normally transmit full torque round corners without letting go in the dry, you have to treat the throttle with much greater respect on a wet road. With so much power on tap, it is hardly surprising that, without some caution, you can break the tail away, especially on roundabouts and slippery town streets. Similarly, the car can understeer straight on during a fast trailing-throttle approach (even under power sometimes). Perhaps it is because the car normally instils such confidence that any sudden loss of adhesion—and it does tend to be pretty sudden—catches you unawares . . .

'The XJ6 is one of the most comfortable cars we have ever tested. The ride is more stable, yet less boulevard, than that of many softly-sprung cars; the resilience is there but none of the wallowy swell. Only a sharp hump taken at speed catches it out, the normal millpond float suddenly being disturbed by a rather sickly sinking as the suspension uses up its long travel. Even when the car sinks to the bump stops, though, it doesn't scrape its belly on the road like the last 420 we tried.'

Next month, June, *Autocar* laid hands on another pre-production XJ6, an automatic model registered PRW890G. They were just as impressed as their colleagues on *Motor*, commenting:

'Throughout the motor industry the whole process of car design is changing in the light of the latest tyre technology. The XJ6 has been built from the tyres up and it shows in the way it behaves on any road in any condition. From our company chauffeur who merely took the test car through city streets to a drive-in car wash to our most blasé tester, every one was impressed immediately with the completely out-of-its-class ride and silence. With certain qualifications, we would say it is the smoothest and quietest car we have driven or been driven in. And that includes cars in the multi-thousand pound bracket like the Rolls-Royce and Mercedes 600.

And after detailed discussion our test staff agreed that the handing was, if anything, better than that of the E type and certainly unmatched by anything in the saloon car class.'

Performance, jerky gearchange included, was inevitably a little more leisurely than the manual car, the automatic recording a 120mph maximum, 10.1-sec 0–60mph and 17.5-sec standing quarter mile times with a virtually-identical 15.2mpg. As ever, the price (£2,687 including tax) was hard to believe: 'As it stands at the moment, dynamically, the XJ6 has no equal regardless of price, which explains those 12-month delivery quotes from dealers and black market prices £1,000 over list.'

John Bolster produced virtually identical figures (save for a 9.8-sec 0–60mph) in his first full road test of a 4.2-litre automatic XJ6, registered MVC204G, reporting for *Autosport* in July 1969:

'The suspension is quite outstanding, contriving to give a level ride over the worst roads while never feeling excessively soft. A car in front of me, travelling at 100mph or so, was flung into the air over a slight hump in the road so that I could see its transmission and rear suspension arrangements, yet I was completely unable to feel any bump at all in the XJ6.'

Motor then had a chance to try an early 4.2-litre automatic, again finding the gear change jerky and returning similar performance figures to *Autosport* except for an even faster 0–60mph time of 9.6secs. But they said, prophetically, in February 1970 of the car registered PRW898G:

'In the nine months since we tested the XJ6 our ardour for it could have cooled; it hasn't. The XJ6 is still a superb car and will remain so for a long time while others struggle to catch up only on value for money but in sheer engineering . . . Just to prove its designers are human, it does have the odd failing, too: the back seat space is not really in the *Financial Times* reading class, unless the boss pushes the passenger's seat well forward; and the switches stretching across the facia are evidence of tradition rather than ergonomic thinking.

'It is customary to call the long-stroke XK unit

dated particularly when an alternative is known to be in the pipeline, but in the XJ6 it takes on a new lease of life for the smooth refinement of its output . . . the engine also feels rather smoother than it used to in the S-series cars and sometimes one can't help wondering why anyone thinks the engine needs replacing—just because it is about 25 years old in basic design?'

Cyril Posthumus tested the same car in Britain for *Road & Track*'s issue of August 1970 because new environmental legislation meant that testing in America would delay quantity imports until the end of the year. His comments were largely similar to those of other British testers, although Posthumus had this to say for the Americans:

'Though the XJ6 has yet to reach the States in quantity it is designed very much with Americans, and their safety regulations, in mind, and it is all there—the reinforced body centre section, the collapsible steering column, generous padding, hazard warning, squashy sun visor, recessed switch gear, snap-off framed mirror, burst-proof locks, flush door handles, etc. There is also provision for safety belts for the rear as well as front passengers . . .

'Altogether this Jaguar emerges pretty much of a paragon in looks, performance, comfort, refinement and value. Time alone will tell how long it will last before decay sets in, but the bodies are carefully rustproofed before painting and the mechanical components are so little stressed that we may expect considerable longevity even though it costs less than a third the price of a Bentley. Is it not significant that the waiting time for an XJ6 in England is now over 12 months, that black market examples regularly command an extra $1,000–1,200, and that recently a group of would-be Swiss buyers flew specially to London to protest to British Leyland headquarters that their market for the car was being discriminated against? It is surely a car worth waiting for.'

Michael Scarlett then managed to borrow Jaguar's well-used prototype, PRW890G, now fitted with the new Borg-Warner model 12 automatic gearbox, for a trip to France, reporting for *Auto-*

car in April 1970:

'The result is a much more useful, responsive and controllable transmission which does change ratio appreciably more smoothly than before, though puzzlingly in view of the weight of the car it still doesn't do so quite as undetectably as the large Americans. Part-throttle downchanges are made with pleasant ease if you are in what one might call a refined hurry. The car will kickdown very willingly to near the top of the rev range, at times almost too much so with such a torquey power unit.'

John Bolster then took a sister car, another 4.2-litre registered PRW898G, to Spa to cover the Belgian Grand Prix, reporting for *Autosport* in August 1970 that the new automatic gearbox was not only much smoother in operation than the old one, but that this car—which had covered 23,000 miles and was well run-in, was virtually as fast as a manual model.

Autocar then summed up a 4.2-litre overdrive

Car and Driver reckoned that the 3.8 litre S-type's directional stability, handling and braking were well in keeping with its performance. Colin Thatcher shows that the higher overall weight is not necessarily so much of a handicap as he leads a 340 and 3.8 litre Mark II in the *Jaguar Quarterly* Pre-1968 Challenge at Oulton Park in April 1990.

car, registered TKV888J, in May 1971 as still offering outstanding value despite price rises of around 50 per cent since the XJ6 was introduced. Deliveries were better, although some dealers were still reporting waiting lists of several months. Detail modifications, such as redesigned extractor vents and the improved cold-starting device, were much appreciated although the engine now seemed harsh about 4,500rpm. But 'in fact, there is seldom any need to exceed 4,000rpm. Such is the engine's flexibility that upward changes are generally made at much lower speeds. With overdrive engaged, 4,000rpm represents 110mph, a speed at which the XJ6 is content to cruise when occasion demands.'

Top speed proved to be 123mph, with an

8.7-sec 0–60mph time and 16.5secs for the standing quarter mile—times that matched the BMW2800 and left Mercedes' 280SE standing. Fuel consumption was heavier than the German pair, however, at 16mpg. The only really disappointing feature was a clutch pedal that was not only heavy to operate but had a very long travel. *Autocar* concluded:

'Perhaps the XJ6's most remarkable attribute is the way in which it adapts to changing moods and circumstances. Gliding along in supreme comfort and silence is only one aspect of its personality. When the occasion arises, it can be transformed into an eager and responsive sports car, capable of showing most of its rivals a clean pair of heels. This is particularly true when the going is twisty.'

Car and Driver had a lot more to say in April 1971 when they had one of the first opportunities to test an XJ6 in America. In fact, their prose was distinctly purple . . .

'A key case sways back and forth as it hangs below the ignition switch . . . and as it does it occasionally brushes against a roll of padding below the dash to produce a rustling sound . . . and you *hear* it in the XJ because there are no other sounds loud enough to hide it.'

Car and Driver liked the precise way in which their 4.2-litre automatic moved: 'Straight down the road, steady as the hand of a sommelier decanting a proud vintage. Steering corrections can be made with vernier accuracy . . .'

And so far as the seating was concerned:

'You are not folded into any three-across econo seat, but in the first-class section . . . You'd be lucky to find anything so hospitable in your den . . . It all suggests "imported"—not in the way a Hong Kong toy does, but in the finest sense of the word, like pungent Havana cigars and mellow, ruby red port from Portugal. It also suggests a time gone by, a time before luxury cars were built on computer-controlled assembly lines . . . You can't help but like it.'

Rivals were viewed with disdain:

'You can turn to Detroit for a Buick or Cadillac or Lincoln or Imperial—it doesn't really matter which. They are essentially alike, competent above question but all oversize variations on the same mindless chrome-and-plastic theme and all screwed together with less attention to detail than you would expect to find in an average pencil sharpener. Or if you are disenchanted with Detroit, there is Germany—Mercedes and BMW. The German cars are cold and aloof, seemingly styled with the same passion that the U.S. reserves for refrigerators . . . They are *machines* and they never let you forget it.

'But there is more to owning a car of this type than hurrying over the face of the earth . . . and it's in these other areas that we hesitate in our glowing discussion. Those men responsible for maintaining Jaguar's traditional, carriage-like level of luxury have also maintained a tolerance toward traditional motoring hardships. The most glaring example of this appeared when it was necessary to add oil to the engine. A simple task—presumably. There in front of you stands a magnificently machined and polished aluminium cap which screws into one of the cast aluminium camshaft covers and a simple twist should unscrew it. But rarely is that the case. The aluminium expands when the engine is hot and it usually requires a *hammer and chisel* to remove the cap. This could be shrugged off as insignificant but various staff members remember the same occurrence on other Jaguars as long as 15 years ago. Jaguar service representatives, on the other hand, are not alarmed. "You can usually get it off if you wrap a rag around it for a little better grip or let it cool off for a while." That's what we'd call tolerance to hardship, and while stiff upper lips may be common among Englishmen, they are a rarity in Yanks.'

Suitably oiled-up, *Car and Driver* heaped more praise on this emission-controlled XJ6, returning a 110mph top speed, with an 11-sec 0–60mph time and 18.3-sec standing quarter mile. Fuel consumption was to the order of 14–16.5mpg. *Road & Track* were a little quicker in February 1972, recording a 115mph top speed, 10.7-sec 0–60mph time and 17.1-sec standing quarter mile, with 15.2mpg in their Model 8 Borg Warner-equipped 4.2-litre. Following initial grumbles along the lines of 'Jaguar Cars,

Coventry, England, is a slow company specialising in fast cars. For years, we've had great difficulty getting their models on test—more than with any other maker—and the fact that this XJ6 wasn't made available to us on home ground until more than two years after its introduction is ample evidence of the fact', they warmed to their task:

'As one might expect from such a slow-moving carmaker, the car is antique in certain ways, sometimes amusingly and sometimes irritatingly so. In other ways, it's as modern as a production car can be . . . and quite outstanding. Everything considered, it's a car with personality and character, as indeed every Jaguar has been.'

They noted, of the antique features, that the engine no longer guzzled oil, but lacked the refinement of the rest of the car at higher revs. But it was more economical than the latest Mercedes V8. Similar comments were applied to the 'clunky' transmission. And with an oblique reference to Mercedes' air suspension, and American reservations about radial-ply tyres, they noted:

'Despite a relatively simple suspension system—by that we mean the XJ has no air springs or automatic levelling—it's one of the best-riding cars money can buy. Even with radial tyres, there's no harshness over small, sharp, bumps such as tar strips; damping is just right and there's plenty of suspension travel to let the XJ glide over really large bumps and dips at speed without bottoming. The car does look rather elevated at the rear when not loaded; this is Jaguar's solution to load-carrying rather than a levelling system. But when loaded, it still rides well and has adequate rear suspension travel.'

Significantly, *Road & Track* also considered the steering—which Jaguar had always insisted was weighted purely for American tastes— was 'a little lighter, with less road feel, than we consider ideal . . . about our only serious criticism of the XJ's road behaviour is that it is unduly sensitive to sidewinds for a front-engine, two-ton, car; perhaps it illustrates the old generalisation than an aerody-

namically clean car may be less resistant to sidewinds than a boxy one.'

It was also significant that the *Road & Track* testers, brought up in a land where drum brakes and hundreds of horsepower were the norm for years, found fault in the XJ6's disc brakes. Quite simply, they found them inadequate, lacking power in simulated panic stops from 60 and 80mph and ultimately resulting in a wheel-locking slide—very much like American 'muscle' cars. Fade tests also revealed a 20 per cent reduction in stopping power. Summing-up, *Road & Track* viewed the XJ6 as:

'A strange and wondrous car. It's one of the most beautiful sedans in the world, and certainly one of the best-handling and best-riding ones . . . elements of greatness, to be sure. Its styling, inside and out, is masterful—combining elegance, graciousness and tradition with a look and feel of speed and sportiness in a way absolutely no other car approaches. But in some respects—rather important ones—it seems to have been designed in a vacuum; it's as though the designers refused to look around them and see what everyone else is doing these days. Is it British pride, or simple British insularity, that lies behind the XJ's ergonomic backwardness? The XJ is a good car, make no mistake, but it's maddeningly short of what it could be if it were designed as competently all the way through as its suspension and bodywork are.'

XJ12 (Series I)

Although the long-awaited XJ12 was announced in July 1972, a prolonged strike delayed deliveries—and road tests by specialist magazines—for several months. But when they finally got their hands on test cars, the reactions were almost universal: praise for the phenomenal performance, and continuing quietness and refinement, but cries of horror at the fuel consumption.

Once again, *Motor*'s Midland editor, by now Philip Turner, managed to land one of the first drives in an XJ12, Jaguar chairman Lofty England's personal car, registered CWK212K, in

John Bolster took a 4.2 litre automatic XJ6 to Spa – where it was pictured at La Source – to cover the Belgian Grand Prix, a journey which confirmed that it was almost as fast as the manual gearbox model.

September 1972. Turner reported:

'Mr England apologised for the lack of a radio but said he had to set an example in economy: "Only the cars of junior management are fitted with stereo and tape decks." However, the Jaguar was not completely basic—it had electrically-operated windows . . .'

An attempt to take it past the historic 126.448mph achieved by an XK120 sports car in a 1949 publicity run along the Jabbekke motorway near Ostend, in Belgium, was frustrated by heavy traffic. But the ventilated disc brakes coped well with sudden demands while cruising at high speed. The big saloon proved equally at home in the narrow winding roads of the Ardennes when Turner had become accustomed to treating the finger-light power steering with a delicate touch. But 'with the kick down, however, there was a perceptible pause before the automatic box changed itself down, and also, with the throttle pressed down to the floor, one had a vivid mental picture of the carburettors taking a great swig of petrol like a man with a bottle at his lips. The fuel consumption overall worked out at 11.74mpg which seems about par for most 140mph cars.'

Apart from the fuel consumption, however, *Autocar* were most impressed when they finally got a road test XJ12, registered CVC446K, in March 1973. They recalled:

'At the time of first appraisal of the XJ6, it may have been difficult to conceive the idea of still further refinement, and the performance with the 4.2-litre engine was already sufficient to outpace most competitors. Yet the gains offered by the new V12 unit in the now-familiar XJ body transcend all expectations, offering a remarkable combination of performance, safety and refinement.'

Maximum performance figures of 146mph, a 7.4-sec 0–60mph and 15.7secs for the standing quarter mile were achieved by holding the lower two ratios to maximum revs, although the acceleration times took less than one second longer when the throttle was floored and the gearbox left to work out its own changing points. But despite the V12's turbine smoothness, *Autocar* felt that the XJ12 was undergeared on a 3.31:1 rear axle ratio and used far too much fuel as a result at an overall 11.4mpg which rose as high as 8mpg during the performance tests—and in heavy traffic.

Philip Turner, who took Lofty England's personal XJ12 registered CWK212K to Belgium in September 1972 was left with an enduring memory of its massive fuel consumption . . .

The new series II XJ had completely revised frontal styling.

John Bolster recorded virtually identical performance figures in the same car and found it a memorable experience on a trip to France for *Autosport* in May 1972:

'Most British cars behave disgracefully on the more difficult roads of Northern France, but the Jaguar rode with that splendid disdain of bumps and potholes which has been almost a French monopoly. As so many Frenchmen ignore their own speed limits, I was not ashamed to drive at 120mph where 69mph is the permitted maximum. On the autoroutes, where the sky's the limit, the astonishing thing about the XJ12 is the way in which its acceleration persists where other fast cars are beginning to struggle . . .

'The splendid surge of power makes overtaking such a safe manoeuvre, especially when the long *camions* with their vast trailers have to be doubled. I would

like to pay tribute to the French lorry drivers, who do everything possible to make the passage of fast cars easy; truly they are the gentlemen of the road . . .'

In distinct contrast to the steering, which could be disconcerting on a wet road, Bolster found that the brakes need quite firm pressure on the pedal: 'For this, they are all the better. No really fast car should have excessively light brakes as the driver may be thrown forward under extreme retardation and involuntarily lock the wheels.'

He described the fuel consumption as the Jaguar's Achilles heel, but summed up:

'The V12 engine has so many theoretical advantages that it is excellent to see them all realised at last, in a car of far from astronomical price. By no means cheap to run, it offers so much that, to the man with the right sort of money it must be just about irresistible.'

By the time Ian Fraser, editor of *CAR*, had CVC446K on test in June 1973, it was running just as sweetly at 24,000 miles. But its directional stability gave him some qualms:

'About 120mph, the car is decidedly edgy. It does not feel completely committed to the course the driver has designed for it and in fact needs very little encouragement to alter direction. You can find yourself involuntarily using a lane and a bit with the possibility of an additional requirement for the rest of the second slot. Just why this should be so is open to conjecture . . . The great urge to make the steering so light that even the most weary executive will feel no strain as he wends his way back after yet another four-hour lunch has imposed too much of a sacrifice in high-speed handling . . .

'Inherently, of course, the Jaguar does understeer. In the dry it never looks like getting out of hand, but in the wet it's a great big handful of a car that will go from the tail quite abruptly thanks in part to the limited-slip differential. The wet-weather roadholding is not bad, but there is a great need to be very careful on the throttle . . .

'Ventilation for the cabin is awful. With the massive, heat-producing engine incarcerated under that tight-fitting bonnet (even the battery box has to have its own electric fan!) the warmth continually seeps back among the passengers and the various vents and slots are powerless to do much about it. On anything approaching a warm day, the XJ12 becomes far too hot inside. There has to be a strong case here for making refrigerated air-conditioning standard equipment. The hinged quarter panes can provide additional extraction of air, but since they also induce extra wind-noise it becomes a matter for exchanging one discomfort for another. I found that careful use of the electric windows at opportune times—when caught up in slower traffic, for instances—was a reasonably satisfactory means of changing the air, but a heavy compromise at best.

'The shortcomings of the XJ12 are more than offset by its low price, but in a world where a four-cylinder BMW costs almost as much, what a pity it is that more money is not spent on the Jaguar to put its wrongs right.'

Car and Driver were in total disagreement the following month:

'On the road, you see pavement flowing quickly and silently under the XJ's long hood. Beneath the wheels a highway melts into a private deep-pile carpet installed solely for your riding pleasure. You track straight and true, boring a perfect one-car-wide hole through the air. The Jaguar's instinctive sense of direction never allows a quiver in your path. It all creates a motoring environment where the destination doesn't seem half as important as the pleasure in getting there. Even a trip to the dentist's office becomes an act of sybaritic indulgence. You leave early for appointments and don't rush in transit because the Jaguar XJ12 could well provide the most pleasurable interlude of the day. Even traffic jams don't seem to matter when you have an honest ten-grand worth of insulation between you and discomfort. The XJ12 is mental therapy on wheels. It soothes the mind by executing the simple task of transportation with such poise that you can't help but relish the experience.'

Why, they even liked the choke . . .

'In a Jaguar, driver involvement is present in the starting procedure. The XJ12 engine comes to life when cold only after a rigidly-prescribed pre-flight countdown. Part of the process requires *manual* operation of the choke. But you won't soil your hands on some mould-scored plastic knob crimped to the end of a stiff cable. Instead, the XJ12 has the world's finest choke control. It's a cast aluminium lever which subtly blends into the shadows of the left-hand lower instrument panel. And as you pull it into action, you feel smooth, precise, resistance. You could be advancing the film in your Nikon. Every millimetre or so there is the added pleasure of a light detent so you can select the choke position with micrometer-like accuracy. Then to complete the manual-of-arms, you engage the starter in the normal way . . . but normal responses do not follow. Instead of the expected thumping and clanking of an engine, all you have is a smooth, even, whine of the constant mesh starter. Surely that 5,343cc V12 has begun to turn over, but suddenly the tach needle moves off its peg, thereby yielding the only irrefutable evidence to the car's occupants that the engine is running.'

With prose as purple as that, and a lot more of it, performance figures might seem superfluous. But they were quite reasonable, considering that this was an emission-controlled car with only 241bhp: 7.7secs for the 0–60mph time, 16secs for the standing quarter mile with an estimated top speed of 125mph (and fuel consumption of 11.5mpg). *Road & Track* had been slightly slower with their car in May 1973, choosing to let the automatic gearbox sort out its own changes rather than use the selector. But they found the car just as impressive, giving the kind of effortless perfor- mance that Americans expected in a luxury saloon—at the same time combined with drive- ability, which was considered no mean feat.

They still considered the steering too light, but were much happier with the brakes, registering notably better stopping distances than they had with the XJ6. And so far as the styling was con- cerned:

'It's one of the most beautiful sedan shapes ever created. And its richly luxurious, traditional (and somewhat busy) interior finish is yet another positive aspect. We'll bet that a large proportion of XJ sales have been and will continue to be won almost solely on its extraordi- nary beauty. Little of that beauty has been lost to the 1973 bumper regulations, either: bulky front bumper guards and slightly larger rear ones add a little to its overall length and subtract little from its aesthetics.'

Daimler Double-Six (series one)

Motor's XJ12 road test was of a rare Daimler Double-Six variant, registered CVC448K, and cost- ing £120 more for the privilege of having a fluted radiator grille and slight differences in trim. Top speed was limited to 136mph (with a one-way 140mph), but acceleration was on form at 7.4secs for the 0–60mph time and 15.7secs for the stand

ing quarter mile—with 11.5mpg. Comments fitted in largely with those of other British testers, although *Motor* did have this to say of the steering:

'Both Jensen and Aston Martin use exactly the same Adwest Pow-a-Rak steering system but, as we've said many times before, eliminate all these defects completely by choosing settings which require a minimum force at the wheel rim of about 8lb for a parking manoeuvre on a dry metalled surface. As a result, their steering arrangements are indistinguishable from good manual systems while remaining light enough to be operated by any woman. Jaguar, please note . . .'

John Bolster had an equally-rare opportunity to try a long-wheelbase Double-Six, registered RVC204M, back-to-back with an air-conditioned automatic XJ6, RVC203M, for *Autosport* in November 1974. He cunningly avoided being drawn into making a decision in favour of either model despite proclaiming 'the object of this test was to find out whether or not the 12-cylinder model really justifies its greater running cost compared with the six!' Reading between the lines, however, he made a strong case for the 14–18mpg XJ6 against the 11–14mpg Double-Six. But his other comments were amusing, reflecting bygone attitudes to fast motoring, and significant in relation to the development of the motor car. Bolster said:

'My road test programme has changed tremendously during the long life of *Autosport*. For our early issues, I donned a leather coat and gauntlet gloves, as most of the cars were open sports models. Since those far- off days, motoring has ceased to be an open-air pastime and pneumonia is no longer an occupational hazard for test drivers . . .

'As petrol becomes more expensive, and even greater price rises are threatened, more and more people are being forced to consider the purchase of very eco- nomical cars. They also like to read about exotic cars far beyond their means, so my continued testing of mil- lionaires' playthings is still viable, I'm glad to say. The two magic carpets in this back-to-back do not fall into either of these categories. There are appreciable num- bers of people who can still afford to buy a Jaguar or

Motor found that the controls of the series II Jaguar were now far easier to use.

Daimler as their best-ever sales figures have just proved
. . .

'Let me say straight away that the longer wheelbase is a great improvement. The difference in comfort and ease of entry for the rear passengers is surprising with such a moderate increase over the original XJ models. The cars have always been good-lookers, but the longer roofline and wider rear doors give altogether better proportions. I also expected the handling to be good because the very long Daimler limousine is an outstanding road-holder, and I was certainly not disappointed.

'It used to be thought that a short wheelbase was desirable for fast cornering, but that's an old-fashioned idea. It was formerly difficult to make a long chassis sufficiently rigid, but integral construction has overcome that problem, for which rear-seat passengers may be duly thankful. The weight penalty is negligible, especially having regard to the massive torque of these two engines.'

So far as the relative top speeds were concerned, Bolster commented:

'Whereas 120mph is an easy speed at which almost anybody can drive, over 140mph is a bit dicey on the public roads with other traffic about. It's different for professional drivers, who keep in practice, but most people do 140mph in the bar much more often than they do

The back seat of the coupe was well up to saloon car standards once the occupants were in place.

The Borg-Warner transmission controlled by this familiar lever was considered 'rather old-fashioned' by *Road & Track*.

it on the road.

'Thus the extra performance of the Double-Six will seldom be used to the full. The XJ6L is so smooth that the V12 could scarcely be smoother and there's little difference in the sound level. Both cars accelerate sufficiently rapidly to be rarely extended, but the reserve of power of the V12 is most enjoyable, even if infrequently exploited. There are certainly many prospective owners who have no need of the extra performance and who will therefore choose the simpler engine on fuel consumption grounds, not to mention price . . .'

At the same time, Bolster found another interesting comparison:

'The Borg Warner transmission is far better than that originally used on Jaguars, but it is not as smooth as some recent systems from Renault and Mercedes . . . I am allowed to be very critical when testing cars of the highest quality and I think that the XJ6L is occasionally let down by a surprising jerk in changing gear. The V12 offends much less in this respect, probably because it is not usually being pressed so hard.'

Philip Turner had again enjoyed an early run in a Series II XJ12, registered EDU872M, for *Motor* in September 1973, reporting that 'even Jaguar company people who are constantly changing from one wheelbase to the other cannot tell

from the handling whether they are driving a long wheelbase or a short wheelbase car.'

He also made an interesting point about the steering:

'Although Jaguar tell me that no alteration has been made to the amount of assistance provided by the power steering, it seemed to me to have more feel to it than previously. Perhaps the constant development programme on the elimination of friction in the system and on improvements to the valving are responsible, but I was by no means the only driver who felt that the steering no longer takes a good many miles to learn to cope with because of its lightness. One is now far more aware of what exactly the front wheels are doing.'

Of the other new features which were more readily apparent, he commented:

'The control layout certainly falls more readily to hand than previously with the wiper and washer switches now embodied in a single steering column stalk on the left and the dipswitch operated by the right-hand indicator stalk instead of by a floor-mounted switch. The abolition of that long row of central tumbler switches has made the car easier to operate . . .'

Motor were also gratified that their grumbling about the heating and ventilation had been heeded, especially as the North East of Scotland—where

But the American magazine congratulated Jaguar on redesigning their heating and air conditioning system.

a yet-to-be-released two-door coupé, registered BWK418M, was also being demonstrated in some secrecy—had unseasonably hot weather:

'Certainly the new air conditioning unit cooled the car rapidly after it had been standing in the sun over lunch and thereafter maintained the interior temperature at a very agreeable figure once this had been selected by the temperature selector rotary switch and with the other switch set to Auto. When the system is working hard to bring down the interior temperature after the car has been standing, the big twin fans running at full chat when the car is stationary are somewhat noisy, but it is probably technically impossible to push around the required volume of air in silence.

'The additional heatproofing on the scuttles of the new cars has also played a part in preventing the considerable amount of heat generated by the big 5.3-litre V12 engine in its somewhat confined bonnet space from creeping back into the car interior. The effect of the additional sound proofing is less obvious, for the XJ6 was indeed a quiet car before the XJ12 excelled it in silent travel.'

Engine development for American Jaguars had been hindered by emission equipment, however, so the XJ12 tested by *Road and Track* was down on performance compared to the earlier and lighter version. The extra 200lb made 0.5secs difference to the 0–60mph acceleration figure of 9.1 secs and 0.8 secs for the 17.3-sec standing quarter mile. But few other cars weighing so much could match that in the United States although, by October 1974, when the test was published, the 11.5mpg which not long before had been the norm for such cars, was considered a heavy fuel consumption. Driveability was considered outstanding, although there was one emission-related quirk:

'During light third-gear acceleration, the car speeds up 2–3mph seemingly of its own will just as the engine passes through 1,600rpm. The editor's BMW 3.0CS exhibits the same behaviour for the same reason: above a preset engine speed, the low-speed spark retard cuts out, allowing full advance and a noticeable improvement to throttle response.'

The 'rather old' Borg-Warner transmission proved disappointing in the way it moved out of first gear too quickly, resulting in sluggish low-speed performance unless the throttle was held wide open relentlessly, but the rest of the car received wholehearted approval. *Road & Track* said:

'Jaguar is to be congratulated for redesigning the instruments and controls without losing any of the old-world charm of the previous dash layout . . . the central climate-control heater and air conditioning system is modelled after the best U.S. designs and is a giant leap forward for comfort and ease of control.'

The extra leg and knee room in the back were welcomed and the only feature in which the long-wheelbase design was considered to suffer could be felt in the larger body cavity leading to more rumbling on rough roads.

The XJ 3.4-litre

Motor had the first test of the 3.4-litre XJ6 in September 1975, finding it far more economical than expected, despite returning a top speed of 115mph with a 0–60mph acceleration time of 11.2 secs and a standing quarter mile in 18 secs which kept the larger-engined cars in sight and made the by-now obsolete 2.8-litre look tame. *Motor* commented on their overdrive model, registered HHP826N, which by now cost more than twice as much as the 4.2-litre when it was introduced six years earlier:

'The price of £4,998 is a disquieting reflection on the ravages of inflation, not an indication that the Jaguar has lost its competitive edge. Far from it. The XJ series is still one of Britain's—and certainly one of Leyland's—world beaters, even though the six-cylinder cars are powered by an engine that's basically 30 years old, albeit one that still does the job remarkably well, combining power with greater refinement than ever before . . .

'The 3.4 incorporates virtually all the many improvements and changes that have been made to the

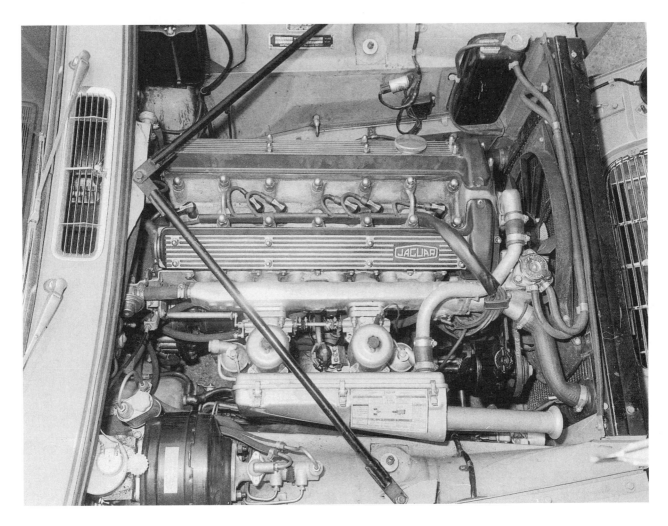

John Bolster considered the six-cylinder XK engine to be 'one of the miracles of the century'.

XJ range since it was launched, although it does not have the electric windows and automatic door locks now fitted as standard to the 4.2, the only significant economies that distinguish the 3.4 from the larger-engined car are those intended: it uses a lot less petrol and it's £400 cheaper.

'The first 4.2 we tested—which was slightly heavier than current XJ saloons even though it was shorter in wheelbase and therefore not as roomy—did 15.3mpg. This 3.4, with identical gearing (other than on first), did 20mpg. Admittedly it was probably driven with greater restraint than we exercised six years ago, but for a big five-seater luxury express that will top 115mph and cruise as quietly as a Rolls-Royce (sometimes even more quietly), anything around 20mpg compares very

favourably with the opposition . . . perfection achieved? Well, no. For a lot less than £5,000 you can buy higher performance elsewhere, though the 3.4 is no sluggard and is certainly much faster than the old 2.8. Many cars—much cheaper ones at that—have more efficient ventilation, others a slicker gearchange or steering that provides better feel.

'Standards have risen a lot since we first assessed the XJ6, yet Jaguar have in the main kept pace with them, especially in the control and interior design departments. Despite detail shortcomings, the combination of many outstanding qualities—among them

The XJ–S outranked the XJ coupé in the publicity stakes, so only *Autocar* were able to test one soon after the launch in 1975. **9/50/51**

They had to wait until November 1975 for the introduction of the fuel injection engine.

the ride, handling, comfort and, above all, quietness—makes the 3.4 something of a bargain, even at today's inflated prices.'

Autocar recorded marginally better performance figures—117mph top speed, 10.9-sec 0–60mph acceleration and the same 18-sec standing quarter mile—with another overdrive 3.4-litre XJ6, registered HHP825N, a week later. They pointed out, however, that although the 3.4-litre manual car could be made just about to match a

Sealing the side windows of the new coupé caused a lot of problems which had not been completely cleared up, said *Autocar*.

4.2-litre automatic on performance, such figures could only be achieved by driving it very hard, as could be seen by a fuel consumption figure of only 16.7mpg. The smaller engine's inferior torque output meant that the driver had to change down more often, although the 3.4-litre engine would pull smoothly from 10mph in top gear, which the 4.2-litre would not.

John Bolster wound his 3.4-litre overdrive XJ6, registered HHP823N, up to 118mph with a 10.8-sec 0–60mph time for *Autosport* in November 1975, but pointed out that it was capable of between 19 and 22mpg with reasonable driving. He liked the idea of using a manual gearbox rather than the automatic normally found in an XJ6, although he agreed with *Motor* and *Autocar* that it had a very heavy gearchange, explaining that 'the synchromesh does tend to baulk on occasion, and those of us who normally handle the lever between forefinger and thumb must take a firmer grip.'

He also welcomed the return of the 3.4-litre engine capacity, saying:

'The twin-overhead-camshaft, six-cylinder Jaguar engine is one of the miracles of the century. Before its appearance, the twin-cam power unit was considered to be indispensable for any thoroughbred racing car, but too noisy and expensive for everyday use. Jaguars confirmed its speed and reliability by their repeated Le Mans and other victories, but they also proved that it could be quieter than the common pushrod job.

'The original XK engine was of 3.4 litres capacity, which is in many ways its most successful size. When reduced below 3 litres, it seems to lack punch, while the larger versions, though plentifully endowed with torque, are not so free-revving. It is therefore pleasant to meet the 3.4 again, now that it has been re-introduced as an economy measure. This is a 3.4 with a difference, however, for it has what is, in effect, an under-bored version of the 4.2-litre cylinder block, which makes the engine run even more smoothly by virtue of its greater rigidity.

'The long throw crankshaft has been retained, but the trend is again in this direction, because short-stroke engines tend to cause greater exhaust pollution. Personally, I prefer the character of a good long-stroke unit, so the dimensions of this engine make sense to me. Above all, the twin-cam Jaguar engine is beautiful and I would like to cover it with a glass bonnet, for it's too nice to hide!'

The XJ 5.3-litre Coupé

Autocar were the only specialist magazine to test an XJ coupé soon after its launch in 1975 as British Leyland aimed to give the XJ-S a clear run when it came to publicity. The launch of the XJ-S also meant that *Autocar* had to wait until November for their coupé test as British Leyland were equally anxious to promote the benefits of the fuel injection which was being phased in on the 12-cylinder saloons. Even then, the car was a pre-production model registered HHP831N, leading *Autocar* to comment on the official reason of trouble with sealing the windows for the two-year delay in putting it into production:

'In the example used for this road test, it cannot be said that the problem has been completely solved since there is certainly some wind noise, but it is low enough not to be in any way annoying and at speeds under 60mph is hardly discernible at all.'

The benefit of the extra power and higher gearing could be felt in the 147mph maximum, at which speed the XJ5.3C ran dead straight with only the slightest lightening of effort at the wheel rim to suggest any front end lift—which *Autocar* found not surprising with more than half the car's 4,095-lb weight over the front wheels. The extra weight and higher gearing increased acceleration times over those recorded by the short-wheelbase XJ12 saloon, however, to 8.3 secs from rest to 60mph and 16 secs for the standing quarter mile. But there was no denying the improvement in fuel consumption: even really hard driving could reduce it only to 12.4mpg, with 15.2 as a good average and as much as 17.9 being achieved with gentle driving.

The roadholding, handling and ride were still the best in the world, in the opinion of *Autocar,* matched only by Mercedes' 450 range at high speed. Only the transmission, with its difficult controls and inability to select low gear at other than low speeds, let the coupé down, along with minor items like the windscreen wipers which had a park control—so beloved of senior Jaguar engineers—rather than the more useful automatic parking plus intermittent wiping now finding its way onto cars in all price ranges. Jaguar's—or more likely Sir William Lyons'—belief that the front seat backs should not be visible from the side view limited shoulder support. *Autocar* commented:

'Now that head restraints [by then compulsory in the United States] are fitted as standard, there is already some of the seat visible above the waistline and so this principle of a short seat back might well be dropped and a longer and better-shaped seat designed.'

Motor had to wait until April 1977 to test a coupé, when British Leyland wanted to publicise the new General Motors 400 Hydramatic transmission and, perhaps, help boost the coupé's flagging sales. Problems with the test equipment used by *Motor* prevented a full set of performance figures being taken on the 5.3-litre coupé registered PWK513R, but they reported:

'The smoothness of the engine is almost matched by the GM Hydramatic box which behaves in exemplary fashion: at small throttle openings it is virtually impossible to tell when a change has occurred, and even at full throttle it is more a change in engine note that tells you that something has happened. Not that it is flawless: kick-down can sometimes be slightly jerky, as can manual downshifts, but the most disappointing facet of its performance is the reluctance to kick down to first at any speed above about 15mph—even selecting low at higher speeds simply brings in second instead. However, most of the time the box behaves as a good one should do—as if it were not there.'

On a prophetic note, they added of the coupé which would be dropped in September that year:

'Compared to a two plus two coupé, the Jaguar XJC is very spacious . . . and makes a comfortable four-seater. It is this extra space that caused more than one member of the staff to query why Jaguar produce both this model and the XJ-S, which is more cramped: since the two cars are so similar in other respects apart from their overall shape, most of us would go for the added interior room of the XJC.'

You could not help thinking that the relative prices, £10,105 for the XJC against £12,367 for the XJ-S, emphasised this point.

The XJ-S

Following so soon after the demise of the E type, the XJ-S invited obvious comparisons—notable in the United States where the most emphasis was given to its launch. *Road & Track*, therefore, was quick to point out in January 1976 that it bore little resemblance to the far more spartan E type, other than for its substantially-similar running gear. The price in the U.S., $19,000 at a time when domestic rivals cost only about two-thirds as much, took it into a completely different bracket as well. The XK120 had sold for around $3,500, which had been within the reach of a large number of enthusiasts; the E type cost relatively more, but not a great deal. But $19,000 put the XK-Ss far from the reach of the average American into the realms of Mercedes and Porsche. They added:

'If one can question the concept of the XJ-S, it is very hard to fault the car itself because it does exactly what it sets out to do . . . be the quietest, most comfortable and luxurious high-performance car on the market.

'The 12-cylinder engine is a delight, partly because it is quite unnecessary (in Detroit, where they make bigger engines, they gave up on 12s decades ago), but Sir William Lyons insisted on a 12 simply because it is exotic, and there is absolutely nothing wrong with that. The only trouble with the 12 in the XJ-S, or in the Jaguar sedans, is that it is so quiet you cannot hear that it is a 12. Ferraris have 12 cylinders (unless they

are Dinos, in which case they are not Ferraris), and you can hear every cylinder working.'

Not surprisingly, *Road & Track* wondered how much better the XJ-S might be with a Detroit-made automatic transmission, rather than the antique British Borg-Warner fitted to their test car. Performance, naturally, fell a little short of the far lighter E type, with a 137mph maximum speed, 8.6 secs for the 0–60mph and 13.5mpg. But the air conditioning was pleasing although 'like most luxury imports, it takes quite a long time to cool the air after the car has been sitting out in the sun.'

The styling failed to excite *Road & Track*'s testers, who concluded:

'It's good, but it's not distinctive like the original XK120, which stunned the motoring world when it was unveiled at Earls Court, and also like the E type, which was totally different but could never be confused with any other car, whether you liked it or not. Previous Jaguars were styled by the late Malcolm Sayers who, like everyone else at Jaguar, did precisely what he was told by one certain gentleman—Sir William Lyons.

'Now Sir William is living in retirement and so is his right-hand man, Lofty England, and his company is part of British Leyland which is in turn in the clutches of the British government. A sorry turn of events, and one that cannot fail to affect the concept and design of the product.'

Patrick Bedard, writing in *Car and Driver* at the same time, liked the XJ-S a whole lot better. He pointed out:

'There is such a shortage of rich men's cars these days. How do you show the world that you've got money to burn? You sure as hell don't do it by buying a Cadillac Seville: a paltry $13,000 on the window sticker, iron-clad warranty, gilt-edged resale value. Nothing chancy about it. It runs like a piece from Tiffany's while you own it and there is always some guy waiting around a used-car lot to take it off your hands for a good price when you grow bored. No extravagance there.

'Now we have the XJ-S, a truly expensive car by every measure. It's priced beyond any American-built car, and for the first few years, you could have a new

Nevertheless, they were more than ready to extend it to maximum speed.

Chevrolet for the cost of its annual depreciation. And if the mechanical and incidental failures we experienced on our car are any indication, it will require frequent maintenance. So you have to be rich. But the beauty of this Jaguar is that it gives you something you can't get elsewhere. It goes to excess.'

Car and Driver then pointed out that extravagance is a car that will happily cruise at 140mph when the speed limit is 55. Even the 7.5-sec 0–60mph time was illegal, let alone a 16-sec standing quarter mile. And so far as their 12mpg was concerned, if you could afford to buy an XJ-S, you could afford to fill the tank. Bedard summed up:

'Those who criticise the XJ-S's styling usually do so on the grounds that such smooth shapes are old-fashioned. Contemporary design centres about rectangular themes and produces broad-shouldered images such as those of current Mercedes cars. This is certainly not this Jaguar. Yet its broad beam, huge tail lights and prominent wheels give it a certain strong character that it shares with no other car on the road. This is a car that will grow on you.'

Autocar considered the XJ-S a world-beater when they tested a manual version registered LDU867P in February 1976, reaching 153mph with a 0–60mph acceleration figure of 6.9 secs and standing quarter mile in 15.2 secs with 15.4mpg. Traction was superb and they found the heavy XJ-S easier to drive in icy conditions than many less-powerful cars because its power was delivered so smoothly. They pointed out:

'If you are feeling lazy in traffic, you virtually have two-pedal control except when you have to stop. You can stay in top down to absurd speeds and still pull steadily away again without the slightest flutter.'

Motor got the 0–60mph time down to 6.7secs later in the month although heavy snow prevented them from taking maximum speed figures with their manual car, registered LDU870P. They commented, however:

'Despite what it is—an outrageously large and heavy two-plus-two—the Jaguar XJ-S is a magnificent car, not just for what it does, but for the way it does it. The XJ-S combines a startling performance with exceptional smoothness and tractability and a standard of refinement that few cars can match. Others may be quicker; some handle better; a Rolls-Royce has more prestige; many have more room; quite a few are prettier. But none (other Jaguars apart) are smoother, quieter or more flexible.

'In concept, the latest Jaguar must be regarded as a splendid anachronism. For a start, it was conceived when there were fewer speed limits, and petrol was relatively cheap and apparently abundant.

'Much the same result could be achieved with less weight, capacity or complication, and thus better fuel consumption—the Lotus Elite shows the way. Yet we don't doubt that throughout the world there are many people who have both the taste and finance to appreciate the skill and technology that has gone into this superb machine, even if it does belong to a bygone era.

'The XJ-S is a classic *gran turismo,* providing not just effortless performance but luxury, comfort, tractability and refinement as well, a species exemplified up to now by such cars as the Mercedes 450SLC, the Aston Martin V8 and the Jensen Interceptor III. At £9,500, it is not cheap, but you have to pay significantly more for any other car with anything approaching the same specification and qualities.'

The XJ-S put John Bolster in mind of the original E type to a certain extent, as he reminisced in *Autosport* in April 1976 about the time 15 years earlier he drove at 150mph on the way to watch a motor race. He was amused to note that at the time none of the grand prix cars were capable of such a speed and that he had broken no laws. But since then the motoring situation had deteriorated so rapidly 'that one could be arrested like a criminal for extending this car on any gear except first.'

Despite the current fuel crisis, people were still queuing to buy supercars, so he made no apologies for enjoying for a week the same XJ-S that was tested by *Motor,* Bolster said:

'If you tell me I could have ridden a moped for six months on the same amount of petrol, you are going to get a very rude answer. I may be a bloated capitalist of the extreme right, but I loved every moment of it, so there!

'Really, to enjoy this V12, it's best to have the manual transmission. Only then can one appreciate the steam-like flexibility of this wonderful engine. It is the first modern car to equal the flexibility of my Rolls-Royce Silver Ghost, running evenly on the top gear at a walking pace and accelerating smoothly from 4mph on that ratio. Where it differs from the 1911 Rolls is

British Leyland's pricing policy put the new XJ-S into the same bracket as a Porsche or a Mercedes in the United States.

that this has approximately double the maximum speed, so there has been some progress in 65 years!

'A sensible choice of gear ratio has been made and though a slightly higher cog would give one the chance of breaking the 160mph barrier, the better acceleration of the existing arrangement is far more valuable. Where this car is so outstanding is in its extraordinary acceleration from 120mph to 140, where most other very fast machines are starting to labour.'

A warning accompanied a picture of the unbelted Bolster exceeding 140mph:

'The man who seldom drives at much more than 100mph should think twice about going up to 140mph [Bolster reached 154mph via a 6.7-sec 0–60 time] without some exploration of intermediate speeds. If things go wrong, it all happens a bit sharpish . . .

Daimler Double-Six Vanden Plas

By the mid-1970s, comparison tests in which cars were pitted against similar products from rival manufacturers, had become the vogue in specialist magazines. Naturally they tended to repeat the findings of individual tests and offer little additional information in a marque book. But there was one relating to the XJ saloons that could not be overlooked—specially when *CAR* magazine declared that Rolls-Royce, which had long proclaimed that it made the best car in the world, had been overtaken by Jaguar! They proclaimed of a Double-Six Vanden Plas, registered POJ798R, in September 1977:

'While we expected the Jaguar (forgive us, but we really can't get used to calling the damned thing a Daimler, or even a Vanden Plas) to have the edge over even the Rolls (Silver Shadow II) in terms of ride quality, overall silence and drive-line smoothness, we did not anticipate that it would not only match the Mercedes [450SEL 6.9, also being tested along with Cadillac's Seville] as a driver's car, but actually better it, although

without such a feeling of excitement. It carried its capabilities more subtly, blending them with more overall refinement than any other car currently made. They are tremendous capabilities, made ever more awesome by the car's price: even in its ultimate form it is £10,000 cheaper than the Rolls and the 450SEL 6.9. Yet, if it was up to us, we would not opt for the top-line Double-Six Vanden Plas but for the standard £10,668 XJ12 with cloth trim for its seating is more comfortable in that form. If motor cars are ultimately a compromise, the XJ12—in whichever form you select to suit you best— is the ultimate compromise . . .'

Not to be outdone, *Autocar* then borrowed an XJ12 registered POJ789R for a road test, commenting that 'in its combination of performance, road behaviour and refinement, it is still unsurpassed. It is a modern classic which no other manufacturer in the world fully matches.'

This was despite price rises which had taken it from 38 per cent of the cost of a contemporary Rolls-Royce Silver Shadow in 1972 to 47 per cent at the time of the test in September 1978. The performance figures reflected its regained power: a 147-mph maximum speed, 7.8-sec 0–60mph time and 15.7-sec standing quarter mile with much-improved fuel consumption of 14.5mpg. The Rolls-Royce could match the Jaguar's fuel consumption, but was left far behind on acceleration (10.6secs 0–60mph) and top speed (116mph). Only Ferrari's 365 GT4 could outrun the Jaguar in the same class on 150mph and it cost twice as much. The Mercedes also lagged on 134mph with a 9.1-sec 0–60mph time, and only BMW's 733i was noticeably more economical on 19.3mpg although it lacked in every other department, especially refinement and performance.

Jaguar XJ6 with Air-Conditioning

Autocar refreshed themselves by testing an automatic XJ6 equipped with various extras like air

Facing page: The 5.3 litre XJ saloons – in plushly-trimmed Jaguar form in the top picture, and with Daimler trim in the bottom picture – were to become recognised as the best cars in the world.

Jaguar had to introduce the fuel-injected engine in the six-cylinder XJ series II without a fanfare . . .

conditioning in October 1977. After deciding that this latest version of Jaguar's famous saloon, registered OOM585R, still set very high standards in performance, handling, and, above all, ride and quietness, they concluded that the power steering was still too light and the seats could be more comfortable. And although the air conditioning—which added more than 100lb to the car's overall weight, taking it to 4,336lb—was a boon in hot weather, its use incurred a considerable penalty. *Autocar* reported:

'In acceleration, the effect was noticeable even without reference to our instruments. Step-off from rest was notably less brisk, with 30mph coming up in 4.2secs instead of 3.9. There was a difference of over a second to 60mph, and 2.8secs to 100mph—in other words, the drag acts progressively. Maximum speed was down from 117mph to 114, which our usual rule of thumb suggests is equivalent to the loss of 12–15bhp, no less. Fuel consumption suffered by around 10 per cent at steady speeds.'

Motor then caught up with OOM585R in March 1978, opining that it needed a higher final drive than the standard 3.3:1 as the engine felt distinctly rough when exceeding 5,000rpm during a maximum speed run of 117.5mph. They recommended the optional 3.07:1 ratio if the automatic gearbox was to be preferred against an overdrive. Higher overall gearing could be expected to improve the 13.7mpg obtained overall while acceleration in the 10.9-sec 0–60mph bracket should not suffer too much. Summing up, they said:

'We'd rate the XJ6 as a superb motor car that sadly still suffers from a number of shortcomings (gearchange, heating/ventilation, interior design). These faults have long been overshadowed by the car's excellence in other respects—particularly refinement—but we wonder how long the situation can continue with rival manufacturers improving their standards so quickly.'

The Fuel-Injected XJ6 Series Two

Magazines in the United States, where Jaguar sales needed a boost due to the rising value of the pound, were encouraged to test the fuel-injected XJ6 only a few months before the series three was launched in Europe. Ever more stringent fuel consumption regulations had threatened to render the carburettor cars unprofitable and, in fact, led to the 12-cylinder models being withdrawn in America the following year. But Jaguar could not wait for the publicity generated by the series three's launch because safety testing would delay its introduction in the United States for more than a year. British magazines did not get the fuel-injection series two because a home market sales boom had caused supply problems which meant that some cars with carburettors were still being produced close to the start of series three production. Editor David E Davis Jnr commented in *Car and Driver* in December 1978:

'The Bosch/Lucas fuel injection is brand new but other than that, this car has been around for a while. The obvious question is how much longer? Difficult to predict because British Leyland works in strange and wondrous ways. Strange, at least. Photos, spy and otherwise, have been floating around for at least five years, so it's obvious somebody has been thinking about a replacement/change. But there's also a good chance the venerable old XJ series will simply slip quietly beneath the corporate waves and be gone forever. BL doesn't sell all that many Jags, after all, and its attention may just turn toward econoboxes and compacts. But drastic change or complete replacement, the writing is on the wall. The car weighs too much: 4,150lb in an era

of 3,500-lb sedans. The fuel injection car is really a last-gasp attempt at meeting emissions and fuel requirements with a hopelessly-outdated engine . . . but let's not worry about things completely out of our control. It's BL's problem. I'll mourn properly when the time comes. Until then, I'll enjoy. Emphasis on enjoy. The XJ6 does everything well. Despite its prodigious weight, it will reach an honest 115mph. It's also capable of handling corners that are white-knuckle for most of us. The XJ6 may well be becoming something of an anachronism. But it isn't there yet. And maybe, just maybe, something will happen to give it several more years of life. I certainly hope so.'

Road & Track had a pleasant surprise in the same month when they realised their fuel-injected XJ6 was capable of 17.5mpg to go with its 116mph, 9.6-sec 0–60mph time and 17.7-sec standing quarter mile. They said:

'As much as we love the V12 and its powerful low-end ability to this heavy car under way, the injected in-line six is so good it nearly makes us forget the lovely sound and strength of the V12.'

The XJ6 Series Three

The series three received a good reception. *Motor* going as far as to say in September 1979 that in many ways it was the best saloon car in the world, and certainly the best value for money in its price range. But it was a pity that some of the old faults remained: the steering, although slightly heavier, was still too light, firmer damping would be appreciated, and the retention of instruments with vertical glazing meant that reflections rendered them illegible in bright sunlight. But the increase in performance of their automatic Daimler, registered DVC787T, as well as the improved fuel consumption, on the higher 3.07:1 final drive ratio, was a shot in the arm: it was more than 10mph faster than their carburettor series two at 128mph, with a slightly better 10.5-sec 0–60mph and much-improved 15.7mpg. The 'model 66' gearbox was

Motor still rated the XJ highly when it went to a series III in 1979.

smoother but still would not kickdown into first above 30mph and the change-up point from first to second at full throttle seemed unnecessarily low at 45mph. 'Both these factors can make the car seem irritatingly sluggish under certain conditions, such as accelerating out of a roundabout,' said *Motor*. The extra headroom and glass area was welcomed, however, making the car feel airier. They also noted:

'The bodyshells of the series three XJs are built at the Pressed Steel Fisher plant at West Bromwich, where what has been described as Britain's best paint shop has recently been completed. The finish of our test car was immaculate, and we liked the alterations which have been carried out, in particular the new bumpers and flush-fitting door handles, which not only improve the appearance of the car but should keep it looking good for a longer time.'

Autocar were even more pleased with the performance of their air-conditioned series three

Jaguar XJ6 in December 1979. They achieved 127mph with 16.8mpg overall in a car registered HRW287V despite leaving the heater on—which in turn worked the air-conditioning pump intermittently—during cold weather. When left to its own devices, the automotive gearbox changed from first to second at 4,300rpm, and from second to third at the ideal 5,000rpm peak power point. But the best acceleration figures were obtained by holding first gear manually till the rev counter hit the red line, then slipping the lever into Drive and leaving the gearbox to sort out its change-points: the result was a 10-sec 0–60mph time with a standing quarter mile in 17.4secs. The greatest effects of the extra power and gearbox modifications were felt at the top end of the range, however, where acceleration times were much faster than before—0–110mph took only 38.5secs, a remarkable 13.3 secs quicker than with an automatic carburettor series two. *Autocar* then issued the sternest warning yet over the Jaguar's automatic gear-change:

'First, there is no detent to stop the driver from pulling the delightfully slender T handle from D straight back into 1 at too high a road speed (fortunately an inhibitor in the gearbox prevents engagement of either gear). More inexplicable is the provision of a detent between 2 and D yet none between D and neutral. Overcoming the 2 to D stop requires the driver to use sideways pressure before moving the selector forward, but it is then free to move through to neutral uninhibited with potentially dire consequences for the engine, or even the car if in full throttle overtaking manoeuvre. Worse still, if the side pressure is not relaxed, the selector can be pushed straight through to reverse. The former mistake would be all too easy for the unfamiliar, or nervous, driver to make, and the latter would certainly send the car out of control and does not bear thinking about. All of this is a pity because in almost every other respect the new XJ is a driver's delight.'

The eight modes employed by the lighting switch came in for similar criticism, but the new AE Econocruise control was much appreciated. After selecting the chosen setting—such as 70mph in Britain or 55mph in the United States—the driver could leave the car cruising at that speed, or use the accelerator to increase speed and then drop back automatically to the cruising speed after releasing pressure on the throttle, before cancelling the speed control by braking or switching it off. *Autocar* said:

'We were particularly impressed by the gentle way the AE Econocruise kept the desired speed, unlike some others which seem to use coarse throttle movements, thus creating annoying surges in acceleration.'

But they considered the new Pirelli tyres to be a mixed blessing. *Autocar* pointed out:

'Without conducting back-to-back tests, we cannot say for certain whether the gains in handling response are worth the increased road noise. The P5s undoubtedly generate more roar and rumble than the optional, previously-fitted, and exceptionally quiet-running Dunlops. This is particularly noticeable over ridged concrete or coarse and uneven surfaces.'

In an exceptionally eagle-eyed test involving former Grand Prix driver and development engineer John Miles, *Autocar* then noted that the increased tumblehome of the new roofline—designed in sunny Italy—meant that a few drips of water could be expected to fall onto the seats when the doors were opened after the car had been standing in rain.

By the time *Road & Track* received their road test series three XJ6 in September 1980, readership surveys had highlighted several years of quality control problems with Jaguars. One third of owners reported cooling problems. Another third had electrical malfunctions. And the rest had engine trouble. *Road & Track* even had to use four cars to keep one running long enough to record all the data they needed for the road test. The best one had a minor fault with the injection system which prevented them from taking accurate fuel consumption readings—although they estimated their car was capable of 15–16mpg. But they obtained a maximum speed of 117mph with a 10.6-sec 0–60mph time and 18.2-sec standing quarter mile. *Road & Track* still loved the way the XJ6 handled, although they noted, with disappointment, that the level of wind noise had increased by four decibels over the previous model on test. They were also puzzled as to why Jaguar should want to change their front seats for the electrically-controlled options normally fitted to Vanden Plas models because they found them less comfortable. *Road & Track* said:

'Summing up the series three is very difficult if one is to be completely fair to both the potential buyer and the manufacturer. British Leyland has a poor reputation in the U.S. for quality control generally, and we must admit that we experienced various problems with the four different Jaguars that passed through our hands during this test. One thing we try to avoid saying about our test cars is "On the one hand this, and on the other hand, that," but in the case of the Jaguar it is inevitable because, on the one hand, it had some outstanding qualities that are equal or superior to some of the finest but, on the other hand, it is haunted by a reputation

Motor reckoned that items such as the new bumpers and flush-fitting door handles should keep the series III looking good for a long time.

for poor quality control and indifferent service and parts facilities, which we have to believe is warranted. Obviously, it is much easier and more pleasurable for us to praise a car wholeheartedly, but unfortunately in the case of the Jaguar, our praises have to be tempered with our reservations.'

By the time *Car and Driver* received their series three XJ6 for test in November 1981—when it recorded an 111mph maximum, with an 11.7-sec 0–60mph time, 18.7-sec standing quarter mile and 16mpg—efforts were being made to rid Jaguar of their reputation for unreliability. They included offering a two-year or 50,000-mile warranty on the power train in addition to the standard 12-month unlimited mileage guarantee on the rest of the car. Michael Jordan reported, however:

'It shows how hard the company are trying, but a warranty doesn't make you feel any better when something breaks. Our test car suffered a cruise-control black-out,

the breakage of a power-window master switch and an apparent oxygen-sensor failure . . . Anyone who drives an XJ6 overlooks a few flaws. This car is still a classic to drive, a symbol of motoring excellence. It's everything a Rolls-Royce tries to be.'

The Series Three XJ12

Meanwhile, Mel Nichols, editor of *CAR* magazine which had been the first to rate an XJ as the best car in the world, became the first British journalist to test the series three—an XJ12—in May 1979. He had already taken some stick for his assertions about the series two—'My friend, David E Davis Jnr of *Car and Driver* attacked me over dinner one night for so praising the XJ12. How could it be the finest car in the world, he said, when everyone knew it was so damned unreliable? Well, we've heard stories and had letters from owners about problems with Jaguars; but we've had plenty more mentioning extremely high bother-free mileages and, on balance, it's our view that the Jaguar appears to be no better nor worse than average.'

His time with the car, registered DVC789T, included a day with four passengers, which thoroughly tested the back seat headroom. It worked well with just four people of more than 6ft, but was cramped when three had to squeeze in the back. Nichols said:

'In the front, the Jaguar is terrifically comfortable—and there is enough headroom for the likes of me to wear even a very large hat. Even without the optional electric height adjustment, the front cushions are excellent; and the new squabs grip you ideally laterally and you can set the enormously-variable lumbar support precisely to your preference. Superb seats, even after the 300 miles that we were to log in just a few hours of thundering through the countryside.'

Nichols found all the XJ12's old qualities as good as ever—even when it was five-up—before summing up:

'Though it be sufficiently intangible to prevent it being spelled out, there is an impression that the Jaguar—despite its new round of modifications and the fact that it is still the saloon by which all others must be judged—is beginning to feel a little dated and that it will need to be replaced (as indeed it will) within three or four years. It does still have flaws, but they cannot detract from a basic excellence sufficient to have kept the car at the top of the tree for 11 years. I may not have recognised the fact once; I certainly do now.'

Cool as David E Davis Jnr might have been over Jaguar's quality control, *Car and Driver's* editor-at-large Patrick Bedard was a rabid enthusiast for the British marque. He reported in July 1979 after being invited to the model's launch in Britain.

'I confess to embarking in a fatalistic mood, as if I were being called in to identify the body of a former sweetheart mutilated in Coventry. Then it became obvious. The new roof definitely pokes up in the air more than the old one. Later, I came upon one of the older Jaguars from the front, and as I walked towards the back, I noticed how weak it is in the rear-roof-pillar area—how the architecture of the roof fails to assert

itself as it sweeps back from the rear doors, instead falling away like a receding chin. And I realised that I had noticed this flaw long before but had dismissed it, wanting to see no warts on such a masterpiece.

'So there is no going back. The series three is here. It's the only car I can think of that makes the previous Jaguar look less than perfect. And in the greater scheme of things, that's probably progress.

'But if this is what happens when artists come back for a touch-up, we'd better keep Leonardo out of the Louvre. Considering the questions that remain unanswered about the original. I don't think the world is ready for a better Mona Lisa.'

Even Bolster was drawn into the quality control controversy when he tested a series three XJ12 for *Autosport* in February 1980. After recording performance figures of 148mph maximum speed. a 7.8-sec 0–60mph and around 15mpg, he commented on the superb handling and ride of his car, registered DVC791T, before saying:

'There remains the question of quality control and it must be admitted that, in the past, the Jaguar reputation has not been all that it might be. The prices were too low and, although the value was fantastic, some owners received cars that were below standard. The manufacturers are well aware of this and quality control is now the first priority, which is much more satisfactory to the customer than the spectacularly low prices of the past. The road test car was very well finished, which I noticed when I washed and polished it, the doors fitted beautifully, and the machine had an air of quality about it that justifies the considerable figure at which it is now sold.'

The XJ-S Revisited

Anxious to test the market reaction to their uprated engine before the May heads were introduced, Jaguar encouraged a series of tests on the interim-model XJ-S *Motor*, which had revealed the existence of the May heads six months earlier, reported on a car registered KRW305V in October 1980:

'If efficiency is the watchword for the 1980s, what hope

is there for the Jaguar XJ-S? Desirable beyond the standards associated with its comparatively modest price, BL's five-year-old flagship is nevertheless conspicuously large, heavy and thirsty for a two-plus-two in the austere 1980s and in danger of being upstaged by mostly more fuel-and-space-efficient rivals from the likes of Porsche, BMW and Lotus. The technology for extracting more miles-per-gallon without compromising power is already at BL's disposal in the form of the May head, though when (or even *if*) the company will play this particular card, it's not saying.

'At £19,187, the XJ-S remains the bargain of the supercar market. Driving this latest version has only served to confirm that while it is possible to buy comparative performance for similar money, it is impossible to buy it with greater refinement and comfort any price. And it is this unrivalled combination of qualities that makes the Jaguar so special even by the elevated standards of the supercar class (though a more sporting ride/handling compromise would make it even better).'

Motor could not fully extend the XJ-S within the confines of the motor industry's test track, MIRA, but estimated it at 145mph (although Jaguar claimed more than 150mph), recording a 7.6-sec 0–60mph time with a 15.8-sec standing quarter mile—slightly down on the by-now obsolete manual version with the earlier engine. Fuel consumption was well up, however, at 13.5mpg.

Autocar ran into problems testing the same car in January 1981—high winds which made them think that it might be possible to better the 141mph maximum speed. Acceleration times were better than those of *Motor,* too, at 6.6secs for the 0–60mph and 14.9secs for the standing quarter mile. Fuel consumption was also far better at 14.3mpg so perhaps the car had benefited from either extra miles or servicing!

Apart from the gear selector, which *Autocar* understood was receiving attention from Jaguar, they mourned the loss of the manual-gearbox version, saying:

'Even more cheering would be an announcement of a revival of either the Mundy-designed five-speed over-drive manual gearbox for the 12-cylinder XJ cars, or the "80mm" manual box. It is a criminal waste of this engine's flexibility and power that no manual option now exists. As it is, the engine is wedded to a transmission that, however good by automatic standards, inevitably dissipates some power and energy in the usual inefficiencies of its breed, and which in this installation is, as before, considerably undergeared, revving at an excessive 13 per cent past its power peak at maximum speed.'

But returning to the positive side of the XJ-S, *Autocar* said that figures were one thing, subjective impressions are the stuff of fast motoring. And so far as they were concerned the XJ-S was superb. So far as rivals like the Aston Martin V8, BMW 635CSi, Ferrari 400i, Maserati Khamsin and Porsche 928, were concerned:

'If one wants more excitement than anything else, then the Aston Martin is the most superficially enjoyable, with its great and rumbling urge, combined with very good road manners. The BMW is exciting, too, with its very fine six-cylinder engine giving pleasing go with handling that is entertaining if not best-behaved. The Maseratis are very pleasing cars, while the 928 is fascinating in its suave performance, spoiled only by the high level of road noise. Ferrari's previous 365GT4 pleased us greatly, too, and has much to recommend it. But overall, the Jaguar XJ-S is top dog: its performance is truly extraordinary for such a car, it has perfect road manners, and it is so quiet. On top of all that, there is its price; of the cars which approach its performance, only the Porsche offers anything near to the same value for money. The slightly cheaper BMW is too slow, and the others cost, apart from the Porsche, between 84 per cent and 56 per cent more.'

The XJ-S HE

Autocar were even more enthusiastic about the XJ-S when they tested an HE model registered RDU928W in April 1982. Their opinions of the opposition were unchanged, although, by now,

But *Autocar* were sternly critical of the perils of the gearchange.

Porsche had progressed to a 928S model: 'For all round satisfaction—a tiger of a car when need be, the most refined, relatively speaking, of grand touring two-plus-twos when driven less hard, let alone gently, and always a gentleman in character—the Jaguar is even more so the paragon, especially now that its fuel economy is so much better than before.'

The overall 16mpg returned by this car had been achieved at no detriment to the performance—the 2.88:1 final drive allowing a higher, 153mpg, top speed, with similar—6.5-sec 0–60mph and 14.9-sec standing quarter mile—acceleration figures. Apart from welcoming the safety aspects of the revised gearchange, *Autocar* found the XJ-S HE every bit as satisfying to drive as its predecessors, considering the raised final drive ratio only slightly undergeared. Restrained driving even managed to take the fuel consumption into the realms of 21mpg! There was a suspicion that the May-headed engine was slightly more noisy than the previous version, but the difference was so small that it could not be confirmed. Road noise had been increased by the new Dunlop D7 tyres, however, but they gave an undeniably better steering response than the previous Dunlop Super Sports.

L J K Setright had similar impressions of the new tyres when he tested an XJ-S HE registered RDU927W, for *CAR* magazine in August 1981. But he pleaded for less compliance from the rubber mountings of the front suspension which led to sluggish turning-in and made it such a contrast to the far more accurate control of the rear suspension. But of the new interior, he said:

'Practically all the time, one just sits there and enjoys the luxury. There is more of it than before, the generally synthetic and moulded interior of the early XJ-S having been superseded by a typically English amalgam of polished burr walnut veneers, sober instrumentation and tasteful expanses of that inimitable and irreplaceable leather so masterfully tanned and curried by Connolly Brothers. The effect of the hide is not wasted: where once Jaguar's intrinsically excellent seats were installed quite wrongly with the seat cushions almost horizontal, so that one went submarining off them into the footwells and even when stationary could enjoy no support of the thighs, the front edges have now been raised so that the left leg need no longer be used continuously as a prop to keep the ischia where they should be.'

John Bolster, predictably, was keen on his XJ-S HE, registered RDU922W, when he tested it for *Autosport* on February 1982, estimating its top speed at 155mph, and recording a 7.3-sec 0–60mph time with 15.6mpg. He commented:

'Perhaps the most delightful feature of this Jaguar is the wonderful reserve of power. One seldom uses more than half throttle and it is all too easy to wander along at 120mph when 70mph was intended, unless the cruise control is employed. An air conditioning system is installed and it is effective if not quite up to Rolls-Royce standards.

'I have previously praised the silence, smoothness and refinement of the car, allied with its extraordinary performance and riding comfort. Perhaps no car is less tiring when driven on a long journey. Yet I must criticise the electric starter, which is no quieter than that of any ordinary car and may be embarrassing in the early hours of the morning. I have owned many cars that started more quietly, notably a Bullnose Morris Cowley.'

Road & Track drove their American-specification XJ-S HE as hard as they knew in December 1982 but could not take it anywhere near the 300-bhp cars on performance, returning 140mph flat out, with an 8.2-sec 0–60 mpg time and 16.3-sec standing quarter mile. Fuel consumption was up to 13.5mpg as well, but *Road & Track* said:

'We blithely blame it on the nature of the car itself. It is simply such a pleasure to deep-foot this machine, especially during one's early relationship with it, that the XJ-S easily routs your resolutions to hoard fuel. We suspect that most drivers' averages would round out to about 14–15mpg in normal driving. We did feel a certain transitory regret over our fuel profligacy but, as one staffer noted, one sweet night of wretched excess is worth years of dull moderation.'

David E Davis Jnr had been to the XJ-S HE launch in Europe for *Car and Driver* and noted in February 1982 that the new model had more torque, better gas mileage and enough horsepower to separate your retinas. The man, who had once called Joseph Lucas the Prince of Darkness, added:

'Perhaps the best news in all this, however, is the fact that Jaguar's new management—a tough, young, team that appears to be loaded with talent and motivation—has publicly put the Joseph Lucas Company's electrical feet on fire. Jaguar's bad reputation for service and reliability is based almost entirely on problems with electrical components—most of which are furnished by Lucas. Now Lucas is on notice. The stuff must work, or Lucas pays a higher percentage of warranty costs than has been the case in the past. More important by far, though, is that Jaguar management has finally recognised the problem and seems determined to do something about it.'

And by the time Patrick Bedard got one to drive in the United States, his opinion, recorded in *Car and Driver* in December 1982, was that 'if Wolfgang A Mozart were alive and well and enjoying the financial fruits of his genius, he'd drive a Jaguar XJ-S. A more Mozartian car does not exist.

It's light on its feet, melodious; so inviting. And yet it's restrained. None of Beethoven's insistence. None of Bach's compulsive mathematics. Like Mozart's work before it, this Jaguar is sure to become a classic.'

Jaguar XJ6 Vanden Plas

There was a happy end to the quality control controversy in July 1984. *Road & Track,* in their thorough way, had been looking into it since surveying owners in 1978 and reporting one of the worst service records ever. Since then Jaguar had reported a turn-round on quality control and, said *Road & Track,* now claimed: 'We've got it whipped. Why don't you try another XJ6?'

This was a Vanden Plas six-cylinder automatic that was 310lb heavier than the series three tested in 1980, with higher gearing, at 2.88:1, rather than the original 3.07 final drive. As a result it was not surprising that the 0–60mph time was up to 12.3secs although the standing quarter mile was not far behind on 18.9secs, with an identical top speed of 117mph. And now that they were able to test the fuel consumption properly it worked out at a highly-commendable 17.5mpg. And so far as the Vanden Plas side was concerned, *Road & Track* said:

'The interior drew mostly raves. Mostly in that there was a consensus concerning the wood, which is perfectly in character. But so far as all that leather was concerned, some thought it a bit too much. The fit and finish struck some as being too perfect, so good it looked like, well, like vinyl. A standard version of the XJ6 drew no such remarks. Plain (relatively) or fancy, most occupants were right at home in their seats.'

And so far as reliability was concerned . . .
'The first example in this test was driven hard for a month. Nothing went wrong. When that one went home, we swapped for another, the XJ6 with a standard interior. That one was used for another 1,500 miles, as long and as hard as good manners allow. It was kept

idling in parking lots, crept through rush-hour traffic, cruised across the desert at unprintable speeds. Nothing went wrong. The needles stayed at the centre of their dials. There were no mysterious noises, no showers of sparks, no puddles of steaming green coolant. This is wonderful news. The XJ6 has always been a driver's car. Now it's one that can be driven there . . . and back.'

Jaguar XJ6 Five-Speed

Jaguar were as reluctant to release cars with the Rover five-speed gearbox for road tests as they were to sell them—the vast majority reaching cus-

tomers being fitted with automatic transmission. This was because, in its early form, the gearbox was at the limit of its capacity to absorb the extra torque produced by the fuel-injection six-cylinder engine. As a result, *Autocar* had to wait until 1983 to be able to test such a car—and then it was a development version registered RDU934W which had covered only 8,600 miles despite being two years old. But it provided them with a great deal of satisfaction by emulating a run from Land's End

Motor were sure that the XJ–S remained the bargain of the supercar market. And Justin Rockett certainly enjoyed driving his in the Hatfield XJ Challenge at Silverstone in March 1990.

to John o'Groats without changing out of top gear achieved by the crew of a Sheffield-Simplex, including an *Autocar* staff member, in 1911!

As supplied, the test car had a 3.31:1 final drive ratio that proved low enough to cope with any gradient on the carefully-selected 900-mile route, starting from rest being achieved by slipping the clutch initially at 1,200 rpm and then fully engaging it on the move from 500rpm. The 0–60mph time by this method proved to be 34.6secs. In a more normal mode, this could be reduced to 8.6secs with a 17.2-sec standing quarter mile and 131mph maximum. These sort of racing-style standing starts were not to be recommended, however, because of alarming tramp that resulted from over-stressing the rear subframe rubbers. Ideally, this XJ6 would have been better geared with a higher final drive and lower first ratio—as near-identical fourth and fifth-gear maximum speeds indicated. Nevertheless, it was a lot more economical than the automatic version, returning 18.3mpg despite the violent standing starts, and reaching figures of 23–25mpg between Land's End and John o'Groats.

The XJ-S 3.6 coupé

With so much interest in the new XJ6 engine, Jaguar could not avoid releasing the XJ-S 3.6 for road tests although they knew they were likely to get a roasting for its lack of refinement compared to the earlier units. Jaguar's need for a lighter engine had been known for so long that they could delay its launch no longer. *Motor* were the first magazine to get an XJ-S 3.6C, registered A190HVC, in March 1984. They commented:

'Capitalising on an upturn in sales of late, the auto-only V12 XJ-S HE lives on and remains remarkable value for those who can afford to run it. Less powerful, but lighter, and equipped with five-speed manual transmission, the six-cylinder cars, though not that much cheaper, step more assertively into BMW/Mercedes/Audi territory.

'Be prepared for a few surprised with the AJ6 engine when you crack on. There's no question that the engine pulls strongly from low revs and with real vigour from about 3,500rpm, but the *quality* of its exertions will come as something of a shock to anyone familiar with the silky urgency of Jaguar's V12 or the gentlemanly refinement of the old XK unit. This engine is afflicted with an underlying roughness present throughout the rev range which isn't only heard, but felt through the toeboard. What's worse, it's prominent in the middle part of the rev band most frequently used in normal motoring. Both BMW and Mercedes make smoother six-cylinder engines. Until the demise of the XK unit, so will Jaguar.

'On the other hand, the AJ6 engine does *feel* potent. Despite that the rather low 5,800-rpm red line, mid-to-upper range punch is such that constant cog-swapping isn't a prerequisite for brisk progress. There again, throttle response isn't as clean as it might be and the injection's overrun fuel cut-off sometimes promotes jerkiness when throttling back, a condition exacerbated by a degree of snatch in the transmission. In short, the AJ6-engined XJ-S has sharp claws, but entirely lacks the seductive purr of the V12 HE.

'Neither is it fast when the chips are down. Jaguar claim a top speed of 145mph for the 3.6 coupé, but we could manage only 136.8mph round Milbrook's high-speed bowl on an almost perfectly still day—a long way short of the claim and, indeed, the 152mph of the V12 HE round the same circuit.'

The fuel consumption of 18.9mpg was equally disappointing for a car with a manual gearbox along with acceleration figures of 7.2secs for the 0–60mph mark and a standing quarter mile in 15.6secs. The spring and damper revisions—in conjunction with the lighter engine—had improved the turn-in however, and the gearchange was adjudged positive although the clutch action was still heavy.

The widely-varying quality of early 3.6-litre cars was emphasised by *Autocar's* test of an XJ-S coupé registered A189HVC in April 1984. This achieved 141mph along a flat road (with 137mph at Millbrook's banked track) with acceleration times of 7.4secs for the 0–60mph and 15.9secs for the standing quarter mile with 17.6mpg—so, presumably, the engines were in a similar state of tune. Yet *Autocar* found little to complain about over harshness. They said:

'We would judge the alloy-blocked AJ6 about as vibrationless as its predecessor at low to middle rpm, and certainly less prone to vibration at its higher limit. It emits a purposeful but still muted growl if driven hard, yet one is inhibited for using over 5,000rpm by the very flat nature of the power curve, and the rather fussy "knitting needle" noises that appear to emanate from the valve gear. It is a minor point, because in all normal and even very fast motoring the engine is smooth and subdued.'

In many other respects, they agreed with *Motor* except the gearchange:

'With the excellent change in Getrag-equipped BMWs

in mind, it was puzzling to find the XJ-S 3.6 shift notchy, heavy and certainly baulky if hurried, or if the heavy-ish clutch was not fully depressed.'

The XJ-S 3.6-litre automatic

Autocar enthused mightily about the XJ-S suspension changes when they tested a 3.6-litre version registered E393HKV in October 1987. They reported on this car, fitted with the new four-speed automatic gearbox:

'At speeds just the right side of recklessness, the car behaved like only a few can. Through sweeping tree-lined bends, it cornered with precision, precious little roll and tenacious grip—like a front-engined Porsche or an M-series BMW . . .

The five-speed manual version of the series III was much more economical than the automatic.

The 3.6 litre XJ-S had to go through a lot of development, despite its performance.

'Jaguar have been criticised for overlight steering in the past, and with good reason—an untimely sneeze resulted in an unplanned lane change. The extra rubber alone on the road would have increased steering effort . . . yet this born-again XJ-S turns into corners like a Volkswagen Golf GTi half its weight. The weighting of the steering at speed is firm and reassuring and a 2.6 turns from lock to lock, the gearing is ideal. Put the big cat on line and it stays there, the P600s doing all you could ask in the dry and the chassis refusing to be deflected from its chosen course by bumps or camber changes. It's the damping performance that's most remarkable, the Boge shock absorbers allowing the springs to absorb the bumps then rebound enough to keep the wheel in contact with the ground under the severest provocation.

'The same property endows the Jaguar with exceptional stability, tracking arrow true at a ton over crests and dips alike. Yet the ride remains relatively smooth and compliant, with hardly any tyre or bump noise transmitted to the cabin—the XJ-S is much better than comparable German cars in this respect.

'The Jaguar's seats are now among the very best—perfectly shaped, firm with body-hugging side cushions that keep you in place during the most enthusiastic bend-swinging. The engine is also now as smooth and refined as the best—certainly there is no trace of the on/off idle roughness of early examples. With the ZF automatic, the 3.6-litre engine performs well enough, but the five-speed Getrag box would be more in keeping with the car as well as delivering a tad more oomph'

Performance figures, however, were quite reasonable on a 134-mph maximum, 7.8-sec 0–60mph and 16-sec standing quarter mile with 18mpg.

Roger Bell had similar opinions to *Autocar* when he took another 3.6-litre automatic XJ-S, registered E396HKV to Norfolk for *Motor* in September 1987. But he had this to say of the new transmission:

'Kickdown is fine for snap overtaking, but manual override is more appropriate and entertaining for maelstrom traffic, never mind for sporting sprints and kinky ascents. The old-fashioned T-bar selector works well, effectively duplicating the left-side slot of the engaging two-plane J-movement selector—the famous Randle Handle—of the XJ6. Detent freedom from D through 3 into 2, unfettered by any inter-ratio jerkiness, makes the lever action swift and easy. Too easy, perhaps. What happens if you overshoot "2" when changing down at 100mph? I will leave to someone else that interesting investigation.'

The XJ-S HE Cabriolet

Motor had the first drive in an XJ-S HE cabriolet, registered B507TAC, during July 1985. It was a delivery run for publicity in West Germany where there was the strongest demand for the new model. Lawrence Pearce thought it a pity that there were only two seats but appreciated the double-skinned hood on a wet, blustery, day while leaving Britain. Averaging 70mph on the way to Frankfurt produced an acceptable 15.2mpg—despite the trip computer's pessimistic figure of 13.5. Then, when the sun came out, the roof-off transformation was complete—although some may criticise Jaguar for not producing a true convertible.

'Now we can do some real motoring in the car that some will see as the successor to the V12 E type. We set our sights on the country roads of the Black Forest, as a contrast to the fast, straight, German autobahns.

'These roads highlight the Cabrio's strengths and reveal a few weaknesses. With the hood down, you get real wind-in-the-hair motoring without excessive buffeting or discomfort, even at 100mph. And unlike many cabriolets, the bodyshell feels very rigid and almost immune from scuttle shake. Rough road travel is smooth and rattle free.

'It is unusual to have an open car fitted with air-conditioning. With the roof lowered, it's best to turn it off—otherwise the system is liable to go mad attempting to cool down all the surrounding air.

'These more demanding roads do not bring out the best in the Jaguar. Uphill gradients and tight overtaking situations reveal that the GM400 automatic transmission is biased more towards smoothness and economy than towards good part-throttle changedown characteristics. So unless full throttle kickdown is used, or the intermediate gears selected like a manual, there's less mid-range urgency than you'd expect.

'Corners betray a chassis set-up that is heavily-optimised for ride comfort. The Jaguar has fine poise and good overall balance, but its languid response and overlight steering do not encourage press-on driving. Competent and safe as it is, it does not feel sporting.

'However, the XJ-S cabriolet is not really meant to be a latter day E type Jaguar, so these dynamic shortcomings are not of major significance.'

The extra weight of the cabriolet and its inferior aerodynamics told against it when *Autocar* tested another HE model in September 1985, recording a 140-mph maximum speed, 7.7-sec 0–60mph time and 15.9-sec standing quarter mile with 14.5mpg. They said:

'In terms of outright performance, there are faster-accelerating cars, notably the Porsche Carrera cabriolet and Aston Martin Volante convertible, but where the Jaguar makes its mark is with its unique, and quite exceptional, blend of power train plus the inherent benefits offered by a cabriolet.'

The XJ-SC received a less-than rapturous

Autocar were wildly enthusiastic about the improvements to the 3.6 litre XJ–S when they tested an automatic version in 1987.

reception in the United States, however, from *Car and Driver*'s executive editor, Rich Ceppos. He commented in August 1986:

'I'm afraid there's nothing but disappointment in the new car for a thrill-seeker like myself. Aside from Jaguar's unconventional means of letting the great outdoors in, time has stood still for this lowrider.

'I've long hoped that Jaguar would firm the XJ-S up into a real sports machine, but, alas, that was not to be. The XJ-SC still uses the pillowy suspension settings that made the XJ6 such a joyous rider—but it's way too loose-jointed for a spirited two-seater. When I call on a hard corner, the body makes like a yo-yo. No change here.

'Then there's the mighty V12, which feels all bottled up at the low end. It's needed a good four-speed automatic to set it free for ages.

'It's been reported that Jaguar has improved its quality control. Unfortunately our test car suffered from a badly-folding top, a climate control that went belly-up, and a bad case of the stalls.

'When I slide into a low-slung, broad-shouldered V12 sports car, I expect a kick in the pants. The XJ-SC may be fine for wealthy men 20 years my senior, but it's far too much of a gentleman for me.'

Performance figures, for the record, on the 262-bhp engine were 135mph flat out, 8.4secs from 0–60mph, with a standing quarter mile in 16.3secs and 14mpg. *Road & Track* returned similar figures—except for a 141-mph maximum—the following month, and repeated how much they liked the XJ-S HE coupé. But they compared the XJ-SC to the late, unlamented, Triumph Stag, and said:

'If Jaguar returns to a lighter, son-of-E type, two-seater in the future, then that might be the more aggressive vehicle that some Jaguar enthusiasts (including us) long for. In the meantime, the XJ-SC is a large, luxurious, two-seater, a fine alternative to a Mercedes or BMW.'

The XJ-S Convertible

Features editor John Simister had the first report on how the new convertible handled in *Motor* during April 1988. He reported from a drive in a French-specification left-hand-drive car registered E829LAC in mountains near the Press launch at the South of France's Juan-les-Pins:

'The Jaguar flowed through the sweeping bends like liquid; only a really bad surface break induced a structural shudder to spoil the serenity. There will be no sport-pack suspension, as fitted to the current 3.6-litre coupé, for the V12 convertible though. It would undo all the careful work that makes the car the refined tourer that it is. Nor will there be a 3.6-litre convertible for Jaguar see only a very limited marked for such a beast.

'Is there a criticism? Hood up, the wind noise is considerable, though far less so than in the Mercedes rival. A bonded windscreen and well designed side window sealing help. It certainly isn't bad enough to drown conversation, even at 100mph.

Autocar managed to get full road test figures on another pre-production left-hand-drive open XJ-S, registered E829LAC, at Millbrook in the same month. They recorded a maximum speed of 144mph with an 8-sec 0–60mph time and a standing quarter mile in 16.3secs with 13.8mpg—commenting that 'the convertible feels positively sedate off the line from a standing start, but it is deceptive due to the three-speed automatic transmission. It really starts to show its mettle only at

the top end.' They added:

'Not only do the Jaguar engineers seem to have made the hood idiot-proof, but they seem to have overcome a major problem when driving convertibles: wind intrusion. Even with the hood and windows down, it is possible to drive the V12 convertible at 70mph without excessive buffeting. This had been achieved by altering the rake and shape of the windscreen after exhaustive wind-tunnel tests at MIRA . . . As far as refinement is concerned, the XJ-S V12 is very accomplished as a convertible. With the hood in place and the windows up, high-speed cruising reveals slight wind intrusion through the seal between the top of the front window and the hood—probably due to suction of the frameless windows—but, unlike many convertibles, there was no hood buffeting. With the hood down there is an obvious increase in wind noise, road and tyre roar and exhaust, but Jaguar has managed to keep wind intrusion to a minimum. Rear visibility is good even with the hood up thanks to the heated glass rear window, but care has to be taken while reversing with the hood down. When folded, it protrudes above the body line, putting the rear three-quarters of the car out of the driver's sight line.

'At £36,000, it may be the most expensive production Jaguar to date, but we feel it is worth every penny.'

The XJR-S 6-litre

The big-engined JaguarSport coupé carried an even-bigger, £45,500, price tag when it was tested by *Autocar* in August 1989—but the car, registered G958SBW, regained much of the original HE's lost performance, recording 150mph (although Jaguar said they had seen 162mph at the Nardo circuit in Southern Italy), with a 7.1-sec 0–60mph time and 15.5-sec standing quarter mile. David Vivian reported:

'There's a greater sense of ease about the Jaguar's work—it feels like a lighter car—but you'll look in vain for the thrill that sends the small hairs on the back of your neck bristling . . . In hard driving, the 6-litre is both more responsive and more forgiving than the

The Jaguar XJ-S convertible flowed through the bends like liquid, features editor John Simister reported in *Motor*.

5.3-litre car it supersedes. Most of the standard car's shortcomings—strong understeer in tight turns, roll oversteer on the limit, sloppy suspension control over crests and dips—have been exorcised from a chassis which will never feel lithe but has always promised greater ability than it's been allowed to display.

'Despite the handicap of steering which remains too light and reticent to communicate, the Jaguar turns in with almost startling agility and precision for such a big car and is better balanced than before, staying neutral for longer. The tail can be punched a little way out of line and easily held or corrected. In steady state cornering on perfectly dry tarmac, the bite of the squat Dunlops is very impressive and the Jaguar feels stable

and secure. In short, the vices have been all but eradicated.

'What's remarkable is that the ride has hardly suffered at all. It feels much firmer but very little harsher. The small loss of absorbency is more than compensated by the huge gains in control.'

The European XJ6 3.6-Litre

The new XJ6 came in for a great deal of acclaim, particularly from *Autocar* which published the first test of a manual example, registered D120KAR, a week after the launch in October 1986. They pointed out that the old XJ6 had been a very hard act to follow but despite the over similarity, the

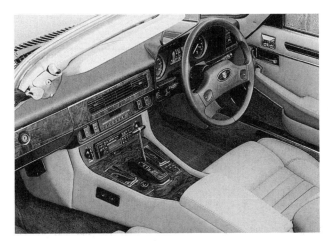

Its interior also came in for fulsome praise.

new car was faster, more economical, handled better and was now well-equipped to fight off German opposition in the same executive market. *Autocar* explained:

'The new car is quicker all the way, but quite dramatically so from its excellent 0–60mph time of 7.4secs [and standing quarter mile in 15.8secs]. In top speed, it is near-enough ideally geared in fifth to achieve the absolute maximum for the power-drag combination. To provide even more relaxed overdrive cruising ability it could easily be geared higher, with the present under-geared fourth made into a proper top, instead of its present status, equivalent to a very high third—the 5,500rpm red-line corresponds to 137mph [with a claimed top speed of 135mph for the 3.6-litre automatic].

'Judged more subjectively, the manual 3.6 is a much more entertaining car to drive quickly than its forerunner. It feels eager, in a way that was not quite so obvious on the 4.2. In spite of its modest tune, and a torque curve which, although kinking upward to return that high-sounding 4,000 rpm peak, is high and near-flat over a long span, this engine is pleasantly and enticingly sporting in its power delivery . . .

'It is backed pleasingly by the Getrag gearbox, which has a delightfully positive, slightly mechanical character to its change. The 34-lb release effort of the clutch is noticeable, although less so than in the series three.'

The effect of 4 per cent less weight, 8 per cent more horsepower and 10 per cent less drag was reflected in 13 per cent better overall fuel consumption at 20.7mpg. Refinement was well up to earlier Jaguar standards although the damping was a little on the firm side by contemporary saloon standards. *Autocar* concluded:

'If our test sounds a trifle enthusiastic, we make no apologies. It is claimed that Jaguar spent £240 million and seven years developing the XJ40—and it shows. They now have a truly worthy successor to the series three, and, more importantly, a world-class luxury saloon range with which to match BMW and Mercedes.'

Gavin Green then commented in *CAR* magazine in November 1986 on a manual 3.6-litre Jaguar, registered D36BRW at the launch in Scotland:

'Where the latest XJ6 really scores over its predecessor is in its behaviour at medium to high speed, and in its ability to go round bends quickly. The new Jaguar does not just control the bumps of a broken urban surface, it also manages, beautifully, to control its body movements as it sprints over undulating country roads. The car's composure in such conditions is truly amazing for its bulk . . .

'Some may still find the steering a touch too light, but the system is still responsive enough to allow the car to be driven with real venom, in sports car fashion.

'The handling is equally inspired: neutral (tending to understeer when pushed hard) and as failsafe as any four-wheeled box could ever be and far less prone to roll than was the more softly-suspended series three . . .

'Jaguar's long-awaited and crucial new car is all that we could have expected. And more . . . Jaguar has just announced what we and plenty of others say is one of the world's finest saloon cars.'

The XJ6 2.9-Litre

Motor were most impressed by the price of the 2.9-litre XJ6—£16,495—when they tested an example registered D40BRW in December 1986, commenting:

'Jaguar's entry-level XJ6 undercuts Rover's Sterling—

The new 3.6 litre XJ6 was faster, more economical, handled better and was more economical than the opposition, *Autocar* were happy to report.

the latest high-profile executive car loaded with equipment—by over £2,000. It's cheaper than the top Ford Scorpio by a similar margin and Jaguar dealers are already experiencing the tidal wave of demand such bold marketing was bound to create. A Jaguar for the price of a Ford had always been a reality on the second-hand market. A brand-new Jaguar for the price of a Ford is something else.'

They found that the 2.9-litre XJ6 could not count performance—a 121-mph maximum speed, with a 9.5-sec 0–60mph time and 17.1-sec standing quarter mile—or economy—16.8mpg—among its attributes and considered the instrumentation poor. But it offered the essentials of luxury motoring at an amazingly competitive price and in some respects—handling, ride and refinement—it had no equal. *Motor* said:

'To derive maximum satisfaction from owning this Jaguar requires a heightened appreciation of the things it does well: its peerless ride/handling compromise, its relaxed refinement, its tremendous braking, its special ambience. In this car the miles simply melt away, involving the driver only as much as he wants to be involved. It handles better than an S-class Mercedes, yet rides more smoothly than a Rolls-Royce. In many ways, it was ever thus. What the new car has done is widen the gap a little further and put behind it the days when the best-engineered car in the world was also one of the worst made.'

The same car was a little slower when tested by *Autocar* in February 1987, but it also used a lot less fuel, returning 19.3mpg. They agreed with *Motor's* findings and commented:

'The overall interior effect is true Jaguar. Plenty of walnut capping and chrome and although the only real leather on XJ6 models is on the steering wheel and gearchange, the leathergrain that covers everything else is a passable substitute.'

The U.S. Jaguar Sovereign

Jaguar did not enjoy the same price differential in the United States however, and suffered from direct comparison with the Mercedes 300E, and the cheaper Audi 5000CS Quattro. *Car and Driver's* associate editor, Arthur St Antoine, complained in June 1987:

'The new XJ6 has been treated to some pretty heady press notices across the pond. Read an English road test and you'll find that the revamped Jag can trounce a big Mercedes sedan and the new BMW 735i with ease. Indeed, more than one British publication has proclaimed the XJ6 the finest sedan in the world.

'Looks to me as though the English pride has run a little amok. A super-creamy ride and an elegant

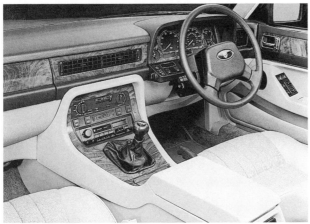

Then they decided that the Sovereign 4 litre was the best XJ6 ever produced by Jaguar.

The reduction in horsepower and high final drive ratio also hit the performance figures, although they were still 10 per cent better than the last of the Federal series three cars: 128mph, 10.8secs for 0–60mph and 18.2 secs for the standing quarter mile. The fuel consumption figure of 15mpg was very much on the high side, however. *Road & Track* managed 17.5mpg during their test in the same month, but had to be content with an 11.5-sec 0–60mph time although their standing quarter mile was virtually the same. Their general comments were a good deal more muted than those of *Car and Driver* and they explained:

'Jaguar doesn't want to pay any more fuel-use penalties than they have to, so mpg is important. At the same time, Jaguar sedans are luxurious . . . and sporting. So there had to be some performance, as much as they could get within the limits imposed by economy and quietness. The Jaguar staff have built a better XJ6. By almost any measure one can thing of, they've done it. For as long as the oldest inhabitant can recall, Jaguar have been a favourite. They've been a gallant underdog, a come-from-behind racing team, offered value for money and even when they had flaws, their mistakes weren't held against them.

'A conclusion here, aided by hindsight and tempered by memory of a good team in bad trouble, goes back to the short and long-term problems and projects. This new car took shape on the drawing boards before the improvements to the old car began to pay off. When the XJ40 was a gleam in the team's eye, how could they have known that the series three could be fixed so well? Or that once its reputation was reversed, the old charmer would climb back onto the sales charts and be the power that put Jaguar in the black?

'What we have here, meanwhile, is an excellent replacement for a car that turned out to be so desirable that it didn't really need to be replaced.'

The Jaguar Sovereign 4-litre

Autocar had absolutely no doubts about the 4-litre Sovereign they tested in September 1989: it was the best XJ6 yet. They returned performance figures

interior do not a world-beater make. The best sedan in the world should move like a leather-lined race car; but compared with the potent German thoroughbreds, this new Jag is a dog . . .

'The new Jaguar fails aesthetically as well. The old XJ6 was perhaps the best-looking sedan in the world, but the new one is nondescript and bland.'

of 140mph flat out, an 8.3-sec 0–60mph time with a 16-sec standing quarter mile . . . and 18.5mpg which bettered the BMW and Mercedes opposition. They said of their car, registered G114WHP:

'The new engine retains the typically "clanky" AJ6 note but it is now notably smoother and quieter in the mid-range and virtually inaudible at motorway cruising speeds. It feels more energetic at low speeds and delivers its urge in a strong steady flow as far as peak power at 4,750rpm. Although its tone becomes slightly frenetic beyond 5,000rpm and power is on the wane, the transmission will take it all the way to 5,500rpm at full throttle.

'Undoubtedly, the new electronically-controlled ZF plays its part in making the car feel more lively. But left to manage itself, change quality is curiously variable. Mostly it shuffles the ratios so smoothly that the only indication is the movement of the rev counter needle but, occasionally, despite the interface between engine and gearbox electronics that momentarily retards the ignition on upshifts, it seems flustered and thumps up or down a gear. This is more noticeable in sport mode when a firm prod of the throttle can cause it to drop two gears for rapid overtaking. Full throttle red-line changes, in contrast, are now as fast as any.

'Jaguar simply couldn't go wrong by fitting a full set of dials. They are a little short on elegance, but much more in keeping with the traditional wood and hide atmosphere. Less obvious, but no less welcome, are the many minor refinements: the simplified trip computer, the conventional indicator stalk and the new locks and catches. While applauding Jaguar's response to criticism, we feel this latest XJ6 is the car which should have appeared at the launch in 1986.'

Strengths and Weaknesses

One of the greatest strengths displayed in recent years among the saloons made by Jaguar has been the depth of integrity in engineering and design which has enabled them to be modified quite readily to suit individual tastes. It is just as well: like so many of their contemporaries, they have always suffered from corrosion problems and one or two other weaknesses.

Sheer old age caused most of the problems in the early cars built on a chassis. Initially, debris thrown up by road wheels lodged under the wings behind the wheels to soak up and retain moisture that came with it. This factor was at its worst when roads were sprayed liberally with rock salt to combat ice and snow—a common occurrence in many parts of Northern Europe, especially Britain, and the east coast of the United States. At first localised repairs would be made, chiefly to the body panels and inner wings, and then to the chassis itself, particularly in the vulnerable rear quarters. Plating the chassis affected stress patterns to such a degree that it was likely to crack, leading to further trouble, especially with any car that survived long enough to become a restoration project. A patchwork quilt of repairs inside the body also, typically, led to distortion and makes the restorer's life so much more difficult. The same great antiquity has meant that many of the more obvious sources of spare parts have dried up, notably transmissions. Tempting as it might be to buy a superficially-attractive restoration project, it is worth waiting until a really good car can be bought and then pay an expert to examine it in the most thorough manner.

A lopsided appearance can be caused by a broken leaf in one of the back springs, which costs little to replace; or it could be that the whole car has been collapsing through corrosion, which may render restoration impractical. The ultimate problem is that the car's value is likely to be far lower than the cost of restoring it properly, so it may never be possible to recoup the cost of the investment should that be necessary.

The unitary construction cars, starting with the Mark I saloon, are more viable because their sporting appeal commands higher prices. This has also generated an industry supplying replacements for the panels that rot away around the perimeter of the car. Good secondhand spares are more common because far more cars were made.

An easy way to spot trouble in what appears to be an immaculate car is to look at the gaps where the doors and other panels shut. These should be neat and consistent in every plane with the panels themselves following smooth rounded shapes without ripples. Rust bubbles around the perimeter, the bottom of the doors, and close to detail fittings like the sidelamp housings, are common and the cost of repairs varies according to the labour needed. But if there is any rust visible, there is likely to be a lot more which the eye cannot detect immediately—so be prepared for a big bill, no matter how shiny the paint and chrome. Again, the major areas for corrosion tend to be behind the road wheels, and—likely on the saloons built on a chassis—around the rear suspension mountings.

Almost anything might have happened to a classic Jaguar saloon mechanically, chiefly through sheer age rather than weaknesses in design or construction. Overheating, caused partly by a lack of maintenance and partly through having a restricted underbonnet airflow, causes the most trouble. Special problems which relate to the independent rear suspension saloons centre on the final drive. Heat soaked up by the inboard mounted disc brakes

An early Jaguar saloon – such as the Mark IX of Richard Ford, seen competing at Oulton Park in 1987 – may perform perfectly well despite suffering from ill-fitting body panels. Making them fit properly can be a very expensive business as virtually the whole car may have to be rebuilt from scratch.

of all but the latest XJ range leads to an early deterioration of the final drive oil seals. These are easy to replace—once the entire rear suspension and subframe has been dropped out of the bodyshell, often leading to an enforced replacement of expensive mounting blocks and exhaust system parts.

Similar general troubles strike the XJ-based saloons, especially the V12 variants with their closely-packed underbonnet areas, but they are usually easier to repair because corrosion is less likely to be so rampant. There is also still a good supply of spare parts, both new and secondhand.

Enthusiastic owners have always exploited the strengths of Jaguar saloons with modifications aimed at improving the performance—in the first instances, chiefly for only competition because the performance was so much higher than that of contemporary rivals on the road in the early years. The first concerted attempt to market a higher-performance Jaguar for road use was by the Surrey dealer John Coombs, using his works-supported racing saloon as an inspiration. The earliest recorded conversion, from a series of around 40 cars built between 1958 and 1967, was to a 3.4-litre Mark I. This car doubled up for competition work, however, running to a similar specification to the cars detailed in Chapter Seven. Later Coombs conversions favoured the 3.8-litre Mark II cars as providing the basic highest performance although the odd conversion was carried out on 3.4-litre examples and an S type. In essence, the work involved rebuilding the engine with balanced and gasflowed parts, lightening the flywheel for

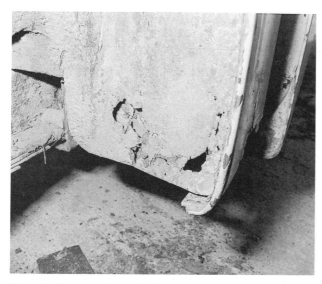

Corrosion is common around the rear spring mountings.

improved response, fitting a freer-flowing exhaust system and higher ratio steering, with adjustable shock absorbers. Cosmetic changes typically included modifying the wheel arches so that the car could run neatly without spats and fitting the woodrim steering wheel from an E type.

The XJ6—and the XJ12 that followed—received little attention at first so far as modifications were concerned. Apparently, owners were quite happy with the cars the way they were—and bodykits to alter the appearance of a car had not yet become established in Europe, whereas in North America, where customisation was quite popular, Jaguars were normally considered so exclusive they did not come in for this sort of treatment.

The first recorded instance of an XJ6 being turned into a convertible was in 1972 when Britain's Queen and Prince Philip visited Mauritius. The mayor of the capital, Port Louis, had the roof removed from his 2.8-litre saloon and the chassis reinforced by local marine engineers, Taylor-Smith Ltd, before the whole car was retrimmed. This meant that the Royal couple couldjd ride in splendour and be readily seen by cheering crowds.

During the late 1960s and early 1970s, when unlimited-capacity sports car racing for the Canadian-American Cup was at the height of its popularity, Chevrolet V8s were developed to give staggering power outputs. It soon became popular too for top power boat racers to run two of these engines at individual capacities of 7.7-litres—to keep within an overall 1,000cu in capacity limit—thus liberating a total of 1,200bhp. The British firm, Forward Engineering, then began developing the Jaguar V12 engine to give competitive power outputs using six downdraught Weber carburettors, gas-flowed cylinder heads, modified camshafts and oil pump. Occasionally these engines found their way into customers' cars as the Turbeau partnership of top power boat designer Don Shead and commodity broker Michael Doxford developed twin turbocharged V12s, a pair of which gave a combined output of 1,600bhp from standard 5.3-litre cylinder blocks. The use of turbochargers meant that the engine capacity was rated at 1.4 times the equivalent of an engine running under atmospheric pressure. This, in turn, meant that they could have gone up to 5.5-litres . . . but 1,500bhp was considered sufficient without risking weakening blocks that were subject to pressures as high as 1.9 bar.

Meanwhile hardly anybody—apart from the designers of *The Avengers* TV series—had tried to alter the appearance of the standard XJ saloon, the styling was considered so good. It was left to the Italian firm of Pininfarina to make the first move while they were producing the facelifted series three XJ bodyshell. They were given an old XJ-S by Jaguar in 1978, and turned it into a concept car to test the reaction to an open XJ-S—or even a new E type sports car—at some time in the future. The resultant Spyder, which had a stubby tail 9ins shorter than that of the XJ-S, attracted a lot of publicity, with Jaguar saying there was no way they could afford to put an open XJ-S into production and Pininfarina saying they would not mind doing it if they changed their minds!

By the mid-1980s, however, there were an awful lot of old XJ Jaguars on the road that still looked very much like later models. What is more, Britain was coming out of economic recession and more people could afford to personalise their cars. It came as no surprise, therefore, that a whole new industry sprang up, making new Jaguars look different from the madding crowd. In the vanguard of this revolution came other developments, such as Jaguar estates for which customers had always cried out, but not in sufficient numbers to interest the factory; and convertibles that really were convertibles, not Targa-topped cars which never look quite like real open cars.

None of this, Targa top aside, had been generated by the factory at the time—but the potential was highlighted when Tom Walkinshaw Racing and Forward Engineering brought out special versions of the XJ-S coupé almost simultaneously early in 1984. At a price nearly double that of a standard saloon, they were joining a field already occupied by Jaguar exponents Duncan Hamilton, with their German Arden conversions using the XJ-S and XJ saloons as a base; Lynx Engineering with their estates and convertibles; and Avon Coachworks, which produced convertibles and XJ-S estates.

The common factor that linked these specialists was that they all marketed new cars with conversions to at least factory standard, as opposed to bolt-on, or rivet-on, attachments of the type used in normal bodykits. It was possible to have existing cars converted by some of the firms, but the cost was likely to be high when they were deprived of the profit generated by selling a new car. But they succeeded where others such as Classic Cars of Coventry had failed. Classic Cars had produced a very attractive convertible Jaguar Mark X, or 420G, received good orders from North America, then could not find enough cars to convert in the late 1970s.

The Arden conversions were typically German, having been based on Mercedes practice. They involved options such as lowering and stiffening the suspension, fitting BMW-style 16-inch wheels with low-profile tyres, along with a front spoiler, rear apron and still coverings. Masses of leather and lamb's wool in the interior predated Jaguar's XJ-S thinking.

Avon's XJ estate car was in harmony with Jaguar thinking in the 1960s, when a solitary Mark II estate prototype was built. Strong competition from Ford's mark two Zodiac estate and the fact that Jaguar could sell every saloon they could make, stopped them putting it into production. Aston Martin had managed to sell a dozen or so DB5 and DB6 estates to hunting, shooting and fishing fans, so Avon aimed for this market. The roof of a series three saloon was sawn in half on a line between the doors, and the horizontal surface of the rear deck removed, complete with boot lid. The roof was then extended to meet a tailgate made up of the vertical part of the boot lid and, amazingly, a Renault 5 rear door! New side panels with extra glazing filled the gap between the roof, rear door, wing tops and tailgate. The standard Jaguar bodyshell took little strength from its rear seat bulkhead in any case, so with the substantial new top, the Avon shell was sufficiently strong.

The practical nature of this conversion was

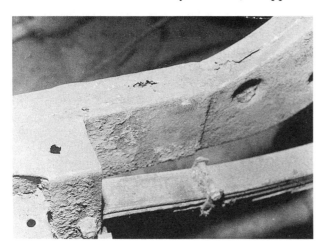

Plated repairs to the rear chassis rails are common – but undesirable. To make matters worse, this plating has corroded through.

emphasised by its massive luggage deck, 6ft 7ins long by 3ft 8ins wide—not quite so big as a Volvo 245, but quite unlike anything else on the market. Avon also produced a convertible version of the XJ saloon, similar to that which had been made by their near-neighbours, Classic Cars of Coventry. But they ran into the same problem; it was based on the obsolete XJ coupé, supplies of which were scarce. It was also expensive because the floorpan needed a lot of work, and looked more like a cabriolet—the hood could not be completely lowered because the rear suspension got in the way.

There were similarities with the cars converted by Lynx Engineering, except that the hoods retracted further, at greater cost. Lynx's convertible version of the XJ-S, called the Spyder, sold well between 1979 and 1982 before they switched emphasis to their Eventer XJ-S estate, expecting Jaguar's cabriolet to be a completely open car. When the Targa-topped machine appeared, the Spyder continued to sell well. So far as the Eventer was concerned, it had not passed without notice that the back seats of the normal XJ-S were distinctly cramped and the flying buttress rear end was not considered one of Jaguar's better efforts. Lynx decided to resolve both problems at once: to make their Eventer big enough to carry, say, two sets of bulky golfing gear and to look as sleek and feline as a Jaguar should, even if it was a hatchback.

With the Lancia HPE for inspiration, and total confidence in their market, Lynx went as far as to commission their own glass—and then found that the back window was the same as the Citroën Ami 8! Freed from glass restraints, Lynx had styling independence when the top was cut off. The fuel tank, sited over the axle to meet American rear-end impact legislation, was replaced by one moulded round the spare wheel so that Lynx could squeeze every last millimetre out of the bodyshell for rear-seat legroom.

Forward Engineering's XJ-S was poles apart from the concept of the Avon and Lynx products. Its conversions came in three stages: one, chiefly

Rust is likely to appear first as pinpricks around the corners of body panels – like the bottom of the bonnet of this XJ6, where the metal behind has been folded for strength, and retains moisture as a result.

bodywork and wheels; two, bodywork, wheels, brakes and a bigger engine; and three, a massive 6.4-litre V12 based on that used in the XJ12 prototype. Their XJ-S conversions, produced with the backing of Brian Lister, who built Jaguar-powered sports racing cars in the late 1950s, cost about the same as the Arden components where they coincided. Stage two of a Beaty conversion involved boring the engine out to 5.7-litres, fitting gas-flowed heads, forged pistons, modified lubrication, a larger water radiator and special exhaust system to give 400bhp with 410lb/ft of torque. The suspension was tied down with reaction bars and massive ventilated disc brakes were fitted all round. More money brought stage three with the bored and stroked 6.4-litre engine giving 440bhp with 450lb/ft of torque linked to a modified General Motors 400 automatic gearbox or a Doug Nash five-speed manual from North American stock car racing.

By 1985, Hamilton was experimenting with the Dutchman Willy Mosselman's supercharging kit on the Arden XJ-S, which also featured American-style twin headlights. The installation of the belt-driven centrifugal supercharger was similar to that evolved for Mercedes cars. Boost was limited to 4.4psi for reliability and to avoid having to modify standard engines, but the American Paxton blower raised the output of the 3.6-litre XJ-S to 285bhp at 5,300rpm with 298lb/ft of torque. Apart from those elements, the chief advantage was seen as a reduction in underbonnet temperatures from those experienced by turbocharged conversions.

Comfort options for TWR included a plush leather rear seat conversion, complete with seat belts, for the XJ-S cabrio as other tuners continued to use TWR bodykits to save developing their own. These included the long-established Janspeed con-

Neglected and oily engine compartments – like this one in a series I 4.2 litre XJ6 – can often spell trouble.

Facing page, top: Cutaway rear spats like those fitted to a Mark II saloon on parade during a Jaguar Drivers' Club meeting at Oulton Park in 1987 were pioneered as a typical part of a Coombs conversion.

cern which began marketing twin turbocharger kits for the AJ6 engine in both Jaguar Sovereign and XJ-S adaptations. Performance was boosted by electronic engine management systems developed by the Coventry firm of Zytek to give 295bhp at 5,000rpm, with 340lb/ft of torque at 4,000rpm— enough to take the six-cylinder cars well into the 12-cylinder performance bracket.

Meanwhile Lister's engine-building operation

Facing page, bottom: Jaguar were one of the first to produce special versions of the XJ6 – like this series II 4.2 litre 'berlina' discreetly modified for the Italian market.

became the province of Laurence Pearce at WP Automotive, and soon took over the bodywork and suspension operation as well. The early V12 cylinder heads were favoured against the later May heads because they gave higher performance breathing, along with gas-flowing, high-light camshafts, forged pistons, special nitrided crankshafts and revised fuel injection. Power outputs of around 440bhp were obtained from 5.3 litres with, initially, the five-speed ZF gearboxes fitted to Aston Martins until the Getrag unit became available. Later modifications with new Marelli-Weber digital electronic fuel injection boosted power to 468bhp at 6,250rpm with 410lb/ft of torque at 4,000rpm, before the stroke was increased to 78mm to give 5,955cc, using a new crankshaft and connecting rods. The capacity was then increased to 6,996cc by combining a 94-mm stroke with an 84-mm bore to give 496bhp at 6,200rpm with 500lb/ft of torque at 3,8509rpm. In this form, these hefty cars proved capable of a 5-sec 0–60mph time with a claimed maximum speed of 188mph.

The wide-wheeled bodywork propagated by *The Avengers* TV series helped inspire Andrew Foster's series III XJ6, seen here racing at Donington.

The Avon estate was one of the more ambitious developments on the XJ6 bodyshell.

Bottom left: Duncan Hamilton marketed various conversions by Arden and Panther on the XJ base.

Bottom right: Some Lister conversions, like this one using an XJ–S as a base, pictured at Oulton Park in 1984, were relatively mild.

Others, such as this slick-tyred XJ–S driven by Roger Mac at Donington in 1986, were more extreme.

Jaguar racing coupés are rarer than rare . . . like this one campaigned by Andrew Hannah at Silverstone in 1988.

Roger Bowman's XJ–S, pictured at Silverstone in 1989, featured extensively lightened glass fibre bodywork.

The JaguarSport concern were proud to picture their XJR 4.0 and XJR–S 6.0 at the Silverstone circuit run by Tom Walkinshaw with the 1990 Le Mans-winning Jaguar designed, developed and run by his organisation.

Restoring a Jaguar Saloon

Classic Jaguar saloons fall into three categories so far as restoration is concerned. There are cars like the Mark VII, Mark XIII and Mark IV that were based on a chassis, the Mark I and II variants, and the Mark X and 420G built in the same era, and, finally, everything developed from the XJ6. Obviously they share common problems, such as the sheer expense of restoring an interior that has deteriorated badly, and there are equally obvious links between the way in which the Mark X, 420G and XJ6 variants were constructed. But the basic divisions are influenced most strongly by the availability of spare parts. Now that old cars, particularly Jaguars, are appreciating rapidly in price, there is nothing that cannot be made—at a price. But the cost may be reasonable only if the spare parts are interchangeable with other contemporary models, such as the XK sports cars, and, to a lesser extent, the E type that followed.

Restoring cars in the first category—those based on a chassis—is likely to be more of a labour of love than anything profitable. Only a small proportion of the 46,477 made have survived in reasonably good condition—possibly around 1,000. Values are also lower than those of the more glamorous Mark II range. These two factors mean that there is little incentive for the large-scale remanufacture of parts peculiar to these cars, which means, in turn, that the costs of setting up such an operation have to be recouped from only a few sales: hence the high price.

On a happier note, if the time and effort can be justified, the large-scale restoration of the more valuable XK sports cars can be of great help. Much of the running gear, such as suspension, steering and brakes—apart from the engine and manual transmission—is directly compatible and there are

many similarities in the chassis. The chassis was also of such agricultural construction that it is possible for skilled fabricators and welders to replace corroded sections—an operation that is not always viable on superficially-similar chassis like those used on M.G. saloons and sports cars from a similar period because they used more-sophisticated double-curvature pressings. The chief problem is that to do the job properly, the body usually has to come off the chassis, which makes any restoration a major venture.

A golden rule to observe before starting a restoration is to make a list of everything that needs replacing: then you have a head start on the long job of obtaining the parts you need. This will be of great help even when you discover, before you start dismantling the car and shotblasting individual panels to find the real imperfections, that the list is growing fast. It is also wise to photograph everything before it is taken to pieces and to make notes about how individual components were assembled—especially in the body. It's no good wondering later whether a window or door had a weather seal; you have to be able to make allowances for such small, and seemingly insignificant, items at an early point during body re-assembly. It is also wise to photograph all the gaps between the body panels to remind you of what they looked like originally. Jaguar's lead-loading of imperfections was not always perfect and can lead to a lot of confusion at later points in the restoration.

So far as the chassis is concerned, the most common areas that are likely to have been subject to earlier repairs are from the front of the rear spring hangers backwards. Corrosion, harboured in debris thrown up by the back wheels, frequently

The bulkhead, pictured being repaired on a bench, is the vital component around which an early Jaguar saloon's body hangs.

ate away the metal well before other parts of the car. Quite often, these areas were repaired by wrapping sheets of steel around what was left of the original chassis. This form of 'plating' is likely to result in cracks caused by the metal of differing ages and thickness reacting adversely under stress. The only answer is to scrap the repaired rear end of the chassis and make new sections which can then be seam welded to the original front legs. The front of the chassis often survives better because Jaguar engines are such renowned oil burners, the crud that results providing a fine protection against corrosion. Body panels are likely to present the biggest problem unless the old parts are sufficiently complete for a panel-beater to copy them accurately or there is another car of identical specification being restored at the same time. In the case of cars that need a total restoration, it is essential to start with a completely straight chassis.

Then the basic body, made up of the front bulkhead, roof and rear quarters, can be mounted on the chassis with some chance of success in the later stages of the restoration. Again, there is a golden rule: leave everything loose until the last

Sill sections frequently corrode and replacement is vital because they, quite literally, hold the body together.

minute before final welding. If pop rivets or screws are used at first to hold panels in place, final adjustments are easy.

Initial work centres on ensuring that the front bulkhead (which supports the scuttle top and windscreen frame) sits full square on the chassis. Although the roof—which is rarely subject to corrosion—does a reasonable job in holding the body together, the scuttle is the focal point because everything must hang around it. In common with

Suspension joints, like this Metalstik-bushed fitting that mounts on the early car's top wishbone, must be kept in first-class condition or replaced.

many other steel-bodied cars, the sills, which run backwards from the bottom of the bulkhead, are a notorious area for corrosion, along with the bottom of the door posts and the floor. Once the sills are removed, or fall off, the body can flex to a marked degree despite the roof holding it together. The movement can be such that it is impossible to get it back into shape. It is essential, therefore, to brace the basic body with temporary internal struts while the doors and bootlid still display good shutlines.

Once it has been established that the bulkhead has been bolted absolutely straight in every plane to the chassis, however, new sills can be fitted. They should be riveted to the bulkhead initially, then be attached by similar methods to the rear door post while the door shut lines are checked, before the central doorpost is screwed or riveted in place. A new or repaired steel floor can then be offered up with further checking of the new, or repaired, doors to ensure that the vital gaps between their edges and the surrounding metal is consistent. The bulkhead will have already been fitted with the front door hinges, pivoting in steel boxes on its extremities. The sills can then be welded in place, starting at the front, moving on to the rear after checking that the shrinkage caused by welding is not a problem, before the central door post is permanently attached. In this way the pressures caused by welding are evenly distributed. The door shut face panels can then be tacked into position and, as each panel is fettled to its final shape, a variety of angled steel straps should be bolted into place so that the doors can be removed again to tidy their surrounds. The process is then repeated for the rear doors.

New, or repaired, rear inner wings are fitted next, either side of the rear panel which sweeps up over the back axle. Again, extreme accuracy of alignment is essential if the rear wings are to follow the doors' waistline when they are fitted. Be prepared for a great deal of fettling. The necessity for such time-consuming adjustments is often the fault

of the car. Good workmen can beat out panels that are almost exactly the same as the patterns, but Jaguar chassis of identical specification can vary wildly in detail. Such problems were overcome during the original assembly at Brown's Lane by bodybuilders having a wide selection of panels from which to choose. If one door did not fit, they could often find another which did, from a selection of seven or eight. Such chassis inconsistencies are likely to be emphasised by earlier repairs to corrosion or accident damage. Each body has to be made individually to suit the car—hardly a task for an amateur.

Once the inner body panels have been welded together, outer panels can be offered up. As these panels are brought into line, the wisdom becomes evident of having made sure that the now-unseen inner wings and door posts are in perfect alignment.

The front wings, linked at their upper rear edges by the scuttle top, are supported like a shroud over the front of the chassis by a fabricated steel hoop. Hinges extend out of the bulkhead to support the back of the bonnet. Again, everything has to hang around the bulkhead to ensure that, quite literally, the lines of the front wings flow through the doors into the back wings in one long, unbroken, sweep.

One of the chief problems when overhauling Jaguar engines is corrosion in the alloy parts, caused by neglect and a lack of anti-freeze. Obviously, the older an engine, or the longer it has been standing, the more serious such problems are likely to be. Items such as the water pump vanes are often corroded—or missing—for the same reason. Because of this inherent corrosion, the actual removal of a cylinder head can be the biggest problem when overhauling an engine. Copious quantities of penetrating oil are likely to be needed around the securing studs. Some machining may also have to be undertaken so that later-specification parts, such as replacement piston rings, can be fitted to earlier engines. But problems

What is should look like ... an engine mounting, and the beam for the front suspension, from an early Mark X Jaguar.

And a fully-repaired shell – from a Mark II saloon – is pictured in primer at XK Engineering in Nuneaton, Warwickshire.

with spare parts are likely to be fewer with the 3.4-litre and 3.8-litre engines fitted to the early saloons simply because there is such a continuing demand from Jaguar enthusiasts whose cars have similar power units. It used to be possible to find replacement engines quite cheaply in most scrapyards because the mechanical components lasted far longer than the bodywork. The sheer age of such units means now, however, that few are to be found and new parts have to be used, which costs more.

The SU carburettors used by Jaguar were produced in such large quantities that spares are relatively cheap and it is still possible to find good secondhand examples.

Although gearbox parts are scarce, the constant demand for replacement parts from all manner of old-car enthusiasts means that there are now small firms who specialise in producing them. Overdrives are an excellent example: at one time, during the 1970s, parts were hard to find, let alone reconditioned units. But now the demand has risen sufficiently, there is no great problem. In general, however, the greatest demand in the classic car world is for the more sporting manual gearbox cars, so supplies of parts for automatic transmissions may never be good.

One of the most common faults with the early

saloons, shared with the Mark II cars, is that the rear axles are often bent. Drivers rarely seem to recognise this problem when the cars are on the road, but when the axle is stripped, it becomes all too readily apparent. It is frequently found that the axle tubes have worked loose, either through an accident, or simply prolonged wear, and distortion has occurred as they have been welded up. This has become such a common problem that specialist firms have made jigs for repairs.

Jigs have also been made to help reassemble parts like the front suspension. Rebushing is made much easier on a jig because the Metalastik joints have to be at the right angle when they are tightened up and it is difficult to insert the split pins in the heavy hubs while they are drooping off a jacked-up car. The rest of the suspension presents

Chrome wire wheels are a popular fitting to early restored Jaguar saloons, although only painted versions are normally allowed in British racing because the chroming process can make the spokes more brittle.

AHH 7325

few problems because it is so primitive with parts that bear a close resemblance to almost every other contemporary car.

The steering column rarely gives trouble, other than for two spider joints which are often worn and can be replaced easily. But most cars benefit from attention to the pedal assemblies. Typical problems in this area centre on fulcrum pins with a grease point that is usually forgotten. This means that the roller bearings and pedal pins on the chassis need to be rebuilt with new spacers and bronze bushes, along with the amazingly agricultural-looking clutch withdrawal mechanism which works so beautifully, despite its appearance.

It is a false economy not to have the braking system completely rebuilt during a major restoration and the similarly with parts used on the XK sports car makes this especially viable. The costs are also relatively low because there is such a big market for replacement parts.

Items like chromework needed to set off a major restoration can be the biggest headache of all. There is nothing that cannot be made by hand, then chromed, but the cost can be very high, so the quality of such original components can make a considerable difference to the value of a restoration project.

The same applies to the interior, although there are so many specialist trimmers that this is likely to present little problem so far as supplies are concerned. The interior of early Jaguars was made of such traditional materials, like leather, cloth and wooden veneers, that replacements are readily available—which is more than can be said for later plastic items which cost far more to put back into production. The big problem with the interior of a Jaguar saloon—particularly that of the Mark VII, Mark VIII and Mark IX—is that there is so much of it; hence the high price. Fortunately there are also a number of small parts which are common with those used in the XK sports car, which eases some supply problems. There is also a strong case for renovation, rather than replacement, because the major areas of trim were hand-made.

Although there is much common ground with the early Jaguar saloons when restoration of unitary construction cars is being considered, they have special problems. The most notable is the way in which the bodyshell can distort when severe corrosion sets in around the bottom of the front wings and in the rear floor pan. Quite simply, the body sags in the middle.

Before a unitary construction car is dismantled, it should be well supported on at least six or eight axle stands—some of which should be placed under the chassis legs—so that the weight is distributed evenly. Major components, such as the engine, transmission, front suspension and rear axle, should be left in place at this point to equalise stresses. If the bodyshell has sagged in the middle it can often be righted at this point by adjusting the height of the stands. An excellent

alternative is to bolt the bodyshell to a crash repair jig, providing the right brackets can be obtained. The only disadvantage in this case is that hiring the brackets can be expensive if repairs take a long time. Good, original, doors and lids can provide invaluable data as locum points are worked out, especially if the alternative method of strapping the bodyshell internally is to be adopted.

The door gaps on the unitary-construction cars are critical, so they should be checked whenever a major component—such as the engine at one end and the rear axle at the other—are removed. A crucial point with such restorations is the 'A' post which supports the front bulkhead and front doors. It is essential that repairs—commonly needed at the bottom—are both accurate and strong, otherwise the panel gaps and rigidity of the bodyshell will suffer.

When replacing the inner and outer sills—both of which are frequently corroded—it is essential to repair at least the bottom part of the front wings which cover the sill's front extension. Repairs to the 'C' post—the one meeting the rear edge of the back doors—and rear valance replacement can be

Chromium-plated components, such as the number plate light in the first picture, and the small badge in the second, can present a major headache if they cannot be readily replaced because they were frequently made from metal that crumbles easily.

completed at the same time. The rear seat pans, which also rot badly, link in with this area. It is often necessary to remove sound metalwork to gain access to the corrosion that it conceals. Typically, it is wise to remove parts of the inner wheel arches to get at the suspension mountings. The attraction here is that subsequent repairs to the inner wheel arches are far less conspicuous than those to the outer panels. Supplies of replacement panels and repair sections, especially for the Mark II-bodied cars, are excellent, and relatively economical, because so many are being restored.

The front wings are rarely replaced, however, unless it is vital, because they are big and expensive. In addition, it can be difficult to make a new wing fit the old surrounding panels. As a result, smaller repair sections, which cover common corrosion areas such as the front chassis legs, are readily available.

The manner in which the sills are replaced is of major importance. A lot of time and money can be saved by using repair sections which cover only the areas most commonly affected by corrosion, rather than the entire sill. But this is unwise because the sills are vital to the integrity of the bodyshell and should be replaced in their entirety—which takes a lot longer. Skilled welding is vital in this area—even though it will not be seen when the car is finished—because untidy work can prejudice the fitting of the outer panels, and the strength of the car as a result. Constant reference to door gaps is vital at this point, of course. It is only when the outer sills have been fitted satisfactorily that subsidiary items, like the jacking points, and sill closing plates can be welded in.

The front suspension crossmember and the 'crow's feet' alongside it, supporting the front body panels, are equally common corrosion areas, but quite easily replaced with repair panels. In many cases, parts—such as wing repair sections meant for the more popular Mark II cars—can be adapted to fit the by-now rare Mark Is.

Mechanical parts are similar to those used on the earlier saloons, although they are often more readily available because of the popularity of the later models and the minor industry which has been established in total rebuilds using a very high proportion of new parts. Beware, however, of bodged repairs from the days when Jaguar saloons were maintained almost exclusively from scrapyards. The British magazine *Practical Classics* revealed:

'As 2.4-litre cars are significantly lighter at the front than 3.4s and 3.8s, the front suspension has to be modified to suit. Jaguar achieved this by using slightly different coil springs. Those for 2.4s will have either a white, blue or green patch painted on the centre coil, those for 3.4s or 3.8s red, yellow or purple. These marks may be covered by tape. Three colours are necessary for each model as there are inevitably slight differences in manufactured length. These are countered by using packing pieces between the spring top and crossmember. Part-way through the production run, there was a slight increase in the "target" manufactured length; later cars with green or purple springs didn't have spacers. If your car doesn't feel right, it might be worth checking that the springs fitted are correct; when Mark IIs were banger transport it wasn't at all unknown for an owner faced with an expensive front suspension overhaul to obtain a beam—complete with all the suspension—from a breaker's yard and fit that; maybe it came from a different model. Alternatively, it is possible that an incorrect secondhand (or new!) coil spring was fitted at the same time to replace a broken one. Check that the same colour-coded spring is fitted to each side.'

Such are the complexities of just the front suspension on just one series of Jaguar saloons, let alone a range that extends from early cars with chassis to an even heavier limousine that is still in production, as well as the modern varieties and lighter interim cars.

Replacement parts for Dunlop braking systems are scarce, but the far more common Girling units and overhaul kits are frequently interchangeable. In the same way, there are a lot of common parts shared by the early independent rear suspension cars with the E type sports models of similar vintage—which are being restored in great numbers—in addition to the later XJ6-based variants. Major problems are likely to occur with the Daimler V8-engined cars, however, because so few were produced and the engine does not react well to a lack of maintenance—notably so far as antifreeze is concerned. In the same way, the sheer complexity of the V12 unit can be a major problem and the repair bills massive if it has been neglected

or allowed to overheat—which is all-too-common. Scrapyard supplies are reasonably plentiful, but, as can be well-illustrated by the example of the earlier six-cylinder engines, these are limited.

Supplies of body panels for the S-type cars are likely to remain good, however, as the increasing popularity of classic cars has rendered it worthwhile producing replacements. This practice is made all the more viable by the fact that many parts are closely related to those used in the Mark II saloons. Other parts, which are peculiar to the S-types, such as the roof pressings, present fewer problems because they do not suffer from the

Concours preparation can involve seemingly endless hours of work.

Beware torn and untidy trim parts like this series I XJ6 door pull . . . they can be extraordinarily difficult to repair or replace.

common perimeter corrosion caused by the saline dressings used on icy roads. But major problems are already being faced by the owners of Mark X, 420G and limousine variants because they share few common body panels with other cars and have always been expensive to repair because they are big, and not so popular with classic car enthusiasts.

Body panels for XJ-based saloons and the XJ-S are relatively cheap and plentiful, however, because sufficient cars have been sold over a long period to make it worthwhile producing replacements. Repairs and restoration are simplified

Tempting starting point for many engine conversions . . . the XJ12 unit, pictured here in early carburettor form.

because they used to be valuable. As a result, when modern universal jigs were established, it was possible to hire the brackets that made it viable to repair bodyshells which, otherwise, would have been scrapped. These brackets are still available, with only the cost of hiring them militating against corrosion repairs. Such repairs are now rendered all the more viable because it is far easier simply to weld in repair sections of fabricated parts for a basic bodyshell that is held rigidly in position.

The major problem faced by the aspiring owners of later cars is that they are so plentiful the overall value is low and the cars frequently suffer from neglected interiors. Many interior parts are not vital to keeping the cars on the road, so they are rarely reproduced—especially because the costs of putting plastic back into production can be far higher than something more immediately rewarding, such as clutch or brake parts. This means that the quality of the interior of later cars is of vital importance to their ultimate value—far more so than even the series one XJ6, which was of a more traditional nature and more easily repaired as a result.

The Personalities Behind Jaguar and Daimler

Just two men have been the power behind Jaguar cars—Sir William Lyons and the more recent knight, Sir John Egan—but they have been supported by an extraordinarily talented rank of lieutenants. Lyons, of course, was the man who created Jaguars, while Egan is the personality who has ensured their survival as an endangered species. The story has often been told of how the young motor-cycle racer, Lyons, started the whole enterprise by taking a partner, William Walmsley, a coal merchant's son who had been building motor-cycle sidecars as a hobby at his family home in Stockport, Cheshire. The sidecars were wonderful-looking devices, shaped like cigars, and they captured the imagination of Lyons when Walmsley's family retired to the seaside resort of Blackpool in 1921. Walmsley was a dreamer—quite different from the far-more-commercial Lyons—and son of an Irish musician. Lyons was only 20 when he went into partnership with Walmsley, 10 years his senior, backed by their fathers. But he was always the dominant partner, taking all the key decisions that saw their company called Swallow expand from producing one sidecar a week to more than 100 within seven years. It was during that time that Lyons learned a lot about styling from the shy, retiring Walsmley.

One of the problems about making sidecars was that selling them was a seasonal trade, so by 1927 Lyons had taken the company into building car bodies. A chronic lack of space and skilled labour led Lyons to relocate the firm in the Midlands, at Coventry, one of Britain's traditional engineering centres. Lyons had already shown an exceptional ability to keep down costs as a result of efficiency rather than skimping. As a result he was able to keep down prices—and because their

special bodies, initially on Austin Seven chassis, were also highly attractive—Swallow rapidly outpaced its competitors. By 1931 Lyons and Walmsley were manufacturing their own cars, called S.S. It has never been revealed what S.S. stood for, but it is widely assumed to be Standard Special because these cars used basic mechanical components mass-produced by Standard. Despite his success at running the company, Lyons never stopped learning from others. He took criticisms to heart. When he was told that S.S. cars looked a lot better than they performed, he fitted them with ever more powerful engines. Profits were high, but so were the overheads and all Walmsley wanted was a quiet life—building bodies. So Walmsley allowed Lyons to buy him out in 1934 so that he could go away and build caravans . . .

One of Lyons's first steps in really going it alone—designing his own bodies as well as running the business—was to hire a bright young engineer from Humber called William Heynes. His task would be to set up a department which would enable S.S. to make all the parts they needed for their cars without having to rely on others. It was one of the best moves Lyons ever made, illustrating not only his foresight but his ability to attract and motivate the right people.

Initially Heynes, who was born in 1904 and was only three years younger than Lyons, wanted to be a surgeon. But, with five brothers to provide for, his father, a cabinet-maker, could not afford that; ambitions to be a veterinary surgeon ran into similar trouble. So the young Heynes, from Leamington Spa, found himself in the motor industry at nearby Coventry. During his apprenticeship at Humber, he designed a four-cylinder motor cycle engine with twin overhead camshafts and hemispherical combustion chambers that was too advanced to put into production. The chance that Lyons gave him to gradually move towards engineering his own car was too good to miss. His immediate priority was to improve the steering and suspension—which he did by using the ball-type kingpin joints which became a universal practice after being fitted to Jaguar's first post-war chassis. This was, in turn, adapted for the Mark VII saloon.

Meanwhile Lyon's cars were becoming ever more adventurous, culminating in the new S.S. sports car. Looking back to the success of the title

The men that made Jaguar . . . on the left, John Egan, and on the right, Sir William Lyons, who started it all, with – behind Sir William – one of his first Jaguars, a 1937 S.S. saloon – and with Egan, later Sir John, his contemporary series III XJ6 on the firm's 60th anniversary in 1982.

Swallow served only to confirm his opinion that the names of birds and animals known for their speed and grace presented an ideal image. He could not think of another one himself, so he found somebody to do it for him. As Wayne Mineau reported in the *Daily Mail*:

'One day in 1935 when the new model was almost ready, Lyons rang his advertising department. "Bring me a list of names," he said, "of insects, animals, birds and fish." On his desk went a typewritten array of 500 creatures that walked, crawled, swam or flew. Within the hour, Lyons made his brilliant choice. "I like the sound of Jaguar," he said. "It has everything we want—power, speed and grace".'

This story has been strenuously denied over the years, but it rings true. Lyons had a reputation for forgetting nothing. He kept a large desk

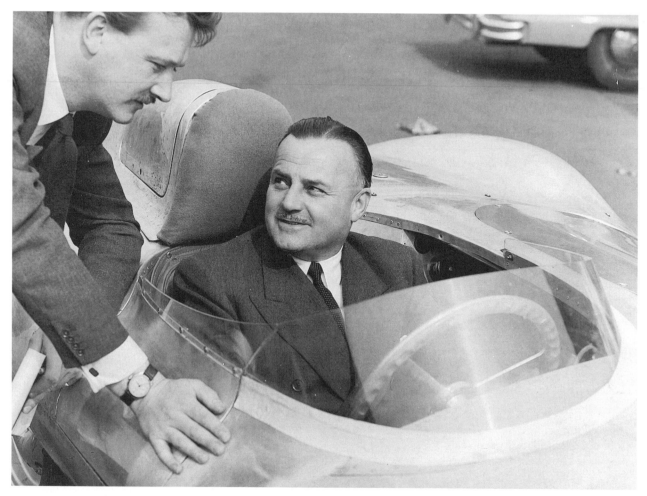

The engineering kinpin behind Jaguars, Bill Heynes, pictured in the cockpit of the prototype D type sports racer.

diary in his rather austere office, in which he noted dates when various jobs should be completed. Then he was on the telephone first thing on the appropriate morning to enquire whether the job had been completed. If it had not, no excuses were acceptable. His people knew that he might be on the phone at any hour of the day, night or weekend expecting to find a ready and co-operative ear.

That is exactly the way that Lyons did everything except styling. He preferred to work in raw material than from a desk or drawing board. For such work he would often commandeer the services of a skilled worker—such as Frank Gardner, in charge of Jaguar's sawmill and the only man he called by his first name—who could reproduce

his ideas in solid form. Even then, the ideas were not necessarily original, the inspiration for Jaguar cars coming from many others. But what made Lyons one of the most brilliant designers of the 20th century was his ability to see that so many diverse elements could be transferred into a harmonious form. Only after mock-ups had been made in the sawmill's experimental bay did they become the basis for drawings.

Lyons' ability to cull the best ideas from all sources could be seen in the XK engine which put the name of Heynes on a pinnacle. His experimental work at Humber led Lyons to visualise a twin

The first Jaguars, like this sensational S.S.100 sports car pictured on the 1948 Alpine Trial, helped establish the company's name.

overhead camshaft engine like that of the great racing cars of his youth, such as the Sunbeam Tiger made in Wolverhampton at the time he was thinking about moving to the Midlands. It was with this sort of engine in mind that Lyons hired Brooklands' tuning ace Wally Hassan as his development engineer and Claude Baily, from Morris Engines, as the third member of his think tank. Hassan recalled:

'Mr Lyons had a great liking for a twin overhead camshaft layout, but Claude Baily and I pointed out that this would be expensive and probably fairly noisy, too. On the evidence of the engines we used pre-war, we felt we could design an engine with a simple bathtub cylinder head combustion space and with pushrod overhead valves, which would give him all the power he wanted. As far as we could see this would be easier, cheaper to make, and quieter. However, this did not satisfy him at all, and if he wasn't completely satisfied with anything he would never agree to it. His new engine would have to be good-looking, with all the glamour of the famous engines produced for racing in previous years, so that when you opened the bonnet of a post-war Jaguar you would be looking at power and be impressed. He got his way, of course—Mr Lyons always did!—but I must admit that the rest of us thought that it was rather a waste of time and money at that time.'

The courage of Lyons's convictions came from having just survived near-bankruptcy when the demand for the new S.S. Jaguars was so great that production methods had to be revised dramatically. Lyons had little choice if S.S. was to grow, than to go over to all-steel bodywork in 1937 in place of the more traditional ash frame and steel panel system, which took longer to assemble. The teething troubles were considerable, but S.S. survived largely through the dedicated efforts of its workforce, inspired by Lyons.

Having come so close to extinction, Lyons never let up in his drive for efficiency. Everybody had to take part in fire-watching sessions after work during the 1939–45 world war, and that's when the XK engine was designed under Heynes.

When the war was over, the initials S.S. were dropped because of their Nazi associations to be replaced, simply, by Jaguar. Lyons concentrated on exports to secure the steel needed to build cars to such an extent that Jaguar have always sold more than half of its cars abroad, 60 per cent of its production eventually going to the United States alone. New staff were hired to supplement the original workforce which had survived the war; the most notable were Frank Raymond Wilton England—known to virtually everybody as Lofty because he was 6ft 5½ins tall—and one of the last employees to join S.S., an apprentice called Bob Knight, hired by Heynes in the drawing office for £7 5s a week.

England, who became service manager, was a legendary racing mechanic in the Hassan mould. He tried to get a job with the local Bentley motors in Cricklewood, North London, like Hassan—but there was not room, so he joined Daimler. As he learned his trade he also demonstrated outstanding driving ability, finishing second in the first RAC Rally with a Daimler Double Six totally unsuited to such an event! He then progressed to looking after Bentley racing cars of the type built by Hassan, before touring Europe with Maserati and ERA racing teams. England recalls of the time

Jaguar began to make its name at Le Mans with the XK120:

'Leslie Johnson was up to third place at Le Mans in 1950 before he had to retire with clutch trouble through using the gears too much to save the brakes. We made sure that didn't happen again by using solid centre clutches! Bill Heynes and I watched the race with Joe Wright, general manager of the aviation division of Dunlop, who made our wheels as well as supplying tyres. He was a great help to Jaguar and motor racing in general.

'So when we returned to Coventry, Bill designed a lighter and more rigid tubular chassis and Malcolm Sayer, who had been an aerodynamicist with Bristol, developed a more streamlined body. Eventually, in December 1950, we got the go-ahead from Sir William and had the cars ready within four months. The test driver, Soapy Sutton, soon left for Alvis and Wally Hassan had gone to Coventry Climax, so I did much of the testing of what would be the C type. Then we were off to Le Mans, our complement being made up of the engine man, Jack Emerson, service engineer Phil Weaver, and myself, each driving one of the racing cars, and two mechanics, John Lea and Joe Sutton, following in a Bedford 30-cwt van with the spares—rather less than Tom Walkinshaw's 110 people at Le Mans the other year!

'But we had help when we got there from Gérard Levecque, the service manager of our French distributors, who was in charge of refuelling and invaluable when dealing with commissaires. A student, Bob Berry, who had been driving his father's Jaguar in rallies, and spoke good French, also turned up and was more than welcome because we had a lot of problems with the cars in practice. But we won, so it came right on the day!'

It was during the racing years, in 1955, that the autocratic Lyons encountered a major setback. He was grooming his only son, John, to eventually take over the business when the young man was killed in a road accident on the way to watch Jaguar win at Le Mans in 1955. Lyons, and his wife, Greta, had two daughters, and one of them—Pat—had shown outstanding organisational ability as the co-driver to her husband, Britain's leading rally driver, Ian Appleyard, a Jaguar dealer from Leeds. Unfortunately the idea of a woman running a major manufacturing business was almost unheard-of in the Britain of the 1950s. The death of John Lyons had little immediate impact on the way in which Lyons ran Jaguar, but it would have a profound long-term effect.

Many of the people hired immediately after the war would play a subservient role in shaping Jaguar, none more so, quite literally, than Sayer. It became his responsibility to complete the designs visualised by Lyons, who was knighted for his services to industry in 1956. It was then that Jaguar quit racing to concentrate on building production cars, chiefly saloons. Heynes recalled:

'Far from being relieved when we pulled out of motor racing, I was more than sorry to abandon success on the track. It had helped me to build up a team of engineers, both in the design office and on the shop floor, second to none in the industry. The effort required

by all the team, and the enthusiasm which spread through the whole factory, I'm sure made a great contribution to the Jaguar successes in production and the world market.'

Sir William, however, had different views:

'Racing was immensely expensive but the main reason we pulled out was the drain on our brains. It employed too many of our engineers and designers, because in racing you have to meet the deadline otherwise you miss the race. Often we had to neglect work which should have been in progress on our bread and butter. We had decided we had to have a new range of production models, and even then we were starting to think about the XJ car.

'Moreover if we had continued racing it would have meant a new car. The D type had done very well but it was beginning to need replacing. We did, in fact, produce a new car so that if we wanted to go ahead we could. The mid-engined car had been developed very slowly and if we had really decided to race, it would have meant a big programme. It would have had to be redesigned in many respects to make it competitive. However, the car was quite a useful exercise and acted as a sort of test bed for the V12 engine in its original twin overhead camshaft form.

'I don't think motor racing today has the impact

The XK engine – shown in the first picture in its early form with tall SU carburettors about to be installed in one of the first Mark VII saloons – and, in the second, with 'squat-pot' SUs in series II XJ6, was so far ahead of its time that it remained at the forefront for more than 30 years.

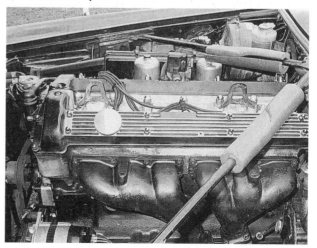

it used to have. The magic and the identification with the manufacturers seems to have gone, all these cars called Player's Please. From the manufacturers' point of view, I really don't think racing has much value today.'

England, who had run the racing team almost as a spare-time job, largely shared Sir William's opinion:

'We had decided to pack in motor racing for just a season, then build something new for 1958. But we had a severe factory fire in 1957 and getting back into production took precedence. We continued to run saloon cars, which were great fun. On one occasion, when John Wyer would not let Roy Salvadori drive John Coombs's Mark II on the same day as his Aston Martin in the British Grand Prix, we got Colin Chapman from Lotus behind the wheel. I read somewhere that he didn't have any friends. To me, he was a great chap as well as a wonderful engineer, and he certainly had one: me!

Jaguar just survived bankruptcy going over to all-steel production with the early S.S. saloons.

'In fact Jaguar nearly bought Lotus in 1964. Chapman was just starting to make his Elan at a small industrial estate in Cheshunt, Herts. He was in terrible trouble over the glass fibre bodies—a similar situation to that in which we found ourselves when we had taken over Daimler two years earlier. He said: "Bring along your chaps and ask any questions you like."

'I told Sir William that Lotus might be going for a song, and he said: "Chapman's a good engineer, go and see what he wants." So we reached a deal with Colin Chapman and his accountant, Fred Bushell, but Sir William had gone to South Africa and by the time he got back, they had written to us saying they had reconsidered the deal and hoped we'd be agreeable to withdrawing. So we let them go, and was I glad. I can't imagine what it would have been like having Colin Chapman with us when Jaguar became involved with British Leyland!'

Lyons and Jaguar had survived during this period by buying up other companies for their production facilities when planning restrictions stopped expansion at Brown's Lane. Guy was also bought to help put Daimler commercial vehicles into profit, and Henry Meadows was acquired not only for their engine building facilities, but, more important, their gearbox production line. The Coventry Climax fork lift truck and engine-building works brought with it a bonus: the return of Hassan to the fold, along with former ERA, BRM and Coventry Climax engineer Harry Mundy, who had designed the Lotus twin cam engine in his spare time from writing for *Autocar* before moving to Jaguar in 1964. Together they developed the V12 engine. As chief engine designer, Mundy—whose curt manner concealed a wry sense of humour—could really put a car through its paces: he was remembered at *Autocar* for being harder than anybody on the machinery he drove! One of his most memorable cars after joining Jaguar was a 6.4-litre V12-engined Mark X saloon which he drove for 150,000 miles while testing his new five-speed gearbox.

Much of Lyons's time during this period was spent wrestling with the twin problems of his first car that looked like being a mistake, the Mark X, and protecting his enterprise from problems with suppliers. It was not economical for Jaguar to produce their own body panels, so they had to rely on Pressed Steel Fisher, part of the British Motor Corporation. As a particularly savage credit squeeze bit in 1966, Lyons fuelled a merger between Jaguar and BMC to protect his body supplies. His rivals in the commercial vehicle field, Leyland—who had taken over his ailing erstwhile engine and chassis suppliers, Standard-Triumph—found themselves short of managerial talent and were alarmed at the BMC-Jaguar joint enterprise, called British Motor Holdings. At the same time, Britain's Labour government were becoming alarmed at the American Chrysler company's imminent take-over of the Coventry-based Rootes Group. Neither Ley-

Lofty England, pictured at his Austrian retirement home, became one of Jaguar's stalwarts.

land, nor BMH, could afford to accede to government pressure to stop Chrysler in view of the credit squeeze's effect on sales. So the seeds were sown for a shotgun marriage between Leyland and BMH with Sir William as one of the prime instigators.

Standard-Triumph chairman Donald Stokes came out on top in a prolonged skirmish for the chief executive's job when the Government-induced merger to form British Leyland took place early in 1968. His new company was the second largest motor manufacturer outside the United States, but he was still short of managerial talent now that men like Sir William—and many of his staff, who had started together in the motor industry—were preparing for retirement. His main problems centred on cars in high volume production, so, initially, Jaguar was left to its own devices for Heynes

to produce his last great work, the XJ6, before retirement in 1969. Hassan stayed on until he was 67 to oversee the introduction of the V12 engine which he wished could have had fuel injection from the start. Then when Sir William retired three years later—after 50 years in business—at the age of 71, he said:

'With hindsight it is possible to say that the Mark X was a little too big. We then concentrated on a much more compact car to give us the volume-seller that we needed to stay in business. I think the XJ6 is an ideal size and that is proving itself by the demand for it. I really think the XJ6 is so very good that it is the best car we have ever made.'

Retirement was not total for Sir William. Until his death in 1985, he maintained an office at Brown's Lane so that he could be on hand to be the focal point of reference on any issue on which the management thought fit to consult him. This could be considerable in the early 1970s as Lofty England took over for the three years before he retired . . . Sir William said:

'I still get all sorts of cars to drive, Americans, Germans, French, Italians, the best of each nationality. I may take one for a day, just drive it home and back or I may keep it for two or three days. They are all good cars, for I am not interested in other than good cars, but I always feel after trying one of them, and getting back into an XJ6 [actually he drove a Daimler Vanden Plas], that the XJ is a better car. I always enjoy driving it more.

'I drove a Ferrari a short time ago and it brought back a little more feeling [Lyons had won his last race in an S.S. Jaguar 100 at Donington in 1938]. It was terrific. It was a fun motor car and I did get quite a bit of fun out of it. But to be honest I would not like to drive it down to my holiday home at Salcombe. I was

almost glad to get back, to be quite honest.'

His views on engineering were of equal importance to those on styling as he continued to propagate anti-lock braking, self-levelling suspension, simplified servicing including electronic diagnosis, improved occupant protection and anything which reduced driver fatigue, in fact anything except unleaded petrol! England recalls:

'The old man was always very keen on the engineering side, saying you can't make a good car without getting that side dead right. One of our biggest problems became how to replace the six-cylinder engine. It was thought that they could get away with a 60-degree V8, but we were misled on that because the original try-out was done on a four-cam engine that did not show up any torsional vibrations. We did all the engine and tooling before we found that we could not stop without having a balance shaft—and we couldn't put the balance shafts in without redesigning the engine, which would have cost another £3 million for tooling. So I had to tell the engine men: "You've made a right Charlie of this, you'd better think up some other ideas."

'So we cut one side off a V12 engine and made the slant six. It should have seen the light of day in the first XJ coupé in 1976, but then there was a big delay. The demand for manual gearboxes was going down and down and down so we couldn't do Harry's five-speed box. What I wanted was an overdrive on an automatic, which you couldn't get in those days. We tried a two-speed axle which would have given you this or a fifth speed on a manual gearbox, but my successors dropped that idea.

'We also had anti-lock brakes ready to go in 1976, but they were dropped too. It was the old story, in that period engineers were never keen to go ahead with anything unless they were dead certain they were going to be a big improvement. What you need is someone running the company who is going to say: "We are going to do that." You've got to know enough not to make a Charlie of it, but after I had gone everybody was fighting a rearguard action in the face of British Leyland's financial problems. I'd say that Sir William was the finest man that I'd known in the motor industry. The only others in his league were William Morris and

Facing page, top: Leslie Johnson's Jaguar, pictured being overtaken by Norman Culpan's Frazer Nash in the 23rd hour, set Jaguar minds thinking at Le Mans in 1950. **12/8**

Facing page, bottom: Lofty England has his back to the camera, partly concealing Malcolm Sayer on his left, and Soapy Sutton, emerging from the cockpit of the record-breaking XK120, on his right. In the background, third from left, is racing mechanic Len Hayden. **12/9**

Colin Chapman. Sir William knew his market so well that there were none of today's clinics, in fact the distributors never saw the car until it was ready to be delivered. He knew exactly what the market wanted. He was also one of the most gifted stylists of his time, along with Sayer who did the E type and ended up on the XJ-S before he died.'

The problems he left behind were considerable, however. One of the great attractions in buying a Jaguar had always been its extraordinarily low price. This was achieved to a large extent by the most amazing economies in production. Concealed hinges in the hand-made bodywork were sometimes bought in bulk from Woolworth's, and as late as 1959 the production line was based on trestles pulled along by chains. When that system became too slow, it was replaced, not with modern equip-

ment, but with a second-hand line bought from another manufacturer which was updating its tracks.

The necessity for Sir William to step down because of his age could not have come at a worse time for Jaguar. He had never been good at delegating ultimate authority, and, although he still had an office at Brown's Lane, he could not give England the political support he needed in turbulent times.

By the mid-1970s, British Leyland faced bankruptcy as the result of soaring inflation and a recession that militated against such seeming luxuries as expensive saloon cars. The work force saw their spending power eroded at the same time and appeared to take it out on the cars. Even as the XJ12 was about to be launched, haggling over wages—related to the changeover from piecework to a flat-rate pay scheme—dragged on for 10 weeks. It was to become almost a tradition that a new

Jaguar's high-performace image was enhanced by the C-type, with the early thoughts of Lyons and Sayers reflected in its radiator grille which led to that on the later Mark I saloons and XK sports cars.

Jaguar chief took over in the face of crisis. But once he had sorted out that problem, England and his chief deputies, Mundy, the former apprentice Knight, now in charge of vehicle engineering, and the young Jim Randle, had the pleasure of seeing their latest offering declared Car of the Year.

England, meantime, was trying to line up his successor. Such was the state of British Leyland, he had a hard time. With yet another British Leyland shake-up on the way, Stokes asked him to be chairman of Jaguar while he brought in a new managing director, Geoffrey Robinson, from British Leyland's Innocenti works in Italy. The 34-year-old Robinson was a dynamic modern manager who inspired considerable support on the shop floor, but even he could not cope with the growing crisis at British Leyland, which was engulfing the still-profitable Jaguar.

As British Leyland faced going under, the Government had little option but to come to their rescue, hoping that the workers would sort themselves out if they still had a job. So they took over more than 90 per cent of British Leyland and Lord Stokes, as he had became, was eased into an honorary chairmanship with managing director John Barber being fired. This super accountant from Ford, who had been hired on even more money than Stokes, had clashed with the Government's troubleshooter, Lord Ryder. At least Barber had been a car man; his successor, Alex Park, was not. It proved a disadvantage as this former Navy officer, late of Rank Xerox, masterminded British Leyland's last-ditch attempt at survival. Robinson was caught up in the tidal wave, and quit to become Labour MP for Coventry North West, representing constituents including the workforces of the two main Jaguar plants! Jaguar then fell under corporate—and distant—control. Starved of investment, made all the more imperative by the years of penny-pinching under Sir William, quality suffered.

There was no doubt that Park was a brilliant accountant, but he was seen to be a comparative novice in the political jungle—so an old hand, all-purpose financier Ronald Edwards was hired to shield him. He died four months later, to be followed by a political appointee, Sir Richard Dobson. As it turned out, he couldn't even shield himself, being felled by the indiscreet use of the word 'wogs' in a supposedly-private speech that was leaked. Former petty officer Park went down with him and the impression was that well-qualified people were not exactly queuing to take over at British Leyland.

Even as Sir Richard was making his fatal speech, however, moves were under way to hire a modern new manager for British Leyland. Ryder's successor at the National Enterprise Board, Leslie Murphy, wanted a tough Scots-born New York

One of the backroom boys . . . service engineer Phil Weaver is pictured on the left.

The Le Mans-winning D type Jaguar, the aircraft-style bodywork of which was pure Sayer, did more than any car to win exports for Jaguar.

businessman, Ian MacGregor, to be chairman of British Leyland, with the fast-rising Michael Edwardes as chief executive. With Dobson's demise, Edwardes's appointment was accelerated and he immediately showed the full force of his personality by insisting that he went on loan from his firm, Chloride Batteries, for five years as chairman and chief executive. There was no other way to do the job, said Edwardes, and MacGregor agreed. It was at this point that the NEB's involvement with British Leyland was about to evaporate, and the savage pruning that might have started with Stokes was really about to begin. Edwardes, later to become

Sir Michael, said:

'In those days there were disputes in half of our 50 British factories day in and day out, and the list often ran to five typewritten sheets. That first day was the start of a period of relentless 70-and 80-hour working weeks, often with breakfast and evening meetings at each end of the day . . .

'In a snatched moment of reflection I made two personal resolutions on Day One of my new job at BL. The first was that I would give up all wines and spirits and that I would only drink beer or, on the right occasion, champagne. The second was that I would play squash four times a week. They were both helpful decisions . . . I certainly needed to keep my mind clear and the pressures were enormous. To start with there were only about three people I felt I could trust in a company of about 198,000 people, and they came with me from Chloride . . . '

The suspicion was mutual. Three men in particular, had fought relentlessly to keep Jaguar as a separate entity, one of them, Brown's Lane plant director Peter Craig, dying tragically at the height of the crisis in 1977. Another was Bob Knight, who, since Hassan's retirement in 1972, had been in charge of Jaguar's engineering. He had been involved in everything since joining S.S., with ever-increasing responsibility. He helped create the prototype chassis for the Jaguar Mark V and XK120 that turned into the Mark VII. By 1948 he was leader of the chassis design section under Baily, with Hassan influencing him over development. Knight took over a lot of Hassan's work when he moved to Coventry Climax in 1950 before forming a close bond with Sayer, who joined Jaguar at that time. He was then deeply involved with the C type and D type racing cars before going on to develop the 2.4-litre bodyshell. Knight recalled:

'We devoted a great deal of effort to the refinement of the 2.4, with the result that when it was finally announced in 1955, it was one of the best unitary construction cars from the noise and vibration point of view. The 2.4 was a milestone in our development and focused attention on the basic lines of action for the future.'

Knight then had to adapt his disc brakes for the 3.4-litre Mark I while developing the E type sports car and Mark X. The active development of the independent rear suspension had begun in 1957 after the rejection of de Dion suspension because it took up too much space. Knight's eventual rear suspension was evolved after he solved serious noise problems caused by a parallel link system produced earlier.

As Heynes's deputy, he started serious design work on the XJ6 in 1964 although Sir William had already been perfecting the styling for years. He had visualised the XJ13 mid-engined sports racing prototypes as a possible replacement for the E type,

but had to give up this line of thought when the American crash testing programme militated against it. When Heynes retired he took his place, eventually to become managing director in 1978. The fact that Jaguar stayed alive at all was due to the quiet, deep-thinking, Knight's great resilence that commanded loyalty.

Autocar's European editor, Peter Robinson, recalled after a meeting in 1979:

'He admitted that the series three XJ6 we had come to drive had been introduced to give Jaguar time to develop a new model. And though I didn't know it at the time, Knight was involved in a desperate fight to get board approval for a new engine for that car, then code-named XJ40, although there were prominent people within Leyland who wanted it known as the LC40—Leyland Cars 40. These were the same tactless individuals who insisted Jaguar became Large Vehicle Assembly Plant No 3 within the BL conglomerate.'

Knight was as passionate as Heynes at holding on to the engineering team created at Jaguar and the very identity of the marque. That's why he told his new masters that the XJ40's engine bay was too narrow to take the Rover V8. It was not worth making it wider to accept the V12, either, because such thirsty power plants were on the way out. Sorry, but they would have to stump up the cash for the new AJ6 engine. Robinson recalled:

'An obstinate, single-minded—some would say narrow-minded—sometimes irascible man, Knight was always an engineer at heart. His skills as a manager of people never really matched his huge talent as a suspension designer, although he was immensely likeable.'

Hard as Knight fought, Jaguar's feeling of detachment came to a head when assembly workers went on strike over pay and grading in 1980. Edwardes's ultimatum was: return to work or lose your jobs. One of his brightest young businessmen, John Egan, like Sir William Lyons a Lancastrian although he was educated at Coventry's famous Bablake School, and who—by happy coincidence—was also an engineer, was offered the

Ian Appleyard not only sold Jaguars and married into the Lyons family but he was a winner on road and track. He is pictured here taking the 1954 Silverstone production car race from fellow works driver Tony Rolt.

job of chairman of Jaguar with the edict: fix it, or shut it! With the V-engine farce in mind, Edwardes had been of the opinion that Knight was more concerned with producing new models and reaching new standards of engineering excellence than with managing the business. Egan, who probably recognised Knight as the perfect number two, offered him a key job. But Knight had had enough of what he saw as political in-fighting and quit. Robinson, the MP, paid tribute in the *Coventry Evening Telegraph*: 'Bob Knight was loyal and dedicated, a man of outstanding integrity and drive.'

Interested observers had tipped former Jaguar publicity chief Bob Berry—the student who joined England's team at Le Mans—to take over Knight's job. His interest in Jaguars had been fostered by his father holding 50 shares in the Blackpool company and owning a Mark V saloon. Berry did not even seek a career with cars at first: with a French mother and English father he had become a gifted linguist who just thought he might be able to help the British team . . . he really wanted to be an airline pilot. But England soon had him working in the service department—which ran the racing team—and Berry recalls:

'It gave me the opportunity to do some fantastic things. I made 19 trips abroad in one year . . . it was an incredi-ble training ground, a small, but highly-active, organi-sation short on manpower.'

As a natural extension to his racing activities, Berry moved on to publicity, under advertisement manager Bill Rankin who had helped create the name Jaguar and lifted the slogan 'Grace, Space and Pace' from a pre-war M.G. campaign to help create the marque's image in the 1950s. Berry recalls:

'He was the most complete publicity, advertising and promotions man I've ever met. He had an instinctive feel for business and I learnt a huge amount from him. There were a lot of people at Jaguar who never got the visibility or credit that they deserved and Rankin was one of them.'

Berry took over from Rankin when he died, and with the acquisition of Daimler, Guy, Meadows and Coventry Climax his responsibilities widened. He recounts:

'The way the business was run then, allowed people with ideas to have considerable impact in areas that were not specifically their own.'

In this way, Berry became deeply involved with marketing, a province that had previously been almost entirely that of Sir William. Lyons had long recognised his abilities, effectively ending a promis-ing racing career following a bad crash in a works-supported car, by issuing an ultimatum: 'It's your job or your racing . . . ' Berry managed to keep his job and continue to race, in one of the light-weight Mark VII saloons, but it was a low-key affair and soon ended.

As Berry fought as hard as any to preserve Jaguar's independence, he enjoyed a special rela-tionship with England, becoming his personal assis-tant when he was chief executive. Berry carried on as marketing director under Robinson before moving around the corporation, finally returning

Facing page: Brown's Lane as it used to be . . . with a production line of D type Jaguars on one side and an assortment of Mark VII Jaguars and XK140 sports cars on the other. **12/14**

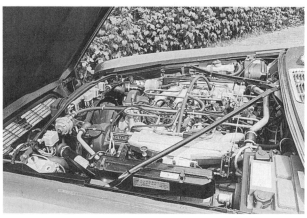

The XJ13 – first pictured at Brown's Lane in 1971 before a line of XJ saloons awaiting delivery – was projected as a racing car but ended up as a test bed for the new 12 cylinder engine in the second picture with the fuel injection Jaguar always wanted.

to Jaguar as European sales director under Egan before taking over as managing director of Alfa Romeo's British operation. Was he disappointed not to have got the top job at Jaguar? he was asked by Roger Bell for *Motor* early in 1981:

'No,' said Berry firmly. 'I never saw myself as Jaguar's boss. When Jaguar lost its independence with the formation of British Leyland, the prospect never struck me

as a possibility. John Egan has the commitment, enthusiasm and drive, and under Sir Michael Edwardes has been given the scope. He has the ability and the climate is right . . . '

It was not always like that. Forty-year-old Egan had spent four months making up his mind before moving into Sir William's old office the year before. He had already spent a lifetime in the transport business: his father ran a Rootes dealership, although Egan chose not to go into it. Instead he took a degree in petroleum engineering at Imperial College, London, in 1961 and spent several years working for Shell in the Middle East. He then took a management course at the London Business School before going to work for General Motors in 1968 as manager of their British parts division, AC Delco. Egan switched to British Leyland in a

The man who could have taken over Jaguar in the 1970s . . . if Jaguar had, first, taken over Lotus, Colin Chapman.

similar capacity in 1971, developing Unipart into a highly-profitable operation, before leaving in 1976 because he opposed the Labour government-inspired Ryder Plan. A devotee of the Conservative party, and particularly its tough leader, Margaret Thatcher, he then joined tractor kings Massey-Ferguson before being lured back to British Leyland and Jaguar.

Egan spent his first weekend at Brown's Lane with assistant managing director Mike Beasley in a hut, negotiating peace with striking shop stewards. Beasley, who had been hired from Ford in 1974 to install a new paint shop at Brown's Lane, but ended up having to instigate it as part of a group operation at Castle Bromwich, had doubled up as plant director. One of his first major problems under Egan was to get the XJ-S back into production. Beasley recalls:

'It had a terrible reputation in 1980, chiefly through

The car that Sir William Lyons favoured to the end . . . a Vanden Plas 12 cylinder saloon.

steering rack and electrical problems. People also thought the all-black cabin was claustrophobic, and half the country seemed to hate the fins.'

So Beasley had a special XJ-S built with interior similar to what would become the HE—and it went down very well with Jaguar enthusiasts, before being sold to David Harvey, then chairman of the Jaguar Driver's Club. But it was not liked by British Leyland's top management, who classed such actions as anarchy. Beasley, however, had the full support of Egan, who was becoming deeply entrenched at Jaguar by forging new relations with the workforce. Beasley recalls:

'John's was a new face and he used it well. He would

say: "That I can guarantee," and mean it. It won him a lot of credibility. But we still had to sit down every week and wonder if we'd be able to pay the bills.'

Part of the reason was the legacy from the days of Sir William's low-cost tooling. Until the XJ40 was launched, a characteristic of Jaguar was that they would never use one panel where two or three would do the job. It saved money on complex tooling but complicated production. As a result, the original XJ6 always had problems with its bonnet, front wings and nose because they were made from numerous pressings welded together.

Below & opposite bottom: Production was hectic at Brown's Lane even as Lyons concentrated on taking over more space.

The need for Egan's first dramatic action, launching an outstandingly-successful campaign to rid Jaguar of its reputation for producing brilliantly-engineered, but very badly-made, cars was highlighted later by Derek Waeland, the human dynamo who became the XJ40's manufacturing chief. He recalled a totally archaic manufacturing facility at Brown's Lane that was starved of investment for years. Panels that just looked right had to be hand-shaped, then filed and finished. It had all become so inefficient under British Leyland as rival manufacturers invested heavily in modern production facilities.

'When I joined Jaguar, the series three saloon was an utter disaster on the production line. We were still designing it on the track, and the first cars were running along before we discovered we couldn't get the air conditioning in. A lot of problems were caused by the wiring harness being held in by bend-over tags. They'd crack, or the wires could get pierced by the rough edges of spot welds. That's why we went over to plastic clips on the XJ40 and began to take the Mercedes 300 as a standard for body production. It's a body man's dream—it looks as if all the body shuts are machined from solid. Going over to mono-side production panels on the XJ40 cost a fortune but it worked wonders with door fits.'

Initially, Egan doubted that Jaguar's plunging sales were entirely due to quality problems. He

Man with many problems . . . Michael Edwardes who saved British Leyland, and, by remote control, Jaguar.

thought that the sales force should take a substantial part of the blame. But Berry mobilised the salesmen, who convinced Egan that there really was a big problem in selling such poorly-made cars. Egan revised his opinions, and found that his biggest problem on quality had been generated at Castle Bromwich. Without Beasley's guiding hand—he had become plant director at Brown's Lane—there were teething troubles so massive that almost every car that left the plant had gross defects in its paint. It was notable that Jaguar output sank from 26,500 cars in 1978 when the plant was commissioned, to 14,000 in 1980.

Body supplies had always been the major strategic problem for Jaguar; it was no good having a brilliant engine if you had no body in which to drop it.

One of the techniques adopted was the Japanese concept of quality circles. These troubleshooting groups operated at each of Jaguar's plants in Castle Bromwich, Brown's Lane and the old Daimler factory in Radford. The members encompassed all relevant disciplines in a particular area with the object of pinpointing problems and working out solutions to them.

Egan's enthusiasm was not only proving infectious, but his ability to keep his problems was soon reflected in improved morale, efficiency and quality despite having to cut back dead wood and restrict pay rises in the run-up to privatisation and

the launch of the XJ40. In 1980, Jaguar had been producing 1.3 cars per employee, a figure that had risen to almost four within six years. Above all Egan showed the ability to make each worker feel personally responsible for the company's success— or failure. His philosophy of giving employees a bonus for good work, or not paying them if a car had to be rectified while being built, took the workforce with him. he was equally tough with suppliers. Any component failures were held to be the responsibility of that supplier and they were made to pay for it.

Quality, of course, was not the only problem. Egan recalled:

'A customer might order a car and then have to wait three months before it came out of our incredible system of jobbing shops, all playing with it to get it right.'

As a result of his personal pressure, several million pounds were spent unscrambling the muddled assembly lines at Brown's Lane and setting up a smoothly-flowing system so that firm delivery dates could be met.

Poor dealership presented further problems. Egan remembers some Jaguar dealers who employed no properly-trained mechanics and others who refused to run demonstrator cars. He reacted by slashing the dealer network in a manner of which Edwardes would have been proud.

As the aggressive Egan—knighted in 1986—wrestled with such myriad problems, Jim Randle, who had joined Jaguar in 1965 from Rover where he was project engineer on the 2000TC, became the effective father of the XJ40. In that crucial year, 1980, he had only 12 engineers working on the new car as the rest battled to improve the quality of the series three. By 1986 Jaguar were still highly efficient although they now had 635 engineers. Although Randle claims credit only for the new rear suspension, he was involved in every decision on the XJ40, even taking overall responsibility for styling. Charged with the suggestion that the XJ40 took a long time to go into production,

Jaguar were hard hit when plant director Peter Craig, pictured present-ing Graig Hinton with his Jaguar Driver of the Year award in 1976, died the following year.

he pointed out:

'Mercedes took seven years with the 300. Look how many people they've got—on the car side alone, over 8,000 engineers, allowing nearly 2,000 per model line. With the XJ40, series three, XJ-S, the limousine and a number of other little things, I am running less than 200 engineers per model.'

And as John Simister recalled in *Motor*:

'Counterparts in rival car companies seem to get worn down by the pressure of developing new cars, yet Randle had withstood enormous pressure to get the quality and reliability of the XJ40 right—and still maintains undiminished enthusiasm for engineering. When he says in his quiet authoritative voice: "Motor cars are abso-lutely fascinating," you know that this is no company technocrat talking.'

As a Jaguar man to the core, Randle could even defend the constant criticism in the motor-ing press of the traditional lightness of the power steering:

'I think it is that our philosophy on steering effort hasn't been developed with respect to U.S. requirements, but has taken into account the tastes of the majority of our customers rather than those relatively few sport-ing types.'

The series III Jaguar was viewed, simply, as a stopgap.

Initially, the series III XJ was a disaster on the production line.

As the gentle, polite, Randle argued Jaguar's case in quiet authoritative tones, the tough-talking Egan received immense support from finance director John Edwards, who had joined Jaguar with him from Massey-Ferguson. Edwards—like Egan, a northerner, from Chesterfield—had studied production engineering at university, but had begun to specialise more and more in finance before moving to Jaguar when he was only 31 years old. It was largely due to Edwards's financial manoeuvres in using Jaguar's cash flow as a hedge against fluctuations in exchange rates that netted the company huge profits before the New York stock market crash in 1987.

Egan and Edwards were matched in aggression only by Tom Walkinshaw, who initially took over the company's competition effort. 'Working for Walkinshaw is a calling rather than a job,' one of his dedicated team told me. They attacked the problems of running the patriotically-green Jaguars with a fervour and attention to detail that left the

There were individuals who wanted Brown's Lane to become the faceless Leyland Assembly Plant No 3.

Mike Beasley's first great work was having to instal Jaguar's new paint shop at Castle Bromwich.

opposition feeling distinctly mortal. Tom Walkinshaw's talent was not limited to his skills as a racing driver and businessman. It was his ability to raise the standards of others to his own dynamic level that was his greatest and winning asset. 'Otherwise they don't work here,' he stated with uncompromising clarity.

Utterances like that, delivered with all the punch of a man who looks disturbingly like a pocket battleship, won Walkinshaw a reputation for being one of the hard men of motor sport—and the retail businesses on which he thrived. This shrewd Scot did nothing to dispel that illusion—until you got to know him better. 'He's never laid anybody off over the winter,' said another member of his team, in an industry accustomed to off-season cutbacks.

In one breath he could be diplomatic. Asked whether his philosophy over the rule-bending that is so much part of motor racing was whiter than white or as black as some would paint it, he merely laughed: 'You'll find everybody wears a grey hat!'

But—with his XJR assembly lines in sight—when he was asked if there really was money in plastic body kits, he exploded: 'Do you think I'm a philanthropist?'

Egan was very much his equal, inspiring every bit as much loyalty and with as good a memory of where it all started. On Heynes's death in 1989, he said:

'He was one of the most talented automobile engineers of his generation. The fact that so many Jaguar cars are owned and cherished by collectors and enthusiasts worldwide is a fine testimony to his genius.'

Egan could equally well have said that of many of the men who made Jaguar. Especially Lyons.

Jaguars as Walkinshaw saw them . . . the XJR 6.0.

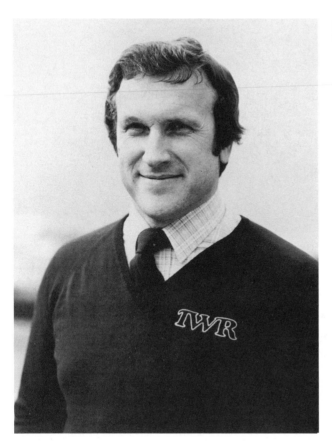

Pocket battleship who put Jaguar back in the front on the track, Tom Walkinshaw.

The Jaguar Clubs

The people who own classic Jaguar saloons, dream of running one, or who are just plain interested in them are extraordinarily well served by specialist clubs. The oldest continuously-active organisation is the Jaguar Drivers' Club, founded in 1955 chiefly by XK sports car owners. Membership declined during the mid-1960s as Jaguars almost vanished from competition and the saloon cars became ever more 'executive' in their appeal. However, when there were enough E types of sufficient age to fulfil a large enthusiast market, and supplement the numbers of XK owners, the club began to grow again and set up registers for a wide variety of interests. These registers, or clubs within the parent club, soon catered for the Mark I and Mark II saloons, the Mark VII, VIII and IX range, plus the 'independent rear suspension' cars.

As membership reached several thousand, the club's *Jaguar Driver* monthly magazine flourished with newsletters for the individual registers endeavouring to help with articles on maintenance, repair and restoration. Spare part sources were highlighted with a full calendar of both local and national meetings, plus races, sprints and hill climbs.

At the same time, the Jaguar Associate Group (JAG) of San Francisco, also formed in 1955, was flourishing, to pioneer a nationwide movement in North America. Because distances are much greater than in Britain, and the Jaguar owners are more widely scattered, the North American Jaguar clubs have a considerably different pattern of existence to that of the Jaguar Drivers' Club, based at Luton, Beds. The North American continent is covered by a large number of relatively small autonomous organisations, each being active on a mainly local basis — although two, one in New York and one in Louisville, Kentucky, are actually branches of the Jaguar Drivers' Club, along with others in Puerto Rico, West Germany, Belgium and Bahrein.

One of the prime movers in the Jaguar club world has been photographer, author and publisher Paul Skilleter, currently producing a superbly glossy *Jaguar Quarterly* magazine alongside his *Practical Classics* monthly at Kelsey House, 77 High Street, Beckenham, Kent BR3 1AN. At the same time, such is the level of interest in classic Jaguars that another arch enthusiast, Les Hughes, has been able to establish a superb, equally glossy, *Australian Jaguar* bi-monthly magazine from his headquarters at 56 Hexham Street, Tarragindi, Queensland 4121, circulating not only in Australia but in New Zealand, the United States and Great Britain.

By the time the XJ saloons and coupés became collectors' cars, membership of the Jaguar Drivers' Club, operating from permanent headquarters at Jaguar House, 18 Stuart Street, Luton, Beds LU1 2SL, had soared to five figures. Inevitably, with so much widely differing interest, a breakaway organisation, the Jaguar Enthusiasts' Club, was formed in 1985, which has rapidly progressed to a membership of several thousand. The enthusiasts' club soon established an extensive range of specialist tools for remanufacturing obsolete parts to their original specification. In company with the drivers' club they organise trips and seminars as well as holding regular meetings and publishing a monthly magazine, the *Jaguar Enthusiast*.

Membership secretaries are Lynn and Graham Searle, of 37 Charthouse Road, Ashvale, Surrey GU12 5LS.

The enthusiasts' club's example was then followed in 1988 by a second breakaway organisation, the Jaguar Car Club, with a strong competition bias. At the same time, the car club — whose

CAR CLUB

HON. SECRETARY:
E. W. RANKIN
44 ST. PAUL'S ROAD
C O V E N T R Y
Telephones:
(DAY)
COVENTRY 88681
(NIGHT)
COVENTRY 8611

AFFILIATED TO THE ROYAL AUTOMOBILE CLUB
President: W. LYONS, ESQ.
Chairman: T. CRUMBIE, ESQ.

EWR/MDH.   June 22nd, 1939.

<u>DONINGTON RACE MEETING.</u>

Dear Member,

　　　　Here are the Regulations for our Third
Donington Meeting. Successful as our two previous
Donington Meetings have been, it is hoped that by holding
this meeting during the early summer, and by widening the
scope of the events, all previous records will be broken.

　　　　This year, instead of the meeting taking the
form of a "knock-out" competition, a series of separate
races has been arranged. This has been done to provide
greater interest for competitors and will enable members
to take part in the meeting with certainty of running in
more than one race if so desired.

　　　　Further interest will be given to this year's
event by the inclusion in certain races of the new
extension to the Inner Circuit bringing in Melbourne
Corner.

　　　　Admission to the track is free to members and
their friends by Members Passes only. Application for
passes should be made to me on form enclosed. Luncheon can
be obtained at Donington Hall adjacent to the track or, if
so desired, members can picnic in the grounds. The Club **cannot**
undertake arrangements for lunches, but members wishing to
lunch at Donington Hall should write making known their
requirements to :-

　　　　　　　J.G.Shields Esq.,
　　　　　　　　Donington Hall,
　　　　　　　　Castle Donington.

　　　　Finally, I would draw the attention of closed car
owners to the events specially reserved for them, and trust
that a good entry of closed cars will result.

　　　　　　　　　　Yours very truly,

　　　　　　　　　　HONORARY SECRETARY.

ENCS.

In the beginning there was the S.S. Car Club, administered by Jaguar publicity chief Ernie Rankin . . .

membership secretary is John Bridcutt, of 23 Worcester Road, Malvern, Worcs WR14 4QY — publishes a monthly newsletter, quarterly magazine, and runs national and international rallies, and race meetings.

As enthusiasts of the Jaguar marque enter the 1990s, their club organisations have never been stronger.

And then members had a wide choice, with badges to match.

Members with a wide range of machines, such as these Jaguars and Daimlers from the Kent area of the Jaguar Drivers' Club, are always happy to meet to help propagate the marques.

Jaguar Mark VII

Introduced October 1950. 20,939 cars built by September 1954. 12,755 right-hand drive from chassis number 710001; 8,184 left-hand drive from chassis number 730001.

Engine

Six cylinders, in-line, twin overhead camshaft, CUBIC CAPACITY 3,442cc; BORE and STROKE 83mm x 106mm; MAX POWER (standard 8:1 compression ratio) 160bhp at 5,200rpm (150bhp at 5,200rpm with optional 7:1 compression); MAX TORQUE (standard 8:1 compression) 195lb/ft at 2,500rpm, (7:1 compression) 185lb/ft at 2,500rpm.

Chassis

WHEELBASE 10ft; WEIGHT 3,850lb; FRONT TRACK 4ft 8ins (4ft 8½ins after May 1952); REAR TRACK 4ft 9½ins (4ft 10ins after May 1952); LENGTH 16ft 4½ins; WIDTH 6ft 1in; HEIGHT 5ft 3ins; FRONT SUSPENSION Independent, wishbones, torsion bars, anti-roll bar; REAR SUSPENSION Live axle, half-elliptic leaf springs; BRAKES Girling hydraulic drums servo-assisted; STEERING Burman recirculating ball worm and nut; GEARING (standard) 4.27:1, 5.84, 8.48, 14.4, (optional automatic transmission from March 1953) 4.27, 13.1-6.12, 21.2-9.9, (optional overdrive from January 1954) 3.54, 4.55, 5.5, 7.96, 13.6; TYRES AND WHEELS Dunlop 6.70 x 16 on 16-inch 5K pressed steel rims (5.5K from late 1952).

Jaguar Mark VIIM

Introduced October 1954. 9,261 cars built by July 1957. 7,245 right-hand drive from chassis number 722755; 2,016 left-hand drive from chassis number 738184.

Engine

As Mark VII except additional 9:1 compression ratio option; MAX POWER (standard 8:1 compression) 190bhp at 5,500rpm, (7:1 compression) 180bhp at 5,500rpm, (9:1 compression) 210bhp at 5,750rpm; MAX TORQUE (standard 8:1 compression) 203lb/ft at 3,000rpm, (9:1 compression) 213 lb /ft at 4,000rpm, (7:1 compression) 193lb/ft at 3,000rpm.

Chassis

As Mark VII except: WEIGHT 3,892lb; GEARING (standard manual) 4.27:1, 5.17, 7.47, 12.73, (automatic) as Mark VII, (overdrive options) 3.54, 4.55, 5.5 or 6.22, 7.96 or 9.015, 13.56 or 15.35

Jaguar Mark VII

Introduced October 1956. 6,332 cars built by December 1959. 4,644 right-hand drive from chassis number 760001; 1,688 left-hand drive from chassis number 780001.

Engine

As Mark VII except: MAX POWER (standard 8:1 compression ratio) 210bhp at 5,500rpm, (optional 7:1 compression) 200bhp at 5,500rpm; MAX TORQUE (standard 8:1 compression) 203lb/ft at 3,000rpm, (7:1 compression) 193lb/ft at 3,000rpm.

Chassis

As Mark VII except: WEIGHT 4,032lb. STEERING Burman recirculating ball worm and nut, power-assisted option on left-hand-drive cars from April 1958, from October 1958 on right-hand-drive chassis.

Jaguar Mark IX

Introduced October 1958. 10,005 cars built by

September 1961. 5,984 right-hand drive from chassis number 770001; 4,024 left-hand drive from chassis number 790001.

Engine

Six cylinders, in-line, twin overhead camshaft, CUBIC CAPACITY 3,781cc; BORE and STROKE 87mm x 106mm; MAX POWER (standard 8:1 compression ratio) 220bhp at 5,500rpm (210bhp at 5,500rpm with optional 7:1 compression); MAX TORQUE (standard 8:1 compression) 240lb/ft at 3,000rpm, (7:1 compression) 230lb/ft at 3,000rpm.

Chassis

As Mark VIII except: BRAKES Dunlop disc all-round, servo-assisted; STEERING Burman recirculating ball worm and nut, power-assisted; GEARING As Mark VIIM except (automatic) 4.27:1, 13.2-6.14, 21.2-9.86.

Jaguar 2.4-litre Mark I

Introduced September 1955. 19,992 cars built by September 1959. 16,250 right hand drive from chassis number 900001; 3,742 left hand drive from chassis number 940001.

Engine

Six cylinders, in-line, twin overhead camshaft, CUBIC CAPACITY 2,483cc; BORE and STROKE 83mm x 76.5mm; MAX POWER (standard 8:1 compression ratio) 112bhp at 5,750rpm (102bhp at 5,750rpm with optional 7:1 compression); MAX TORQUE (standard 8:1 compression) 140lb/ft at 2,000rpm, (7:1 compression) 130lb/ft at 2,000rpm. From November 1956, optional stage one conversion MAX POWER 119bhp, stage two conversion MAX POWER 131bhp, stage three conversion MAX POWER 150bhp.

Chassis

WHEELBASE 8ft 11.375ins; WEIGHT 3,024lb; FRONT TRACK 4ft 6.625ins; REAR TRACK 4ft 2.125ins; LENGTH 15ft 0.75ins; WIDTH 5ft 6.75ins; HEIGHT 4ft 9.75ins; FRONT SUSPENSION Independent, wishbones, coil springs, anti-roll bar;

REAR SUSPENSION Live cantilever axle, radius arms, Panhard rod, half-elliptic leaf springs; BRAKES Lockheed hydraulic drums servo-assisted (Dunlop disc brakes, servo assisted, all round from November 1957); STEERING Burman recirculating ball worm and nut; GEARING (standard to June 1956) 4.55:1, 6.22, 9.01, 15.35, (optional overdrive to June 1956) 3.54, 4.55, 6.22, 9.01, 15.35, (standard from June 1956) 4.27, 5.84, 8.46, 14.4, (optional overdrive from July 1956) 3.54, 4.27, 5.84, 8.46, 14.4 (automatic transmission option from November 1957) 4.27, 13.2-6.14, 21.2-9.86; TYRES AND WHEELS Dunlop 6.40 x 15 on 15-inch 4.5K pressed steel rims (5K x 15ins 5K wire wheels optional from September 1957, track front and rear plus 0.5ins with wire wheels).

Jaguar 3.4-litre Mark I

Introduced March 1957. 17,405 cars built by September 1959. 8,945 right-hand drive from chassis number 970001; 8,460 left-hand drive from chassis number 985001.

Engine

Six cylinders, in-line, twin overhead camshaft, CUBIC CAPACITY 3,442cc; BORE and STROKE 83mm x 106mm; MAX POWER (standard 8:1 compression ratio) 210bhp at 5,500rpm (200bhp at 5,500rpm with optional 7:1 compression, 220bhp at 5,500rpm with optional 9:1 compression); MAX TORQUE (standard 8:1 compression) 216lb/ft at 3,000rpm, (7:1 compression) 206lb/ft at 3,000rpm, (9:1 compression) 226lb/ft at 3,000rpm.

Chassis

As 2.4-litre Mark I except: WEIGHT 3,192lb; GEARING (standard) 3.54:1, 4.54, 6.58, 11.95, (optional close-ratio) 3.54, 4.28, 6.20, 10.55, (standard gearbox with optional overdrive) 2.93, 3.77, 4.836, 7.01, 12.73, (optional close ratio gearbox with overdrive) 2.93, 3.77, 4.56, 6.60, 11.23, (optional automatic transmission) 3.54, 10.95-8.16, 17.6-7.08.

Jaguar 2.4-litre Mark II

Introduced October 1959. 25,173 cars built by September 1967. 21,768 right-hand drive from chassis number 100001; 3,405 left-hand drive from chassis number 125001.

Engine

As 2.4-litre Mark I except: MAX POWER (standard 8:1 compression ratio) 120bhp at 5,750rpm (110bhp at 5,750rpm with optional 7:1 compression); MAX TORQUE (standard 8:1 compression) 144lb/ft at 2,000rpm, (7:1 compression) 134lb/ft at 2,000 rpm.

Chassis

WHEELBASE 8ft 11.375ins; WEIGHT 3,136lb; FRONT TRACK 4ft 7ins (4ft 7.5ins from September 1960); REAR TRACK 4ft 5.375ins (4ft 5.875ins from September 1960); LENGTH 15ft 0.75ins; WIDTH 5ft 6.75ins; HEIGHT 4ft 9.75ins; FRONT SUSPENSION Independent, wishbones, coil springs, anti-roll bar; REAR SUSPENSION Live cantilever axle, radius arms, Panhard rod, half-elliptic leaf springs; BRAKES Dunlop disc brakes all round, servo assisted; STEERING Burman recirculating ball worm and nut, power assistance optional on left-hand-drive cars, then right-hand-drive chassis also from September 1960; GEARING (standard) 4.27:1, 5.48, 7.94, 14.42, (optional overdrive until September 1965) 3.54, 4.55, 5.84, 8.46, 15.35, (overdrive from September 1965) 3.54, 4.55, 5.84, 8.46, 15.36, (optional automatic transmission) 4.27, 13.2-6.14, 21.2-9.86; TYRES AND WHEELS Dunlop 6.40 x 15 on 15-inch 4.5K pressed steel rims, 5K from September 1960 (5K x 15ins 5K wire wheels optional, standard track front and rear plus 0.5ins with wire wheels before September 1960).

Jaguar 3.4-litre Mark II

Introduced October 1959. 28,666 cars built by September 1967. 22,095 right hand drive from chassis number 150001; 6,571 left-hand drive from chassis number 175001.

Engine As 3.4-litre Mark I

Chassis

As 2.4-litre Mark II except: WEIGHT 3,304lb; GEARING (standard) 3.54:1, 4.54, 6.58, 11.95, (close ratio option 3.54, 4.28, 6.20, 10.55), (overdrive) 2.93, 3.77, 4.84, 7.01, 12.73, (close ratio option 2.93, 3.77, 4.56, 6.60, 11.23), (automatic) 3.54, 10.95-5.08, 17.6-8.16.

Jaguar 3.8-litre Mark II

Introduced October 1959. 30,141 cars built by September 1967. 15,383 right-hand drive from chassis number 200001; 14,758 left-hand drive from chassis number 210001.

Engine

Six cylinders, in-line, twin overhead camshaft, CUBIC CAPACITY 3,781cc; BORE and STROKE 87mm x 106mm; MAX POWER (standard 8:1 compression ratio) 220bhp at 5,500rpm (210bhp at 5,500rpm with optional 7:1 compression, 230bhp at 5,500rpm with 9:1 compression ratio); MAX TORQUE (standard 8:1 compression) 240lb/ft at 3,000rpm, (7:1 compression) 230lb/ft at 3,000rpm, (9:1 compression) 250lb/ft at 3,000rpm.

Chassis

As 3.4-litre Mark II except: WEIGHT 3,360lb.

Daimler 2.5-litre V8

Introduced November 1962. 3,997 cars built by July 1967. 3,376 right hand drive from chassis number 1A 10001; 621 left-hand drive from chassis number 1A 20001.

Engine

Eight cylinders, V-formation, single central camshaft, pushrods and rockers, CUBIC CAPACITY 2,548cc; BORE and STROKE 76.2mm x 69.25mm; MAX POWER (standard 8.2:1 compression ratio) 140bhp at 5,800rpm; MAX TORQUE 155lb/ft at 3,600rpm

Chassis

As Jaguar 2.4-litre Mark II except: WEIGHT 3,046lb; GEARING (standard automatic transmission) 8.54-4.27:1, 12.38-6.19, 20.41-10.20, (optional manual gearbox with overdrive from February 1967) 3.54, 4.55, 5.84, 8.46, 15.36.

Jaguar 240

Introduced September 1967. 3,716 cars built by September 1968. 3,716 right-hand drive from chassis number 1J 1001; 730 left-hand drive from chassis number 1J 30001.

Engine

Six cylinders, in-line, twin overhead camshaft, CUBIC CAPACITY 2,483cc; BORE and STROKE 83mm x 76.5mm; MAX POWER (standard 8:1 compression ratio) 133bhp at 5,500rpm (123bhp at 5,750rpm with optional 7:1 compression); MAX TORQUE (standard 8:1 compression) 146lb/ft at 3,700rpm, (7:1 compression) 136lb/ft at 3,700rpm.

Chassis

As 2.4-litre Mark I except: WEIGHT 2,941lb; LENGTH 14ft 11ins; GEARING (optional overdrive) 3.54:1, 4.55, 5.78, 7.92, 12.19; WHEELS AND TYRES (pressed steel only) Dunlop RS5 6.40 x 15 or SP 185 x 15 on 15-inch 5K rims.

Jaguar 340

Introduced September 1967. 2,800 cars built by September 1968. 2,265 right-hand drive from chassis number 1J 50001; 535 left-hand drive from chassis number 1J 80001.

Engine

Six cylinders, in-line, twin overhead camshaft, CUBIC CAPACITY 3,442cc; BORE and STROKE 83mm x 106mm; MAX POWER (standard 8:1 compression ratio) 210bhp at 5,500rpm (200bhp at 5,500rpm with optional 7:1 compression); MAX TORQUE (standard 8:1 compression) 216lb/ft at 3,000rpm, (7:1 compression) 206lb/ft at 3,000rpm.

Chassis

As 240 except: WEIGHT 3,109lb; GEARING (standard) 3.54:1, 4.54, 6.58, 11.95, (overdrive) 2.93, 3.77, 4.84, 7.01, 12.73, (automatic) 3.54, 10.95-5.08, 17.6-8.16.

Daimler V8 250

Introduced July 1967. 782 cars built by August 1969, right-hand drive from chassis number 1K1001.

Engine

As Daimler 2.5-litre V8.

Chassis

As Jaguar 340 except: WEIGHT 2,841lb; GEARING (standard automatic transmission) 4.27:1, 13.2-6.14, 21.2-9.86, (optional overdrive) 3.54, 4.55, 5.78, 7.92, 12.19; WHEELS AND TYRES (pressed steel only) Dunlop SP 185 x 15 on 15-inch 5K rims.

Jaguar 3.8-litre Mark X

Introduced December 1961. 12,977 cars built by August 1964. 9,129 right hand drive from chassis number 300001; 3,848 left-hand drive from chassis number 350001.

Engine

Six cylinders, in-line, twin overhead camshaft, CUBIC CAPACITY 3,781cc; BORE and STROKE 87mm x 106mm; MAX POWER (standard 8:1 compression ratio) 255bhp at 5,500rpm (245bhp at 5,500rpm with optional 7:1 compression, 265bhp at 5,500rpm with 9:1 compression ratio); MAX TORQUE (standard 8:1 compression) 260lb/ft at 4,000rpm, (7:1 compression) 250lb/ft at 4,000rpm, (9:1 compression) 260lb/ft at 4,000rpm.

Chassis

WHEELBASE 10ft; WEIGHT 4,172lb; FRONT AND REAR TRACK 4ft 10ins; LENGTH 16ft 10ins; WIDTH 6ft 4ins; HEIGHT 4ft 6.75ins; FRONT SUSPENSION Independent, wishbones, coil springs, anti-roll bar; REAR SUSPENSION Independent, wishbones, radius arms, coil springs;

BRAKES Dunlop disc brakes all round, servo assisted; STEERING Burman recirculating ball worm and nut with power assistance; GEARING (standard automatic transmission) 3.54:1, 10.95-5.08, 17.6-8.16, (optional manual gearbox) 3.54, 4.54, 6.58, 11.95, (optional overdrive) 2.93, 3.77, 4.83, 7.01, 12.73; TYRES AND WHEELS Dunlop 7.50 x 14 RS5 on 14-inch 5.5K pressed steel rims.

Jaguar 4.2-litre Mark X

Introduced October 1964. 5,680 cars built by December 1966. 3,720 right-hand drive from chassis number 1D 50001; 1,960 left hand drive from chassis number 1D 75001.

Engine

Six cylinders, in-line, twin overhead camshaft, CUBIC CAPACITY 4,235cc; BORE and STROKE 92.07mm x 106mm; MAX POWER (standard 8:1 compression ratio) 255bhp at 5,400rpm (245bhp at 5,400rpm with optional 7:1 compression, 265bhp at 5,400rpm with 9:1 compression ratio); MAX TORQUE (standard 8:1 compression) 283lb/ft at 4,000rpm, (7:1 compression) 273lb/ft at 4,000rpm, (9:1 compression) 293lb/ft at 4,000rpm.

Chassis

As 3.8-litre Mark X except: GEARING (standard automatic transmission) 7.08-3.54:1, 10.33-5.16, 17-8.5, (optional manual gearbox) 3.54, 4.70, 6.98, 10.76, (optional overdrive) 2.93, 3.77, 5.00, 7.44, 11.46. TYRES AND WHEELS Dunlop SP41 7.50 x 14 RS5 on 14-inch 5.5K pressed steel rims.

Jaguar 420G

Introduced October 1966. 6,554 cars built by June 1970. 5,429 right hand drive from chassis number G1D 5537720; 1,125 left-hand drive from chassis number G1D 76961

Engine

As 4.2-litre Mark X.

Chassis

As 4.2-litre Mark X.

Daimler Limousine

Introduced 1968, production by special order.

Engine

Six cylinders, in-line, twin overhead camshaft, CUBIC CAPACITY 4,235cc; BORE and STROKE 92.07mm x 106mm; MAX POWER (standard 8:1 compression ratio) 235bhp at 5,500rpm (225bhp at 5,500rpm with optional 7:1 compression), MAX TORQUE (standard 8:1 compression) 283lb/ft at 3,750rpm, (7:1 compression) 273lb/ft at 3,750rpm.

Chassis

As Jaguar 420G except: WHEELBASE 11ft 9ins; WEIGHT 4,816lb; FRONT AND REAR TRACK 4ft 10ins; LENGTH 18ft 10ins; WIDTH 6ft 5.5ins; HEIGHT 5ft 3.75ins.

Jaguar S type 3.4-litre

Introduced September 1963. 6,554 cars built by June 1970. 5,429 right-hand drive from chassis number G1D 5537720; 1,125 left-hand drive from chassis number G1D 76961

Engine

As 3.4-litre Mark II.

Chassis

WHEELBASE 8ft 11.5ins; WEIGHT 3,584lb; FRONT TRACK 4ft 7.25ins; REAR TRACK 4ft 6.25ins; LENGTH 15ft 7ins; WIDTH 5ft 6.25ins; HEIGHT 4ft 7.75ins; FRONT SUSPENSION Independent, wishbones, coil springs, anti-roll bar; REAR SUSPENSION Independent, wishbones, radius arms, coil springs; BRAKES Dunlop disc brakes all round, servo assisted; STEERING Burman recirculating ball worm and nut with power assistance; GEARING (standard) 3.54:1, 4.54, 6.58, 11.95, (overdrive) 2.93, 3.77, 4.84, 7.01, 12.73, (automatic) 3.54, 10.95-5.08, 17.6-8.16, optional from December 1964, standard from September

1965, GEARING (standard automatic transmission) 4.27:1, 13.2-6.14, 21.2-9.86, (optional overdrive) 3.54, 4.55, 5.78, 7.92, 12.19; TYRES AND WHEELS Dunlop RS5 6.40 x 15 or SP 41 185 x 15 on 15-inch 5K rims (5K wire wheels optional).

Jaguar S type 3.8-litre

Introduced September 1963. 15,135 cars built by June 1968. 9,717 right-hand drive from chassis number 1B 50001; 5,418 left-hand drive from chassis number 1B 75001.

Engine

As 3.8-litre Mark II.

Chassis

As 3.4-litre S type except: WEIGHT 3,696lb; GEARING (standard) 3.54:1, 4.54, 6.58, 11.95, (overdrive) 2.93, 3.77, 4.84, 7.01, 12.73, (automatic) 3.54, 10.95-5.08, 17.6-8.16, (from September 1964), (standard automatic transmission) 4.27:1, 13.2-6.14, 21.2-9.86, (optional overdrive) 2.93, 3.77, 5.01, 7.39, 11.46.

Jaguar 420 and Daimler Sovereign

Introduced October 1966. 9,801 Jaguars built by August 1969. 7,172 right-hand drive from chassis number 1F 1001; 2,629 left-hand drive from chassis number 1F 25001, unidentified number of right-hand-drive Daimlers.

Engine

Six cylinders, in-line, twin overhead camshaft, CUBIC CAPACITY 4,235cc; BORE and STROKE 92.07mm x 106mm; MAX POWER (standard 8:1 compression ratio) 235bhp at 5,500rpm (225bhp at 5,500rpm with optional 7:1 compression, 245bhp at 5,500rpm with 9:1 compression ratio); MAX TORQUE (standard 8:1 compression) 283lb/ft at 3,750rpm, (7:1 compression) 273lb/ft at 3,750rpm, (9:1 compression) 293lb/ft at 3,750rpm.

Chassis

WHEELBASE 8ft 11.75ins; WEIGHT 3,696lb;

FRONT TRACK 4ft 7.5ins; REAR TRACK 4ft 6.5ins; LENGTH 15ft 7.5ins; WIDTH 5ft 7ins; HEIGHT 4ft 8.25ins; FRONT SUSPENSION Independent, wishbones, coil springs, anti-roll bar; REAR SUSPENSION Independent, wishbones, radius arms, coil springs; BRAKES Girling disc brakes all round, servo assisted; STEERING Burman recirculating ball worm and nut with power assistance; GEARING (standard automatic transmission) 2.0-1.0:1, 2.92-1.46, 4.80-2.40, (optional overdrive) 2.93, 3.77, 5.0, 7.44, 11.46, (optional manual non-overdrive) 3.54, 4.70, 6.97, 10.76; TYRES AND WHEELS Dunlop RS5 6.40 x 15 or SP 41 185 x 15 on 15-inch 5.5K rims (5.5K wire wheels optional).

Jaguar and Daimler XJ6 2.8-litre

Introduced September 1968. 19,426 Jaguars built by May 1973. 13,301 right-hand drive from chassis number 1G1001; 6,125 left-hand drive from chassis number 1G 50001; 3,068 Daimlers, all right hand drive, from chassis number IT 1001.

Engine

Six cylinders, in-line, twin overhead camshaft, CUBIC CAPACITY 2,791cc; BORE and STROKE 83mm x 86mm; MAX POWER (standard 8:1 compression ratio) 170bhp at 6,000rpm (160bhp at 6,000rpm with optional 7:1 compression, 180bhp with optional 9:1 compression); MAX TORQUE (standard 8:1 compression) 172lb/ft at 3,750rpm, (7:1 compression) 162lb/ft at 3,750rpm, (9:1 compression) 182 lb/ft at 3,750rpm.

Chassis

WHEELBASE 9ft 0.75ins; WEIGHT 3,668lb; FRONT TRACK 4ft 10ins; REAR TRACK 4ft 10.5ins; LENGTH 15ft 9.5ins; WIDTH 5ft 9.25ins; HEIGHT 4ft 6ins; FRONT SUSPENSION Independent, wishbones, coil springs, anti-roll bar; REAR SUSPENSION Independent, wishbones, radius arms, coil springs; BRAKES Girling discs all round, servo-assisted; STEERING Rack and pinion, power-assisted; GEARING (standard manual gearbox with overdrive) 3.54:1, 4.55, 6.33, 8.67, 13.32, (optional automatic) 4.27-8.54, 6.19-12.38, 10.2-20.41, (optional manual non-overdrive gearbox) 4.27, 5.93, 8.14, 12.5; TYRES AND WHEELS Dunlop E70 VR-15 SP Sport on 15-inch 6K pressed steel rims.

Jaguar XJ6 4.2-litre and Daimler Sovereign

Introduced September 1968, 58,972 Jaguars built by July 1973. 33,467 right-hand drive from chassis number 1L1001; 25,505 left-hand drive from chassis number 1L 50001; 10,893 Daimlers, all right-hand drive, from chassis number IU1001.

Engine

Six cylinders, in-line, twin overhead camshaft, CUBIC CAPACITY 4,235cc; BORE and STROKE 92.7mm x 106mm; MAX POWER (standard 9:1 compression ratio) 245bhp at 5,500rpm (225bhp at 5,500rpm with optional 7:1 compression, 235bhp at 5,500rpm with optional 8:1 compression); MAX TORQUE (standard 9:1 compression) 283lb/ft at 3,750rpm, (7:1 compression) 263lb/ft at 5,500rpm, (8:1 compression) 273lb/ft at 3,750rpm.

Chassis

As 2.8-litre XJ6 except: WEIGHT 3,696lb; GEARING (standard automatic transmission) 2.0-1.0:1, 2.9-1.45, 4.78-2.39; (manual gearbox with overdrive) 2.94, 3.77, 5.23, 7.18, 11.04, (optional manual non-overdrive gearbox) 3.54, 4.92, 6.74, 10.38.

Jaguar XJ12 Series I

Introduced July 1972. 2,492 cars built by August 1973. 720 right-hand drive from chassis number 1P 1001; 1,762 left-hand drive from chassis number 1P 50001.

Engine

Twelve cylinders, V formation, single overhead camshafts, CUBIC CAPACITY 5,343cc; BORE

and STROKE 90mm x 70mm; MAX POWER 253bhp at 6,000rpm; MAX TORQUE 302lb/ft at 3,500rpm.

Chassis

As 4.2-litre XJ6 except: WEIGHT 3,920lb; GEARING (standard automatic transmission) 23.0-1.0:1, 2.90-1.45, 4.80-2.40.

Jaguar XJ6L and Daimler Sovereign

Introduced October 1972. 584 Jaguars built by July 1973, 583 right-hand drive from chassis number 2E 1001, 1 left-hand drive chassis number 2E 50001, 393 Daimlers, all right-hand drive, from chassis number 2D1001.

Engine

As XJ6 4.2-litre except:

Chassis

WHEELBASE 9ft 4.75ins; WEIGHT 3,808lb; LENGTH 16ft 2.75ins.

Jaguar XJ12L, Daimler Double Six and Daimler Double Six Vanden Plas

Introduced October 1972. 753 Jaguars built by August 1973. 750 right-hand drive from chassis number 2C 1001; 3 left-hand drive from chassis number 2C 50001, 523 Daimlers, all right-hand drive, from chassis number 2A 1001; 336 Vanden Plas, all right-hand drive, from chassis number 2B 1001.

Engine

As XJ12 except:

Chassis

WHEELBASE 9ft 4.75ins; WEIGHT 4,032lb; LENGTH 16ft 2.75ins.

Jaguar XJ6 and Daimler Sovereign Series II

Introduced September 1973. 12,370 Jaguars built by November 1974. 7,463 right-hand drive from chassis number 2N 1001; 4,907 left-hand drive from chassis number 2N 50001; 2,312 Daimlers, all right-hand drive, from chassis number 2M 1001.

Engine

As 4.2-litre series I.

Chassis

As 4.2-litre series I.

Jaguar XJ6L (XJ 4.2 from May 1975), Daimler Sovereign and Vanden Plas Series II

Introduced September 1973. 50,912 Jaguars built by February 1979. 26,236 right-hand drive from chassis number 2T 1001; 24,676 left-hand drive from chassis number 2T 50001; unidentified number of Daimlers, all right-hand drive, from chassis number 2S 1001; unidentified number of Vanden Plas from chassis number 3C1001.

Engine

As 4.2-litre XJ6L series one except: MAX POWER 170bhp at 4,500rpm; MAX TORQUE 231lb/ft at 3,500rpm; GEARING (optional manual non-overdrive gearbox from April 1975) 3.54, 4.92, 6.74, 10.38. GEARING (manual non-overdrive gearbox from October 1978) 2.76, 3.31, 4.62, 6.91, 10.99.

Jaguar XJ12L (XJ 5.3 from May 1975) and Daimler Double Six Vanden Plas Series II

Introduced September 1973. 14,226 Jaguars built by February 1979. 4,157 right-hand drive from chassis number 2R 1001. 10,069 left-hand drive from chassis number 2R 50001; unidentified number of Daimlers, all right-hand drive, from chassis number 2P 1001.

Engine

As XJ12 except: (from May 1975) MAX POWER 285bhp at 5,750rpm; MAX TORQUE 294lb/ft at 3,500rpm.

Chassis

As XJ12 except: GEARING 3.07:1, 3.55-1.48, 5.95-2.48.

Jaguar XJ6C (XJ 4.2C from May 1975) and Daimler Sovereign coupé

Introduced September 1973. 6,505 Jaguars built by November 1977. 2,606 right-hand drive from chassis number 2J 1001; 3,899 left-hand drive from chassis number 2J 50001; 1,585 Daimlers, all right-hand drive, from chassis number 2H 1001.

Engine

As XJ6 series II.

Chassis

As XJ6 series II except: WHEELBASE 9ft 0.75ins; WEIGHT 3,724lb.

Jaguar XJ12C (XJ 5.3C from May 1975) and Daimler Double Six coupé

Introduced September 1973. 1,873 Jaguars built by November 1977; 604 right-hand drive from chassis number 2G 1001. 1,289 left-hand drive from chassis number 2G 50001, 371 Daimlers, all right-hand drive, from chassis number 2F1001.

Engine

As XJ12 series II and XJ 5.3 saloon

Chassis

As XJ12 series II and XJ 5.3 saloon except: WHEELBASE 9ft 0.75ins; WEIGHT 4,032lb.

Jaguar XJ 3.4

Introduced April 1975. 6,490 Jaguars built by February 1979. 5,004 right-hand drive from chassis number 3A 1001; 1,486 left-hand drive from chassis number 3A 50001; 2,343 Daimlers, all right-hand drive, from chassis number 3B 1001.

Engine

Six cylinders, in-line, twin overhead camshaft, CUBIC CAPACITY 3,442cc; BORE and STROKE

83mm x 106mm; MAX POWER (8.8:1 compression ratio) 161bhp at 5,000rpm; MAX TORQUE 189lb/ft at 3,500rpm.

Chassis

As XJ 4.2 except: WEIGHT 3,717lb; GEARING (standard overdrive) 2.75:1, 3.54, 4.91, 6.75, 11.45, (automatic) 2.0-1.0, 2.90-1.45, 4.80-2.40.

Jaguar XJ-S and XJ-S HE

Introduced September 1975. 9,913 cars built by December 1990. 3,999 right-hand drive from chassis number ZW 1001; 5,914 left-hand drive from chassis number ZW 50001.

Engine

Twelve cylinders, V formation, single overhead camshafts, CUBIC CAPACITY 5,343cc; BORE and STROKE 90mm x 70mm; MAX POWER (compression ratio 9:1) 285bhp at 5,750rpm; MAX TORQUE 294lb/ft at 3,500rpm, (from October 1980, compression ratio 10:1) MAX POWER 300bhp at 5,400rpm, MAX TORQUE 318lb/ft at 3,900rpm, (from July 1981, compression ratio 12.5:1) MAX POWER 300bhp at 5,400rpm, MAX TORQUE 318lb/ft at 3,900rpm, (from September 1985), MAX POWER 291bhp at 5,400rpm.

Chassis

WHEELBASE 8ft 6ins; WEIGHT 3,892lb; FRONT TRACK 4ft 10.5ins; REAR TRACK 4ft 10ins; LENGTH 15ft 11.75ins; WIDTH 5ft 10.5ins; HEIGHT 4ft 2ins; FRONT SUSPENSION Independent, wishbones, coil springs, anti-roll bar; REAR SUSPENSION Independent, wishbones, radius arms, coil springs, anti-roll bar; BRAKES Girling discs all round, servo-assisted; STEERING Rack and pinion, power-assisted; GEARING (standard automatic) 6.14:1-3.07, 8.92-4.46, 14.68-7.34, (from July 1981) 5.76-2.88, 8.37-4.18, 13.77-6.89, (manual until May 1979) 3.07, 4.26, 5.85, 9.94; TYRES AND WHEELS Dunlop 205/70 VR15 or Pirelli P5 205VR on 15-inch 6K rims, (from July 1981) Dunlop D7 215/70 VR 15 on 15-inch 6.5K rims.

During the 1970s a new computerised numbering system was introduced which made it impractical to extract details of individual models produced.

Jaguar XJ 3.4 Series III

Built between March 1979 and April 1987 from chassis number JAAL A 3CC.

Engine

As XJ 3.4 series II.

Chassis

As XJ 3.4 series II except: WEIGHT 3,892lb; LENGTH 16ft 2.75ins; GEARING (standard manual gearbox) 2.95:1, 3.54, 4.94, 7.38, 11.8, (automatic) 8.14-3.54, 11.9-5.17, 19.55-8.50.

Jaguar XJ 4.2 Series Three, Daimler Sovereign and Jaguar Sovereign

Built between March 1979 and April 1987 from chassis number JAAL P 7CC.

Engine

As XJ 4.2 except: COMPRESSION RATIO 8.7:1; MAX POWER 200bhp at 5,000rpm; MAX TORQUE 236lb/ft at 2,750rpm.

Chassis

As XJ 4.2 series two except: WEIGHT 3,965lb; LENGTH 16ft 2.75ins; GEARING (standard automatic transmission) 7.37-3.07:1, 11.05-4.61, 18.42-7.68, (manual) 2.76, 3.31, 4.62, 6.91, 10.99.

Jaguar XJ 5.3 Series III and Daimler Double Six

Introduced March 1979 from chassis number JBAL W 3CC.

Engine

Twelve cylinders, V formation, single overhead camshafts, CUBIC CAPACITY 5,343cc; BORE and STROKE 90mm x 70mm; MAX POWER 285bhp at 5,750rpm; MAX TORQUE 294lb/ft at 3,500rpm.

Chassis

As XJ 4.2 series III except: WEIGHT 4,228lb.

Jaguar XJ-S 3.6

Introduced September 1983.

Engine

Six cylinders, in-line, twin overhead camshafts, CUBIC CAPACITY 3,590cc; BORE and STROKE 91mm x 92mm; (compression ratio 9.6:1) MAX POWER 225bhp at 5,300rpm, (from June 1986) 221bhp at 5,000rpm; MAX TORQUE, 240lb/ft at 4,000rpm, (from June 1986) 248lb/ft at 4,000rpm.

Chassis

As XJ-S except: WEIGHT 3,584lb; REAR SUSPENSION Independent, wishbones, radius arms, coil springs, (from October 1987) REAR SUSPENSION Independent, wishbones, radius arms, coil springs, anti-roll bar, GEARING (standard manual transmission), 2.78:1, 3.54, 4.93, 5.59, 7.11, (automatic option from February 1987) 2.58, 3.54, 5.24, 8.78; TYRES AND WHEELS Dunlop D7 215/70 VR 15 on 15-inch 6.5K rims, (from October 1987) Pirelli 225-60VR15 on 15-inch 6.5K rims.

Jaguar XJ-SC 3.6

Built between September 1983 and October 1986.

Engine

As XJ-S 3.6.

Chassis

Cabriolet version of XJ-S 3.6

Jaguar XJ-SC V12

Built between July 1985 and December 1987.

Engine

As XJ-S HE

Chassis

Cabriolet version of XJ-S 5.3.

Jaguar XJ6 2.9

Built between October 1986 and September 1990.

Engine

Six cylinders, in-line, twin overhead camshafts, CUBIC CAPACITY 2,919cc; BORE and STROKE 91mm x 74.8mm; MAX POWER (compression ratio 12.6:1) 165bhp at 5,600rpm; MAX TORQUE 176lb/ft at 4,000rpm.

Chassis

WHEELBASE 9ft 5ins; WEIGHT 3,662lb; FRONT TRACK 4ft 11ins; REAR TRACK 4ft 11ins; LENGTH 16ft 4.4ins; WIDTH 6ft 6.9ins; HEIGHT 4ft 2ins; FRONT SUSPENSION Independent, wishbones, coil springs, anti-roll bar; REAR SUSPENSION Independent, wishbones, radius arms, coil springs; BRAKES Discs all round, servo-assisted; STEERING Rack and pinion, power-assisted; GEARING (standard automatic) 3.01:1, 2.75, 3.77, 5.58, 10.29, (optional manual transmission) 3.77, 3.07, 5.16, 5.82, 7.34; TYRES AND WHEELS Dunlop TD Sport 220/65VR 390 on 15.3-inch 7K rims.

Jaguar XJ6 3.6

Introduced October 1986.

Engine

Six cylinders, in-line, twin overhead camshafts, CUBIC CAPACITY 3,590cc; BORE and STROKE 91mm x 92mm; MAX POWER (compression ratio 9.6:1) 221bhp at 5,000rpm; MAX TORQUE 248 lb/ft at 4,000rpm.

Chassis

As XJ6 2.9 except: WEIGHT 3,718lb; GEARING (standard automatic) 2.58:1, 3.54, 5.24, 8.78, (optional manual transmission) 2.78, 3.54, 4.93, 5.59, 7.11.

Jaguar XJ-S convertible

Introduced March 1988.

Engine
As XJ-S V12.
Chassis
As XJ-S V12 except: WEIGHT 4,112lb; WHEELS AND TYRES Pirelli 225-60VR15 on 15-inch 6.5K rims.

Jaguar XJ6 4.0

Introduced September 1989.
Engine
Six cylinders, in-line, twin overhead camshafts, CUBIC CAPACITY 3,980cc; BORE and STROKE 91mm x 102mm; MAX POWER (compression ratio 9.5:1) 235bhp at 4,750rpm; MAX TORQUE 285lb/ft at 3,750rpm.

Chassis
As XJ6 3.6.

Jaguar and Daimler XJ6 3.2

Introduced October 1990.
Engine
Six cylinders, in-line, twin overhead camshafts, CUBIC CAPACITY 3,239cc; BORE and STROKE 91mm x 74.8mm; MAX POWER (compression ratio 9.5:1) 200bhp at 5,250rpm, MAX TORQUE 220 lb/ft at 4,000rpm).

Chassis
As XJ 3.6.

Index

Index of Illustrations

Picture credits

The author is grateful to the following photographers, firms and libraries for allowing their pictures to be used:

Autocar 101, 103
Barker, Harold 105 bottom
Barnes, Owen Colour plate 6, black and white pages 8 top, 11
Biddeleux, Ricky 29 bottom, 256
British Leyland Heritage 224
Express Newspapers 249 top
Hamilton, Duncan 215 bottom left
Harvey, Chris Cover, Colour plates 2, 3, 4, 5, 8, 9, 10, 11, 13, black and white pages 7, 12 top, 14, 19, 22, 25, 26 bottom, 27, 30, 31 left and right, 32 top and bottom, 33 top and bottom, 34, 37, 39, 40, 44 top left and top right, bottom left and bottom right, 68, 71, 88, 89 top left, top right, bottom, 91, 92 top, 104 bottom, 105 top, 106 top, 107, 109 bottom left, 112, 113 top and bottom, 117 top and bottom, 119 top, 120 top and bottom, 121, 122 left and right, 123, 125, 126 bottom, 127 bottom, 128 top and bottom, 129 top, 130 top and bottom, 132, 133 top and bottom, 134 top and bottom, 141, 145, 149, 152, 154 bottom, 156, 158, 163, 167, 170 top and bottom, 175 right, 183, 185 bottom, 186, 195, 197, 211, 212, 213 top, 215 top and bottom left, 216 top and bottom, 217 top, 223, 225 left and right, 228 top, 237, 244
Harvey, Mary Colour plates 14, 15, 16, 18, 20, 22, black and white pages 16, 48 bottom left and right, 49, 50 top, bottom left and bottom right, 51, 52 top, 53 left and right, 54 bottom, 56, 57, 60, 65 right, 84, 85 bottom, 86 left and right, 87, 90, 126 top, 127 top, 129 bottom, 131, 138 bottom, 153 top and bottom, 154 top, 161, 164, 175 left, 178 top and bottom, 179 top, 208, 214 top and bottom, 227, 228 bottom, 235 right, 246 bottom, 230, 259, 260
International Publishing Corporation 233, 238 top and bottom, 240 bottom, 241, 242
Jaguar Cars Colour plates 12, 21, 23, 24, 25, 26, black and whites pages 8 bottom, 9 top and bottom, 14 bottom, 17, 28, 29 top, 36, 41, 46, 48 top, 54 top, 58, 59, 61 right, 62, 63 top and bottom, 65 left, 66, 67, 70, 72, 73 top and bottom, 74, 75, 77, 79, 92 bottom, 93, 94, 95 top and bottom, 96, 97, 98 top and bottom, 104 top, 109 top right, 110 top, 171, 174, right, 185 top, 190, 198, 200, 202, 203, 205 top and bottom, 213 bottom, 217 bottom, 222 top, 231, 235 left, 245, 246 top, 247 bottom, 248, 249, 250, 252 top and bottom, 253, 254, 255 top and bottom
Lotus 247 top
Motor (The) 13, 23, 24 top and bottom, 38, 42, 52 bottom, 55, 61 left, 64, 69, 102, 106 bottom, 108, 110 bottom, 111 top and bottom, 115 top and bottom, 116, 118, 119 bottom, 138 top, 174 top left, bottom left, 177, 179 bottom, 182, 193, 232
Skilleter, Paul Colour plates 1, 7, 17, 19, black and white pages 15, 26 top, 43, 83, 111 bottom, 124, 209, 210, 219, 220 top and bottom, 258